Learning
Python with
Raspberry Pi

Learning Python® with Raspberry Pi®

Alex Bradbury & Ben Everard

WILEY

This edition first published 2014

© 2014 Alex Bradbury and Ben Everard

Registered office

John Wiley & Sons Ltd, The Atrium, Southern Gate, Chichester, West Sussex, PO19 8SQ, United Kingdom

For details of our global editorial offices, for customer services and for information about how to apply for permission to reuse the copyright material in this book please see our website at www.wiley.com.

The right of the author to be identified as the author of this work has been asserted in accordance with the Copyright, Designs and Patents Act 1988.

A catalogue record for this book is available from the British Library.

ISBN 978-1-118-71705-9 (paperback); ISBN 978-1-118-71703-5 (ePub); 978-1-118-71702-8 (ePDF)

Set in 10 pt and ChaparralPro-Light by TCS/SPS

Printed simultaneously in the United States and the United Kingdom

To Kat for her continuing support, Mum and Dad for encouraging me to learn to program on the Commodore 64, Zappa for coping with continual disruption, and every single free and open source software developer for being awesome.

—Ben

Publisher's Acknowledgements

Some of the people who helped bring this book to market include the following:

Editorial and Production

VP Consumer and Technology Publishing Director:
Michelle Leete

Associate Director–Book Content Management:
Martin Tribe

Associate Publisher:
Chris Webb

Executive Commissioning Editor:
Craig Smith

Project Editor:
Kezia Endsley

Copy Editor:
Kezia Endsley

Technical Editor:
Paul Hallett

Editorial Manager:
Jodi Jensen

Senior Project Editor:
Sara Shlaer

Proofreader:
Linda Seifert

Editorial Assistant:
Annie Sullivan

Marketing

Marketing Manager:
Lorna Mein

Marketing Assistant:
Polly Thomas

About the Authors

BEN EVERARD is a Linux geek with a penchant for writing. He's a founder and director of Linux Voice (http://linuxvoice.com), and his musings can be found on the pages of their magazine and in their podcast. Previously, he's worked as a technical editor at Linux Format, and as a country manager for NoPC, where he oversaw the testing and deployment of computers to schools in Tanzania. Once upon a time, he was an IT consultant, but that was so long ago he can't remember it.

He's moved house and country so many times in the past six years, he's practically nomadic, although these days he can usually be found in the West Country, England. This is his first book.

ALEX BRADBURY is a compiler, hacker, Linux geek, and Free Software enthusiast. His involvement with the Raspberry Pi started when the first alpha boards were produced. He quickly got sucked in, leading Linux software development efforts for the platform. Still a steady contributor, he's currently focusing on finishing his PhD at the University of Cambridge Computer Laboratory on compilation techniques for a novel many-core architecture. He's on Twitter as @asbradbury, or else you can email him at asb@asbradbury.org.

Acknowledgments

Many people have helped make this book possible. At Wiley, Kezia Endsley and Craig Smith saw the book through from its inception. Thank you also to Erin Zeltner for making the words look fantastic and making sure they fit on the pages properly.

There are so many more people that also deserve a huge thank you. There couldn't be a programming book without a programming environment. Python on the Raspberry Pi is the work of literally thousands of programmers, many of them unpaid. They all deserve acknowledgment, but because of space, we'll only mention three—Guido van Rossum, Linux Torvalds, and Richard Stallman.

Of course, the software needs hardware to run on, so we'd also like to extend thanks to Eben Upton and the entire Raspberry Pi Foundation.

Any and all mistakes are, of course, the sole responsibility of the authors.

Contents

Introduction

COMPUTERS AREN'T JUST beige square things we use for work, they're everything that has a programmable processing unit at its heart. Games consoles, smartphones, GPS units, tablets and a mind-boggling range of other devices all work in the same way. They're all computers, and they've taken over the world. They're the things we use for work, for communications, and for relaxation. In fact, it's hard to think of an area that hasn't been taken over by computers.

Marketing people like to tell you that devices with embedded computers are smart (smartphones, smart TVs, smart watches, and so on), but the truth is they're not. The processing units are just bits of silicon that follow a set of instructions. The "smart" in a smartphone doesn't come from the computer chips, but from the people who program them.

Computers are the most powerful tools mankind has ever created, yet they're under-utilised because few people know how to unleash their full potential. In a world where everything is a computer, the most important people are the programmers who can realise their full power. Programming, then, is an essential skill that's only going to become more and more important in the future.

What Is Programming?

Computers, as we've said, aren't smart. They just follow a simple list of instructions one-by-one until they reach the end. That list of instructions is a program. *Programming*, then, is the process of taking a task, splitting it up into steps, and writing it down in a language the computer can understand.

The Raspberry Pi can understand many languages, but in this book, you'll learn about Python 3. It's a powerful language, and easy to learn.

This book is for people who want to learn about computer programming and who have a Raspberry Pi. You don't need any special skills or prior experience to work your way through this book, and it doesn't matter if you're not a classic geek who reads comics and watches Sci-Fi, and it doesn't matter if you are. As long as you fit those two basic criteria, this is the book is for you.

By the end of this book, you'll have a good grasp of Python 3, and you'll be familiar with many of the most useful modules (add-ons). Using these, you'll be able to control almost every aspect of your Pi. You'll make it interact with the world around through the General Purpose Inputs and Outputs (GPIOs), and communicate over the Internet. You'll give it vision so it can snap photos and know what it's looking at. You'll make games and manipulate three-dimensional worlds. In short, this is a book about how to utilise your Raspberry Pi to its fullest potential.

Why the Raspberry Pi?

There are a few things that make the Raspberry Pi a great device on which to learn programming. Firstly it's cheap. At around a tenth of the price of a low-end PC, it's cheap enough to have in addition to your main computer. This is useful because programmers tend to tinker with their development machine, and tinkering can break things. Generally this doesn't damage the machine itself, but it can require you to reinstall the system, which can mean a bit of lost data, and it can put the machine out of action for a few hours. If you have a Pi that's used just for development, this isn't a problem; however, if your only computer is shared with a few other people, they may be a bit put out by this.

Secondly, the Pi is raw. It doesn't come hidden away in a box, or in a complete system. This means that you get to decide what sort of system you want to make. You can enclose it in a case should you wish, or you can run it naked. You have access to GPIOs that many machines don't have. Most computers come pre-packaged for a particular purpose (a tablet for surfing the web or playing games, a games console for watching movies or playing games, a laptop for working or playing games, and so on). A Raspberry Pi can turn its hand to any of these things with just a little technical know-how.

Thirdly, the Raspberry Pi runs Linux. This is an operating system a bit like Windows or Mac OS X. It provides a windowing system and a text-based interface for controlling the Pi. If you haven't used Linux before, you'll notice a few differences between it and the system you're used to. For budding programmers, though, the most important difference is that Linux is far more flexible than the alternatives. Just as the physical design of the Raspberry Pi encourages experimentation, so does the operating system.

How Does this Book Work?

Chapters 1–3 are all about getting started with Python on your Raspberry Pi. At the end of them, you'll have a pretty good idea of what Python programming is about. The rest of the book is split into chapters that deal with different uses, such as games or multimedia. These chapters deal with different areas of Python, so generally, you don't need to have read one chapter to understand the next (there are a couple of times where we refer back to something, but we make it clear what's going on when we do).

This means that you can go through this second part of the book in whatever order you want. For example, if you have a particular interest in multimedia, you can skip ahead to that, and then come back and read the others later.

Learning to program is all about actually getting your hands dirty and programming. This means that you can't learn it by just sitting down and reading a book; you actually have to do some yourself. Throughout this book we challenge you to put what you've learned to the test. Sometimes it's through specific exercises designed to train your skills, other times it's through taking the programs we've introduced and adding your own features to them. An important part of programming is the creativity to decide what you want the program to do, so you don't have to follow our suggestions. In fact, we encourage you to treat our suggestions and code as a starting point to creating your own digital works of art.

Chapter 1
Getting Up and Running

WELCOME TO *Learning Python with Raspberry Pi*. In this book, you'll learn how to unlock the full power of the tiny computer, from 3D graphics to games programming to controlling electronics to tweeting. You'll see what's going on under the hood and learn how to create programs that take advantage of every feature of this minuscule computer.

Setting Up Your Raspberry Pi

To follow this book, you'll need a few bits of equipment:

- Raspberry Pi
- USB keyboard
- USB mouse
- SD card
- Monitor
- Power supply

There are also a few optional bits of kit that may help:

- Powered USB hub (highly recommended)
- Camera module
- USB webcam
- USB WiFi dongle

It is possible to do everything in this book with a model A Raspberry Pi. The real advantage of a model B as far as programming is concerned is the network port. This port will make it easier to connect to the Internet, which you'll need to do to install some software.

Any USB keyboard and mouse should work fine. Most SD cards should work, although there are a few that will cause problems. If you're unsure, buy one from a Raspberry Pi online shop (there are links to a few on `http://raspberrypi.org`).

The Raspberry Pi has a HDMI (high-definition multimedia interface) video output, but most monitors have VGA or DVI input. If at all possible, use a monitor that has DVI or HDMI input. A HDMI-to-DVI converter should cost only a few pounds/dollars and shouldn't detract from the image quality. HDMI-to-VGA converters are available, but they're more expensive and can cause problems, so use them only if you have no other option.

Most micro USB power supplies from reputable manufacturers should work; however, some cheap ones from no-name companies have caused problems, so if possible, don't skimp too much on this. You could use a USB cable from a normal computer to power your Pi.

Powered USB hubs are recommended for the power-related problems described later in this chapter. Not all USB hubs are powered, so make sure that whatever one you get plugs into the mains electricity to get extra power.

We talk more about camera options in Chapter 9 on multimedia. The only thing to say here is that if you do choose to get a USB webcam, make sure it's compatible with the Raspberry Pi. There's a partial list of working web cams at `http://elinux.org/RPi_USB_Webcams`.

You'll need to connect your Pi to the Internet to install the software you need in this book. You can do this either by plugging your Pi into your router with a network cable or by using a USB wireless dongle, which will add WiFi connectivity.

Solving Problems

The most common problems with the Raspberry Pi are power-related issues. Not all micro USB power sources can provide enough power, and it becomes more of a problem as you connect peripherals to your Pi, or when you overclock it (see Chapter 5 for more details). Power-related problems will usually manifest themselves as the computer crashing, so if you find that your Pi becomes unstable, this is the best place to start. A good way to get around such issues is to connect your Pi to one power source and connect all the peripherals (keyboard, mouse, and so on) via a powered USB hub.

The second most common cause of problems with Pis is the SD card. These issues can be caused by power supply problems, or they can be problems with the cards themselves. It's important to take preventative measures here to ensure that your data is safe, and that means backups! You can use a service such as Google Drive (although this runs slowly on the Pi), or you can simply keep extra copies of any work on a USB memory stick. SD card issues will usually manifest themselves by the Pi displaying error messages when you try to start it. Most of the time you can solve the problem by reinstalling Raspbian, but if this doesn't work, you'll need to get a new SD card.

If neither of these help, then you'll need to dig a little deeper. The most useful places to look are the kernel buffer and the system log file. The kernel buffer is usually best if you're having problems with hardware, such as a USB device not working. If you open LXTerminal and type:

```
dmesg
```

It will output all the messages from the Linux Kernel. The last ones are the most recent and should show any problems.

The system log file (often called syslog) can be displayed with:

```
cat /var/log/syslog
```

Again, the most recent messages will be at the end. The information in both of these can be somewhat cryptic. If you still can't work out the problem after reading these, the best place to go is the Raspberry Pi forums at `www.raspberrypi.org/phpBB3/`. There's a community of helpful people who should be able to point you in the right direction.

A Quick Tour of Raspbian

This is a book about programming, not about generally using Raspbian, so we won't dwell on it too much, but you'll find it useful to know a bit about what's going on.

There are a few operating systems available for the Raspberry Pi, but the instructions in this book are all based on Raspbian, which is the default operating system, and the best choice for a new user. If you have some experience with Linux, you could use Arch or Fedora if you like, but you'll have to change the apt-get commands to ones suitable for your package manager.

The easiest way to install Raspbian on your Pi is using NOOBS, which is available from `www.raspberrypi.org/downloads`. You'll also find a quick start guide at that website that will tell you everything you need to know to get up and running.

There are two different ways of interacting with Raspbian—from the terminal and using the graphical system (LXDE).

Using LXDE (Lightweight X11 Desktop Environment)

The Lightweight X11 Desktop Environment is the standard windowing system for Raspbian. Its basic setup is the same as most versions of Windows pre-Windows 8. There's a button in the bottom-left side of the screen that opens an applications menu, and currently running applications are displayed in the bar along the bottom (see Figure 1-1).

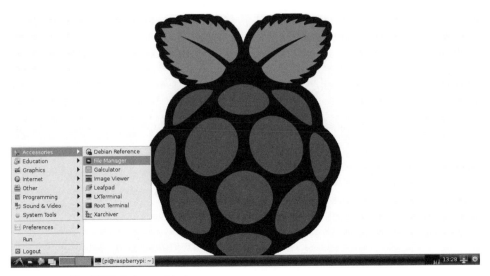

FIGURE 1-1: The LXDE desktop with the menu open.

If you get a black screen with white text asking you to log in when you boot up your Pi, it means that you haven't set it up to start LXDE automatically. Don't worry; just log in with the username pi and the password raspberry, and then type the following:

```
startx
```

You can set it up to boot into LXDE automatically using raspi-config (see the next section).

Using the Terminal

LXDE is great for many tasks, but sometimes you'll need to use the command line. This is an incredibly powerful interface that's accessed through the terminal. In LXDE, that means opening the LXTerminal application.

When you open LXTerminal, you should see the following line:

```
pi@raspberrypi~$
```

This signifies that you are using the username pi on a computer called raspberrypi, and you are in a directory called ~.

In Linux, all directories start from / or root. This is the base of the directory tree and every directory is located in some subdirectory of this. You can move between directories using the cd (change directory) command. Start by moving to this root directory with:

```
cd /
```

You should now seen that the command prompt has changed to

```
pi@raspberrypi/$
```

You can list the contents of this directory with the command `ls`. One of the subdirectories is called `home`. This is where every user on the system has his `home` directory. Move into it and view its contents with:

```
cd home
ls
```

There should only be one directory called `pi`. The command prompt should now have changed to show that you're in the directory `/home`. Move into the only subdirectory with:

```
cd pi
```

Now the command prompt will have reverted to:

```
pi@raspberrypi~$
```

This is because the character ~ is a shorthand for the current user's home directory. When you type ~ in the terminal, the computer converts it to `/home/pi`.

There is much more to learn about the command line. So much so that it would take another book this size to cover it with any semblance of completeness. However, you don't need to know everything to start using it, and whenever we tell you to use LXTerminal, we tell you exactly what to type.

If you are interested in learning more about the Raspberry Pi, or Linux in general, the command line is an excellent place to start, and there's loads of information about it both online and in print. The Linux command-line book, which you can browse for free online, is an excellent place to start. See `http://linuxcommand.org/tlcl.php`.

TIP

We'll leave you with two pieces of advice. Firstly, don't be afraid of the terminal. It can be a bit daunting at first, but the only way to learn how to use it is to use it. Secondly, almost all commands have built-in help that you can access using the flag `--help`. For example, if you want to learn more about how to use the command `ls`, you can enter:

```
ls --help
```

This will output:

```
Usage: ls [OPTION]... [FILE]...
List information about the FILEs (the current directory by
default). Sort entries alphabetically if none of -cftuvSUX nor
--sort is specified.
```

It then goes on to list all the various flags you can use with the command.

Changing Configurations with Raspi-Config

Raspbian comes with a tool to help you set up the hardware on your Raspberry Pi; it's called `raspi-config`. To start it, open LXTerminal and type:

```
sudo raspi-config
```

Here, you'll find options to start LXDE automatically when you boot up, overclock your Pi, and other things. Overclocking your Pi will make a few things in this book run a little better, most notably, installing new software.

Installing Software

You can install new software on your Raspberry Pi using the `apt-get` command in the terminal. Before installing anything, it's a good idea to update all your software to the latest version. You can do this with:

```
sudo apt-get update
sudo apt-get upgrade
```

Then you can use `apt-get` to install whatever you want. For example, if you want to use `iceweasel` (a re-branded version of Firefox), you need to open LXTerminal and type:

```
sudo apt-get install iceweasel
```

If you prefer to do this using a graphical program, you can get the program synaptic with:

```
sudo apt-get install synaptic
```

When you want to install something, you can start it with:

```
sudo synaptic
```

From there you'll be able to search for whatever you want.

> Whenever you install software, you need to use the word **sudo** before the command. It tells the computer that you want to make a system-wide change and gives the program sufficient permissions to do this. **NOTE**

Python 3

In this book, you'll learn how to use the Python 3 programming language. In Raspbian, there are a couple of ways to use this language.

The Python Interpreter

There are two ways of using Python, from the shell and saved programs. The shell executes each instruction as you type it, which means it's a really good way of trying out things and doing experiments. Saved programs are bits of Python code that are saved in a text file and run all at once. It's easy to tell which environment you're in because in the shell, all the lines will start with three chevrons:

```
>>>
```

Most of the time in this book, we'll deal with saved programs, but there are some occasions (particularly early on) when we tell you to use the shell. To make it clear which bits of code are for which, we've started every bit of code for the shell with three chevrons.

Running Python Programs

There are two different ways you can write programs for Python. You can create text files that contain the code, and then run these files with Python, or you can use an Integrated Development Environment (IDE) such as IDLE 3. Either way will result in the code being run in the same way and it's just a matter of personal preference.

If you want to write the programs as text files, you need to use a text editor such as Leafpad. A word processor such as LibreOffice's Writer is unsuitable because the various formatting it uses will confuse Python. As an example, open Leafpad and create a new file that just has the line:

```
print("Hello World!")
```

Once you've created your file, just save it with the extension .py; for example `testfile.py`. You can then run it by opening LXTerminal and navigating to where the file is saved. Then you run `python <filename>`. You can use the `cd` command to move to different directories. For example, if you save the file in a folder called `programming` in your `home` directory, you could run it by typing the following into LXTerminal:

```
cd programming
python3 testfile.py
```

If everything has worked correctly, you should see the following line appear on the screen:

```
Hello World!
```

The second way is a little simpler. Using an IDE, the text editor and Python interpreter are in the same program. For example, open IDLE 3 (make sure to use the one with the 3), and go to File⇨New Window. In the new window, enter this code:

```
print("Hello IDLE")
```

Then go to Run⇨Run Module. It will prompt you to save the module, so select a filename. Once you've done this, it will switch back to the Python interpreter and display the following:

```
Hello IDLE
```

It doesn't really matter which one you use, so just go with the way you feel most comfortable with.

Summary

After reading this chapter, you should understand the following a bit better:

- You'll need a few extra bits of hardware to get the most out of your Raspberry Pi.
- Insufficient power is the most common cause of problems.
- If you're having problems, `dmesg` and `syslog` are the best places to find out what's going on.
- Raspbian uses the LXDE desktop environment.
- The terminal provides the most powerful way of interacting with the underlying operating system.
- The `raspi-config` tool lets you configure your Raspberry Pi.
- Use `apt-get` to install new software.
- You can run Python either through the interpreter or by running saved programs.

Chapter 2

A Really Quick Introduction to Python

IN THIS CHAPTER, you'll dive right into some code examples. Don't expect to grasp all the details yet. This chapter is meant to give you a taste of programming. You'll learn how to draw on the screen, and even how to make a simple game. Along the way you'll pick up some basic programming concepts, but don't worry if you don't understand every line of every program you create in this chapter. You'll learn more about the details in later chapters.

Drawing Picture with Turtles

It's time to get programming! We strongly recommend that you enter the code into IDLE 3 as you read along, as it will help you understand what's happening. So, without further ado, open IDLE 3, go to File➪New Window, and enter the following:

```
import turtle
window = turtle.Screen()
babbage = turtle.Turtle()
babbage.left(90)
babbage.forward(100)
babbage.right(90)
babbage.circle(10)
window.exitonclick()
```

Then go to Run➪Run Module or press F5 to execute the program. A dialog will open and ask you to provide a filename. This name can be whatever you want, although it helps if it's descriptive so you'll remember it in the future (we used `chapter2-example1.py`).

Each of these lines is an instruction to Python. Python goes through them one-by-one and executes them in the order it finds them. The result of the computer following all these steps is to draw a line with a circle on top, as shown in Figure 2-1. You might think the drawing looks like a lollipop, but actually, it's the first part of a flower. If you don't get this result, go back and check that everything is typed correctly and try again.

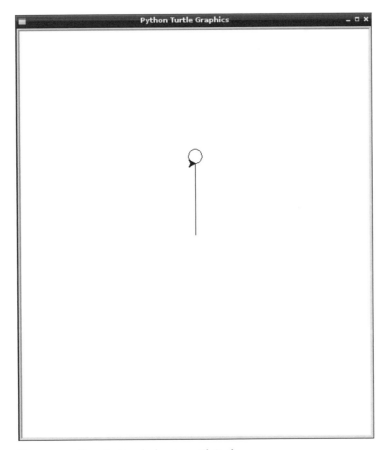

FIGURE 2-1: Your first turtle drawing with Python.

Let's take a closer look at what Python's doing as it goes through the code.

```
import turtle
```

You'll often see several `import` lines at the start of Python programs. They bring extra features into programs a bit like add-ons or plug-ins in other software. These features are grouped into modules. You'll learn more about how to use the `import` command in the following chapter. This time we're importing the turtle module, which lets us draw graphics.

The next portion of the code is

```
window = turtle.Screen()
...
window.exitonclick()
```

This creates a new window that we can draw onto, and set it to close when it's clicked.

The next line uses the turtle module that you imported in the first line to create a new turtle, named *babbage* (after Charles Babbage, who invented the concept of the computer):

```
babbage = turtle.Turtle()
```

Babbage has a number of *methods*, or things you can tell it to do. For example, in the line:

```
babbage.left(90)
```

You're using the method `left()` which turns `babbage` left a certain number of degrees. Parameters are added in the brackets after the method and you can use them to send certain bits of information to control how the method runs. In this case, you passed the parameter 90, so `babbage` turns left 90 degrees. The following lines use the methods `forward()`, `right()`, and `circle()`.

```
babbage.forward(100)
babbage.right(90)
babbage.circle(10)
```

The first method moves the turtle forwards 100 pixels, the second turns it right 90 degrees, and the final one draws a circle with a radius of 10 pixels.

Now it's time to add a petal. Edit the code so that it reads as follows (changes are in bold):

```
import turtle
#create window and turtle
window = turtle.Screen()
babbage = turtle.Turtle()
#draw stem and centre
babbage.left(90)
babbage.forward(100)
babbage.right(90)
babbage.circle(10)
#draw first petal
babbage.left(15)
```

```
babbage.forward(50)
babbage.left(157)
babbage.forward(50)
#tidy up window
window.exitonclick()
```

Run this now. You should see that the flower now has a solitary petal. You'll notice that we've added some lines that begin with a # symbol. The computer ignores any line that starts like this, so you use them to leave little comments to yourself (or anyone else who looks at the code). These make the code more readable, and mean that if you come back to the code in a few days, weeks, or even years, you can easily see what it's doing.

Using Loops

You should find the section that draws the petal quite easy to understand (we calculated the angles of the two left turns using trigonometry, but don't worry, we won't be going into the maths here).

You could now add a block of code to draw a second petal (there'll be 24 in total). It will be exactly the same as the first petal, and directly below it, so with a bit of copy and paste, you'll get the following:

```
#draw second petal
babbage.left(15)
babbage.forward(50)
babbage.left(157)
babbage.forward(50)
```

And then do the same for the next 22 petals … Okay, hang on here. As a general rule of thumb, when programming, you should never repeat identical code. Suppose you decided to change the size of the petal; you'd have to change it 48 times (twice for each petal), and if you forgot any one, you'd get a wonky picture. Instead, you can use a *loop*, which is a piece of code that tells the computer to repeat a certain section of code over and over again.

Instead you can replace all the code from #draw first petal downwards with the following code:

```
#draw all petals
for i in range(1,24):
    babbage.left(15)
    babbage.forward(50)
    babbage.left(157)
    babbage.forward(50)
window.exitonclick()
```

We'll deal with exactly what the first line (after the comment) means in the next chapter, but for now, it's enough to say that it repeats the block 24 times, then the computer moves on to the instructions after this block.

Code blocks like loops (and others that you'll explore later) always follow the same layout in Python. The first line ends with a colon, and every line after it is indented. Once the tabbing/indention stops, Python considers this code block over. If you've programmed in other languages before, you'll probably have noticed that they do things a little differently.

Try running the code. You should find that babbage runs round drawing all the petals, and we finish with a complete flower, as shown in Figure 2-2.

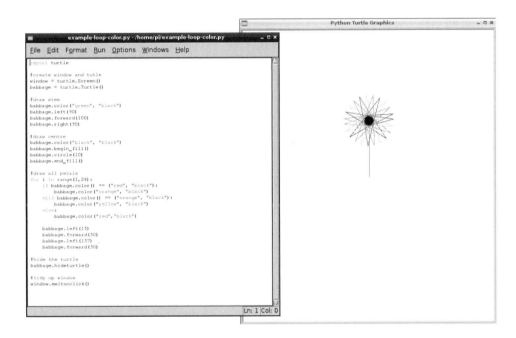

FIGURE 2-2: Loops make drawing flowers a breeze.

Not bad for just 13 lines of code! Of course, not many flowers are all black, so it would be better if you could add a little colour to the picture. The Python turtle module does include some methods that allow you to change the colour of your drawing. Amend the first half of your program so it reads as follows (changes are shown in bold):

```
import turtle
#create window and turtle
window = turtle.Screen()
babbage = turtle.Turtle()
#draw stem
```

```
babbage.color("green", "black")
babbage.left(90)
babbage.forward(100)
babbage.right(90)
#draw centre
babbage.color("black", "black")
babbage.begin_fill()
babbage.circle(10)
babbage.end_fill()
```

As you can see, we're using the color(colour1, colour2) method (Brits should notice the American spelling of the method), where colour1 is the pen colour and colour2 is the fill colour. When you start the centre circle of the flower, you tell the computer to fill in the circle with the begin_fill() method. Afterwards, we used end_fill() so it doesn't keep filling in all the petals.

Conditionals: if, elif, and else

Now type the second half of the flower-drawing program into IDLE 3:

```
#draw all petals
for i in range(1,24):
    if babbage.color() == ("red", "black"):
        babbage.color("orange", "black")
    elif babbage.color() == ("orange", "black"):
        babbage.color("yellow", "black")
    else:
        babbage.color("red","black"))
    babbage.left(15)
    babbage.forward(50)
    babbage.left(157)
    babbage.forward(50)
#hide the turtle
babbage.hideturtle()
#tidy up window
window.exitonclick()
```

We've used a little artistic licence and decided that the flower should have petals with three different colours: red, orange, and yellow. As this book is in black and white, you'll have to run the program on your Raspberry Pi, or you can take a look at flower.png on the companion website, to see the result in living color. To alternate our petal colours, we've used an if .. elif .. else block. This is a way of telling Python how to make decisions about what to do based on certain data. The basic structure is as follows:

```
if <condition> :
    code
```

where `<condition>` is a statement that can be true or false. In this case, we're using the following condition:

```
babbage.color() == ("red", "black")
```

`babbage.color()` (note that now this method doesn't have any parameters) tells the program what colour our turtle currently has. This is a little different to the methods you've seen so far because it sends information back that you can use. This return value is a pair of colours—the first is the drawing colour, and the second is the fill colour (which hasn't changed since you set it to draw the centre of the flower, so it will stay the same for the whole of the program). The double equals sign (==) means 'is equal to'. You use a double equals here because a single equals is used differently, like when you created the window and the turtle.

If the condition is true (in this case, if the turtle's colour is (`"red"`, `"black"`)), then Python executes the code. However, if the condition is false, Python moves on to the `elif` (`elif` is short for *else if*). This has the same structure as the original `if` condition.

If the condition in the `elif` is false, then Python moves on to the `else`. If it gets this far (that is, if the conditions for the `if` and `elif` are both false), Python will execute the code. `else` doesn't have a condition. Figure 2-3 shows the flow of this logic.

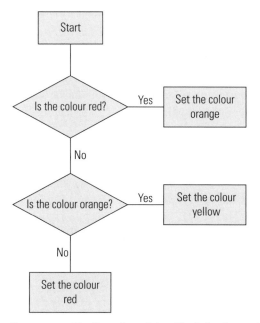

FIGURE 2-3: The flow of conditional logic for determining the colour of each flower petal.

This `if` clause then, will alternate the colour of the pen after each petal is drawn. The final alteration is to add the following line to the end of the program:

```
babbage.hideturtle()
```

This simply makes the turtle (cursor) invisible so it doesn't obscure our picture. There you have it; your very first Python program finished completely!

Using Functions and Methods to Structure Code

Before we dive in and start our second Python program, we're going to pause for a second to talk a bit more about methods. As you've seen, methods are really useful for controlling parts of our program. In the previous example, you used them to move turtles, change colour, and create windows. Each time, you called them on something. For example, you called `forward(50)` on `babbage` with `babbage.forward(50)` and `exitonclick()` on window with `window.exitonclick()`. Each time, the methods run bits of code that are stored in the Python modules. Python has another similar feature called *functions*. These work in a fairly similar way, but they're not called on anything. For example, in your Python interpreter, type:

```
>>> print("Hello World")
```

This runs the `print()` function that simply outputs its parameter to the screen. Remember when we said that you shouldn't repeat any code in your programs? We explained that loops are one way of reducing repetition, and functions are another. As an example, think of a program that deals with circles and often needs to calculate the area for a given radius. If you listened in maths classes, you should know that the area of a circle is 2 × pi × the radius (if you didn't listen in maths class, then you'll just have to take our word for it). Rather than repeat this every time you need to calculate the area of a circle, which could lead to problems (if you mistype the value of pi somewhere, it could cause all sorts of problems and be hard to find), you can create a function to do it. In Python this would be:

```
def circlearea(radius):
    return radius * 3.14 * 2

print(circlearea(1))
```

Here we've used two functions nested together. `circlearea(1)` calculates the area of a circle with a radius of one, and `print()` sends this number to the screen.

As you can see, you define your own functions using the word `def`, followed by the name of the function, followed by the parameters enclosed in brackets. You can then use the name of the parameter inside the function where it will act with the value that's passed to it. The word `return` tells Python what value you want to send back. So, in the previous example, when Python gets to the phrase `circlearea(1)`, it runs the code under `def circlearea(radius)`, but instead of `radius` it substitutes the number you passed across (`1`). Then it returns the value of that calculation (`6.28`) to the `print` function. You'll see later that you can nest methods in the same way so that one method sends information straight to another one. This can be a really useful way of getting data to flow in the right way between different sections of your program.

A Python Game of Cat and Mouse

Now, let's move on to our second Python program. This time you're going to make a game of cat and mouse. The player will control the mouse using the arrow keys, and she has to stay ahead of the cat (controlled by the computer). The longer she stays ahead, the higher score she gets.

Most of the longer code examples in the book are available for download from the book's **NOTE** companion website at `www.wiley.com/go/python-raspberrypi`. To avoid potential typos, you can download and copy and paste the text into your IDE or code editor. The code for the following example is `Chapter2-catandmouse.py`.

Open a new window in IDLE 3 and type the following code:

```
import turtle
import time

boxsize = 200
caught = False
score = 0

#functions that are called on keypresses
def up():
    mouse.forward(10)
    checkbound()

def left():
    mouse.left(45)
```

```python
def right():
    mouse.right(45)

def back():
    mouse.backward(10)
    checkbound()

def quitTurtles():
    window.bye()

#stop the mouse from leaving the square set by box size
def checkbound():
    global boxsize
    if mouse.xcor() > boxsize:
        mouse.goto(boxsize, mouse.ycor())
    if mouse.xcor() < -boxsize:
        mouse.goto(-boxsize, mouse.ycor())
    if mouse.ycor() > boxsize:
        mouse.goto(mouse.xcor(), boxsize)
    if mouse.ycor() < -boxsize:
        mouse.goto(mouse.xcor(), -boxsize)

#set up screen
window = turtle.Screen()
mouse = turtle.Turtle()
cat = turtle.Turtle()
mouse.penup()
mouse.penup()
mouse.goto(100,100)

#add key listeners
window.onkeypress(up, "Up")
window.onkeypress(left, "Left")
window.onkeypress(right, "Right")
window.onkeypress(back, "Down")
window.onkeypress(quitTurtles, "Escape")

difficulty = window.numinput("Difficulty",
    "Enter a difficulty from easy (1), for hard (5) ",
    minval=1, maxval=5)

window.listen()
```

```
#main loop
#note how it changes with difficulty
while not caught:
    cat.setheading(cat.towards(mouse))
    cat.forward(8+difficulty)
    score = score + 1
    if cat.distance(mouse) < 5:
        caught = True
    time.sleep(0.2-(0.01*difficulty))
window.textinput("GAME OVER", "Well done. You scored:
    "+ str(score*difficulty))
window.bye()
```

That's quite a lot of code, but before you look at it too deeply, play the game a few times to get a feel for it. This will also help you make sure that you've entered it correctly. If you get any errors, check your typing, and then try again. Take a look at Figure 2-4 to see it in action.

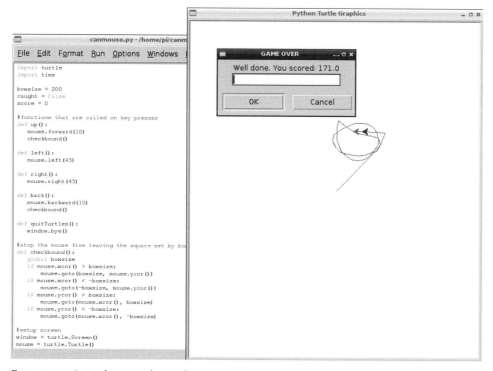

FIGURE 2-4: A simple game of cat and mouse.

Understanding Variables

The first two lines just bring in modules for using turtles and time, and then the following three lines are

```
boxsize = 200
caught = False
score = 0
```

These lines use something that we've touched on, but haven't really talked about: *variables*. Variables are places where you can store values you want to use later. For example, in the first line, you store the value 200 in the variable boxsize. After you've set them up like this, you can simply put in boxsize and Python will substitute the correct value. These constructs are called variables because they can change. In this particular program, boxsize will stay the same, but both caught and score will vary throughout it. Each time you want a new value, you simply use the single equals sign. This is the same thing you did in the first example with window and babbage; there the variables held the screen and the turtle. We'll cover variables, and what exactly you can store in them in the next chapter.

Defining Functions

The next part of the code defines some functions that you'll use in the program. In the function checkbounds(), you'll notice that there's the following line:

```
global boxsize
```

This line is needed because functions don't automatically get access to variables defined outside of them. This line tells Python that we want to use the boxsize variable in this function, and it's declared outside of the function itself.

Perhaps the most confusing section is

```
#add key listeners
window.onkeypress(up, "Up")
window.onkeypress(left, "Left")
window.onkeypress(right, "Right")
window.onkeypress(back, "Down")
window.onkeypress(quitTurtles, "Escape")
```

This code tells the window what to do when various keys are pressed. For example, the first line says to run the function up (which we've already defined) whenever the key "Up" (which corresponds to the up arrow on the keyboard) is pressed.

Looping Through the Game

Next you get to the main loop that runs the game:

```
while not caught:
    cat.setheading(cat.towards(mouse))
    cat.forward(8+difficulty)
    score = score + 1
    if cat.distance(mouse) < 5:
        caught = True
    time.sleep(0.2-(0.01*difficulty))
```

This code uses a different type of loop. The `while` loop take this form:

```
while condition:
    loop code
```

They keep on looping the code as long as the `condition` is True. In the initial list of variables at the beginning of the code, you set the variable `caught` to `False`:

```
caught = False
```

Thus in this case, `not caught` is the condition (and it's true at the start since `not False` is `True`), so the program keeps running until you change it to true because `not True` is `False`. It all sounds a bit complex when phrased like this, but an easy way to think of it is that the word not just swaps `True` and `False` around.

`time.sleep()` tells Python to stop for a certain number of seconds. In this case you reduce the amount of time it sleeps as the difficulty level (which is a variable set to a number that the user enters) increases. You should also be able to see that the distance the cat moves increases with difficulty.

At this point you may be wondering how on earth you're supposed to remember all the
methods that are associated with the various modules. For example, how did you know to
use `forward(10)` instead of `forwards(10)` or `move_forwards(10)`, or for that matter,
how did you know there was a method to move forwards at all? Well, you don't have to have
superhuman memory to use Python; you just need to know where to look. When you're in
IDLE 3, press F1 to open your web browser and display the Python documentation. There's
some really useful information here and it's well worth exploring. For information on the turtle
module, just enter `turtle` into quick search, and then select the top response. You'll see that
we've only touched on its methods here.

TIP

Summary

This brings us to the end of our really quick tour of Python. Hopefully the programs made some sense to you. Don't worry if you didn't understand a hundred percent of everything, because we're going to look at the different parts of Python in a bit more detail in the next chapter. However, hopefully you now understand the following:

- Python programs consist of a series of instructions and they run from top to bottom.

- You can control the way Python moves through your program using loops and if statements.

- You don't have to do everything yourself. You can import modules and use methods to take care of much of the work.

- Functions allow you to reuse code, which makes your programs easier to understand and maintain.

- Variables allow you to store information so you can use it later.

- It's really easy to draw flowers and make games in Python.

Remember, when programming there's often more than one way to do something, and if you can pick the right way (or at least, not the wrong way) you'll make your life easier. However, it's not always easy to know if a way is right or wrong, so we'll finish this chapter with Python's own advice on the matter. In your Python interpreter, type:

```
>>> import this
```

`this` is a special module that outputs some useful Python advice when it's imported. Now that you have a feel for Python, let's move on and dig into the code a bit deeper.

Chapter 3
Python Basics

IN THE PREVIOUS chapter, we got straight into programming in Python. Hopefully that gave you a good idea of what Python is, but you probably have quite a few questions about how it all worked. In this chapter, we'll aim to answer those questions, and go into detail about exactly how to create your own programs in Python. Then, in later chapters, we'll look at the specific features of Python that help you write particular types of programs for the Raspberry Pi.

Variables, Values, and Types

In the last chapter, we saw that variables can store data we want to use elsewhere. They're one of the most powerful tools programmers can use, and now we'll look at what they actually are. If you've programmed before in a different language, you may notice that Python does things a little differently here.

In the Python interpreter, enter the statement:

```
>>> score = 0
```

All this does is tell Python that you want to use score as a new name for the value 0. After this point, whenever Python sees score, it will insert the value 0. To demonstrate this, try entering the following:

```
>>> print(score)
```

Remember that Python executes our instructions in order, and you must give score a value before you use it. Otherwise, Python will produce an error.

If you want `score` to point to some other value, you just assign it a new one, such as:

```
>>> score = 1
```

Now, Python will substitute 1 every time it sees the word `score` (you can verify this by running `print(score)` again). You can update a variable using its own value:

```
>> score = score + 1
```

Variables can have almost any name you want, but they must start with a letter or an underscore, and it can't be the same as a word that's used elsewhere in Python (such as `if`, `for`, and so on). The convention in Python is to name variables in lowercase and to separate individual words with an underscore, like so:

```
high_score = 1000
```

In the previous examples, the values have all been numbers, but this doesn't have to be the case. They can also be text, such as:

```
player_name = "Ben"
```

We can even switch a name between numbers and text, such as:

```
>>> our_variable = 1000
>>> print(our_variable)
>>> our_variable = "Some Text"
>>> print(our_variable)
```

However, the value that a variable currently points to has a particular type.

Values Have Types

When you see a number 3, you probably just see that, a 3. It doesn't matter if it's in a sentence or a sum, 3 always means 3. Python, however, sees it differently. Every piece of data has to have a type associated with it so it knows what it's dealing with. You can find out what type Python has associated with a bit of data by using the `type()` function. In a Python interpreter, enter:

```
>>> type(3)
<class 'int'>

>>> type("3")
<class 'str'>
```

The first one, Python will inform you, is an `int` (short for integer—basically a whole number), whereas the second is a `str` (short for string—a piece of text). That is because Python sees the number three differently from the character 3. To see the difference, enter these two lines:

```
>>> 3+3
6

>>> "3" + "3"
33
```

The first will add the two numbers together whilst the second will join the two pieces of text together. As you can see, it's vitally important that you don't mix up your types or you could get some pretty interesting results. To discover some more types, enter:

```
>>>type(3.0)
<class 'float'>

>>>type(3>2)
<class 'bool'>
```

The first will give you `float` (a floating-point number, which is any number with a decimal point). The second gives you `bool` (a Boolean, which can take just one of two values: `True` and `False`).

Storing Numbers

The type of a particular piece of data affects what Python can do with it. We'll start with numbers (both `int` and `float` types, but not strings even if they contain numbers). There are two types of operations we can do with numbers: comparisons and numerical operations. Comparisons, as listed in Table 3-1, take two numbers and return a `bool`.

Table 3-1   Comparison Operators for Numerical Types

Operator	Meaning	Example
<	Less than	3<2→`False`
>	Greater than	3>2→`True`
==	Equal	3==3→`True`
<=	Less than or equal to	3<=3→`True`
>=	Greater than or equal to	3>=4→`False`
!=	Not equal to	3!=4→`True`

Meanwhile, numerical operations return a numerical data type and are shown in Table 3-2.

Table 3-2   **Numerical Operators**

Operator	Meaning	Example
+	Addition	2 + 2→4
-	Subtraction	3 – 2→1
*	Multiplication	2 * 3→6
/	Division	10/2→5
%	Divide and take the remainder	5%2→1
**	To the power	4 ** 2→16
int()	Convert to integer	int(3.2)→3
float()	Convert to float	float(2)→2.0

You can test any of these operators by typing them into the Python interpreter. For example:

```
>>> 3!=3
False
```

If you're using numerical operators in your program, you'll usually want to capture the value they return in a variable. For example:

```
>>> number_1 = 10
>>> number_2 = number_1**2
```

Keeping Text in Strings

The `string` type allows you to store any chunks of text that you need. To create a string, simply enclose the data in either single or double quote marks. As far as Python is concerned, either type of quotation is fine. We prefer to use double quotes because this doesn't cause problems when creating strings that have apostrophes in them, but this is by no means universal and some programmers prefer single quotes because they're easier to type.

This data type is a little different from the others because, in many ways, a string isn't a single piece of data but a collection of letters. The name comes from the fact that they are a string of characters.

As with numbers, Python gives us operations we can perform on them. Table 3-3 shows a few of the most useful.

Table 3-3 　**String Operations**

Operator	Meaning	Example
string[x]	Get the xth character (starts from 0th)	"abcde"[1] → "b"
string[x:y]	Get all the characters from the xth to the yth	"abcde"[1:3] → "bc"
string[:y]	Get every character up until the yth	"abcde"[:3] → "abc"
string[x:]	Get every character from the xth to the end	"abcde"[3:] → "de"
len(string)	Return the length of the string	len("abcde") → 5
string+string	Join two strings together	"abc"+"def" → "abcdef"

Boolean: True or False

The last data type that we'll look at here is bool. This is the simplest because there are just two values it can take: True and False. Note that in Python, these values must always have a capital first letter and aren't surrounded by any quotation marks. Although this data type isn't often stored in variables (although it can be as we saw last chapter), it is often used in conditions for if statements and loops, which we'll cover in more detail a bit later in this chapter. The main operators on this are and, or, and not.

not simply switches the value, so:

```
>>> not True
False

>>> not False
True
```

and takes two bools and returns True if they are both True, and False otherwise, so:

```
>>> True and False
False

>>> False and False
False

>>> True and True
True
```

or also takes two bools, but it returns True if either one of them is True, so:

```
>>> True or False
True

>>> True or True
True

>>> False or False
False
```

Converting Between Data Types

It is possible to convert between data types using the functions int(), float(), and str(). They convert other data types to integers, floating-points, and strings, respectively. However, these can't just change anything to anything. If you change a float to an int, Python will round down any fractions. Strings can be converted to numbers only if they contain only digits. On the other hand, more or less anything can be converted into a string. Take a look at the following examples:

```
>>> print(int(3.9))
3

>>> print(str(True))
True

>>> print(float("Three point two"))
Traceback (most recent call last):
  File "<stdin>", line 1, in <module>
ValueError: could not convert string to float: 'Three point two'
```

Test Your Knowledge

Following are a series of Python statements. See if you can work out what each of them means to Python. When you think you know, type them into a Python interpreter to check. Hint: some will produce errors.

- int("two")

- print(str(3+3) + "3")

- type(3=3)

- "4" == 4

- `"Python"[4]`

- `(3 > 2) or (2 > 3)`

- `not "True"`

- `2345[2]`

- `str((not True) and (not False))`

- `10 % 3`

Exercise 1

What are the variables, what values do they hold, and what are the types of these values in the following program? The answers are at the end of the chapter. If you're unsure, try typing them into Python and inserting `print` statements in various parts of the code to see what's going on. This is an excellent way of finding out what a particular piece of code is doing when it's not running as you expect.

```python
prompt_text = "Enter a number: "
user_in = input(prompt_text)
user_num = int(user_in)

for i in range(1,10):
    print(i, " times ", user_num, " is ", i*user_num)

even = (user_num % 2) == 0

if even:
    print(user_num, " is even")
else:
    print(user_num, " is odd")
```

Storing Values in Structures

As well as the simple data types, Python allows us to bring data together in various ways to create structures. The simplest structures are called *sequences*. These store information one piece after the next. There are two sorts: lists and tuples. In many ways, they're very similar. Take a look at the following example:

```python
>>> list_1 = [1,2,3,4]
>>> tuple_1 = (1,2,3,4)
>>> list_1[1]
2
>>> tuple_1[1]
2
```

You create a list by enclosing it in square brackets, whilst tuples are surrounded by round ones. So far, they seem to be working the same. You can retrieve an individual item from either by putting square brackets after it with an index. Note that indexes start at 0, so `list_1[0]` and `tuple_1[0]` will retrieve the first item in either sequence.

The difference between lists and tuples comes when you try to update them:

```
>>> list_1[1]=99

>>> list_1
[1, 99, 3, 4]

>>> tuple_1[1]=99
Traceback (most recent call last):
  File "<pyshell#35>", line 1, in <module>
    t1[1]=99
TypeError: 'tuple' object does not support item assignment
```

As you can see, you can update an item in a list, but not in a tuple. However, whilst you can't update a tuple, you can simply overwrite the lot. In this case, you're simply telling Python to point the variable `tuple_1` to a new tuple and discard the old one.

```
>>> tuple_1
(1, 2, 3, 4)

>>> tuple_1=(1,99,2,4)

>>> tuple_1
(1, 99, 2, 4)
```

In the previous section we covered strings. These are just sequences of characters, and the operations you can perform on them you can also perform on lists and tuples. For example, continuing to use `list_1` and `tuple_1`:

```
>>> len(list_1)
4

>>> tuple_1[:3]
[1, 99, 2]
```

You can flick back to Table 3-3 for a recap on the string operators we can use here.

The individual items in lists and tuples can be any data type, including lists and tuples themselves. If you so wish, you can have a list of lists of lists of lists; although if you do, the chances are that your code is going to be pretty hard to understand. Having a list of lists, however, can often be very useful. You can think of this a bit like a table, so:

```
>>> list_2 =
  [["a","b","c"],["d","e","f"],["g","h","i"],["j","k","l"]]
```

You can get items out of it by indexing both the main list and the sublist:

```
>>> list_2[2][0]
'g'

>>> list_2[0]
['a', 'b', 'c']

>>> list_2[0][1:]
['b', 'c']
```

Take a look at Table 3-4 to see how this corresponds to a table.

Table 3-4 An Illustration of a Two-Dimensional List

list_2[0][0] = "a"	list_2[1][0] = "d"	list_2[2][0] = "g"	list_2[3][0] = "j"
list_2[0][1] = "b"	list_2[1][1] = "e"	list_2[2][1] = "h"	list_2[3][1] = "k"
list_2[0][2] = "c"	list_2[1][2] = "f"	list_2[2][2] = "i"	list_2[3][2] = "l"

There are a few operations that we can carry out to manipulate lists. Some of the most useful are listed in Table 3-5.

Table 3-5 Operations on Lists (in All the Examples, Use list_3 = [3,2,1])

Operator	Meaning	Example
list.append(item)	Add item to the end of the list	list_3.append(0) → [3,2,1,0]
list.extend(list_2)	Join list_2 to the end of list	list_3.extend([0,-1]) → [3,2,1,0,-1]

continued

Table 3-5   **continued**

Operator	Meaning	Example
`list.pop(x)`	Return and remove the xth item	See below
`list.insert (x, item)`	Insert item at the xth position	`list_3.insert(99,1)` → `[3, 99, 2, 1]`
`list.sort()`	Sort the list	`list_3.sort()` → `[1,2,3]`
`list.index(item)`	Return the position of the first occurrence of item in list	`List_3.index(2)` →1
`list.count(item)`	Count how many times item appears in list	`list_3.count(2)` →1
`list. remove(item)`	Remove the first occurrence of item in list	`list_3.remove(2)` → `[3,1]`

Most of these examples are a little different to the ones we've given before, because each of them (except `index()` and `sort()`) changes the value of `list_3` rather than returning anything. So, for example, to run the first one in the Python interpreter, you'll also need a line to show the final value of `list_3`.

```
>>> list_3 = [3,2,1]
>>> list_3.append(0)
>>> list_3
[3, 2, 1, 0]
```

`index()` and `count()`, however, return a value, so:

```
>>> list_3.index(2)
1
```

`pop(x)` is a little unusual as it does two things. Firstly, it returns the value at the xth position, but it also removes it from the list. Try out the following example to get a feel for what it does:

```
>>> list_3 = [1,2,3]
>>> out = list_3.pop(1)
>>> out
2
>>> list_3
[1, 3]
```

As mentioned, tuples are a lot like lists except that they can't be changed. Any of the list operators that don't change the value can also be used on tuples, so:

```
>>> tuple_2 = (1,2,3)
>>> tuple_2.index(2)
1
>>> tuple_2.sort()
Traceback (most recent call last):
  File "<pyshell#91>", line 1, in <module>
    tuple_2.sort()
AttributeError: 'tuple' object has no attribute 'sort'
```

Non-Sequential Values in Dictionaries and Sets

You can think of lists and tuples as groups of items that each have a number associated with them as an index. For example, in the list `["a", "b", "c", "d"]`, a has the index 0, b has the index 1, and so on. However, what if you want to use an index that isn't a number? For example, perhaps you wanted to create a data structure that linked your friends' nicknames to their real names. It could work like this:

```
>>> real_name["Benny"]
'Benjamin Everard'
```

In Python, you can do this using *dictionaries*, and you create them using curly braces. You can create the `real_name` dictionary using:

```
>>> real_name = {"Benny" : "Benjamin Everard",
                 "Alex" : "Alexander Bradbury"}
```

Items in a dictionary are known as key/value pairs, where the first part (in this case, the nickname) is the key and the second part (the full name) is the value. You can add a new item to a dictionary by simply specifying a new key and giving it a value:

```
>>> real_name["Liz"] = "Elizabeth Upton"
>> real_name
{'Alex': 'Alexander Bradbury', 'Benny': 'Benjamin Everard',
    'Liz': 'Elizabeth Upton'}
```

You may be wondering why you need indexes or keys at all. In fact, you don't. Python also allows you to just lump a load of data together with no indexing or ordering using the set structure. For example:

```
>>> herbs = {'thyme', 'dill', 'corriander'}
>>> spices = {'cumin', 'chilli', 'corriander'}
>>> "thyme" in herbs
True
```

As you can see, Python has the in operator to test if a particular value is in a set. There are also a few operators that are specific to sets. Take a look at Table 3-6.

Table 3-6   **Operations on Sets (Examples Use the Sets Previously Defined)**

Operator	Meaning	Example
set_1 & set_2	Return the items that are in both sets	herbs & spices→'corriander'
set_1 | set_2	Combine the items in both sets	herbs | spices→{'dill', 'thyme', 'chilli', 'corrian-der', 'cumin'}
set_1 - set_2	The items in set_1 that aren't in set_2	herbs – spices→{'dill', 'thyme'}
set_1 ^ set_2	The items that are in set_1 or set_2, but not both	herbs ^ spices→{'dill', 'cumin', 'thyme', 'chilli'}

Test Your Knowledge

What do you think the following will do? Try to work it out, then enter them into the Python interpreter to find out. Remember, some of them will produce errors.

- ```
["a", "b", "c"].index("c")
```
- ```
(3,2,1).pop(2)
```
- ```
{1,3,5} & {2,4,6}
```
- ```
{1,2,3} & {1}
```
- ```
3 in {1,2,3} ^ {3,4,5}
```
- ```
"abcde".remove("c")
```
- ```
3 not in (1,2,3)
```

# Controlling the Way the Program Flows

while loops are the simplest kind of loop. They have a condition that can be anything with a bool data type, and they will continue looping until that condition is False. If that condition never becomes False, then they will simply keep looping forever. For example:

```
>>> while True:
    print("Ben is awesome")
```

Hopefully, you'll remember this code block from the previous chapter. There's a colon after the condition, and then the next line is indented. Anything that is indented is considered
```

part of the code block. To run this in the Python interpreter, you'll need to press Return after the print line, then backspace to remove the automatic tab, then Return once more. This lets Python know that the code block has finished and you want to execute it.

If you find yourself stuck in an infinite loop like this, you can stop it by pressing Ctrl+C.

The condition can be as complicated as you like, as long as it comes back to either `True` or `False`. However, in order for it to eventually terminate, it will have to include one or more variables that can change inside the loop. For example, take a look at the main loop in the following number-guessing game.

```
import random
secret = int(random.uniform(0,10))
print("I'm thinking of a number between zero and ten."
      , "Can you guess what it is?")
guess = 11

while guess != secret:
    guess = int(input("Take a guess: "))

print("Well done!")
```

Note that this program will throw an error if you enter text that isn't a number. We'll look at how to fix that shortly, but first we'll take a look at a different type of loop.

Moving Through Data with for Loops

`for` loops are used to move through pieces of data, and perform the instructions in the loop on each piece of data in turn. These are commonly used with `range(x,y)`, which moves through every number between x and y. For example, you can calculate the 12 times table with:

```
>>> for i in range(1,13):
    print(i, " times twelve is ", i*12)
```

`range()` can take another parameter that sets the gap between two numbers. For example, if you change `range(1,13)` to `range(2,14,2)` it will go through all the even multiples of 12. We can also use for loops to move through any of our sequence data types (including strings) and sets, so the following are also all valid:

```
>>> for i in [1,2,3,4,5,6,7,8,9,10,11,12]:    print(i, " times 12 is
  ", i * 12)
>>> for i in (1,2,3,4,5,6,7,8,9,10,11,12):
```

```
   print(i, " times 12 is ", i*12)
>>> for i in {1,2,3,4}:
   print(i, " times 12 is ", i*12)
>>> for i in "123456789":
   print(i, " times 12 is ", int(i)*12)
```

Although the last one is a pretty good example of using the wrong data type for a task. The set is a little different from the others because you can't specify the order—it's just a bunch of items. The following will produce the same result.

```
>>> for i in {1,2,3,4}:
   print(i, " times 12 is ", i*12)

>>> for i in {4,3,2,1}:
   print(i, " times 12 is ", i*12)
```

Dictionaries are the odd data type out because they don't just hold items, but key/value pairs. You can still use `for` loops to move through them, but you have to do it in a slightly different way:

```
>>> real_name = {"Benny": "Benjamin Everard",
                 "Alex": "Alexander Bradbury"}
>>> for key,value in real_name.items():
   print("The real name of " + key + " is " + value)
```

As with sets, you can't specify the order that the loop goes through the data in. In fact, caring about the order the loop goes through the data is a pretty good indication that you should be using a sequence data structure such as a list or tuple rather than an unordered data structure like a set or dictionary.

In the previous examples, `i`, `key`, and `value` are just variable names and can be changed to whatever you want.

Going Deeper with Nested Loops

When programming, you often have to go through more than one thing at a time, such as in the following program, which calculates all the prime numbers between 1 and 30.

```
for i in range(1,30):
    is_prime = True
    for k in range(2,i):
```

```
        if (i%k) == 0:
            print(i, " is divisible by ", k)
            is_prime = False
    if is_prime:
        print(i, " is prime ")
```

Note how the indent level is increased, so inside the first loop there is one indent, then inside the second loop there are two. This is important so Python knows which bits of code belong to which code blocks and where each block ends.

When nesting loops like this, you do need to be a little careful to avoid slowing down your programs too much. The previous example runs quite quickly, but if you try to calculate all the prime numbers under 3,000 (simply add an extra two zeros to the 30 in the first line) then it takes much longer. Not only because there are a hundred times as many outer loops, but as you get into the higher numbers, each inner loop takes longer as well. The whole thing quickly grinds to a crawl (if you try this out, remember Ctrl+C will stop the program). Fortunately, there are a couple of things you can do. Try out the following:

```
for i in range(1,3000,2):
    is_prime = True
    for k in range(2,i):
        if (i%k) == 0:
            print(i, " is divisible by ", k)
            is_prime = False
            break
    if is_prime:
        print(i, " is prime ")
```

The first thing this does is skip over all the even numbers using `range(1,3000,2)`. Of course, this will miss the first prime number, but we already know that one. Straight away, this saves half the time. The second thing we did, though, saves far more. You'll notice the line containing just `break` in the `if` block. Since we're calculating prime numbers, we don't care about all the factors of a number, so once we've found one we know that the number's not prime. The `break` statement then ends the current loop, in this case the inner one, and continues execution from the bottom (at the line `if is_prime:`). These two optimisations allow the program to run much faster.

Branching Execution with if Statements

As well as looping round sections of code, you can also control the flow of a Python program by branching off and executing different pieces of code depending on a condition. This is done using the `if` statement that you've already seen quite a few times, but we'll briefly recap it. `if` statements, like `while` loops, take a condition that has to have the `bool` data type. They can also have additional `elif` (else-if) statements, and an `else` statement. For example:

```
num = int(input("enter a number: "))
if num%2 == 0:
    print("Your number is divisible by 2")
elif num%3 == 0:
    print("your number is divisible by 3")
elif num%5 == 0:
    print("your number is divisible by 5")
else:
    print("your number isn't divisible by 2,3 or 5")
```

`if` statements only execute at most one block. Once Python finds a condition that is `True`, it'll execute that block and then exit the `if` statement. So if you entered 10 as your number, it will only say it's divisible by 2, and won't test if it's divisible by 5 (if you wanted to do that, you'd need to use a separate `if` block, not an `elif` statement). The `else` block is executed if none of the conditions are `True`. As you've seen in other examples, if blocks don't have to have `elif` or `else` statements. If there's no `else` statement, and none of the conditions are `True`, then it simply exits the `if` block without executing anything.

Catching Exceptions

If you happen to be a mischievous sort of person, you may have noticed that the previous example will throw an error if you enter anything other than a digit. This is because Python can't convert arbitrary strings into numbers and so doesn't know what to do. Whenever Python doesn't know what to do, it throws an exception. So far, we've been letting these go, and when they do, they crash the program.

However, if you know that a particular section of code is likely to throw an exception, you can tell Python to look out for it, and let the program know what to do if it encounters such a problem. This is done in the following way:

```
try:
    code where there might be a problem
except type_of_error:
    code to run if there's an error
```

You can tell what type of error it is, because Python will tell you. For example:

```
>>> num = int(input("Enter a number: "))
Enter a number: dasd
Traceback (most recent call last):
```

```
  File "<pyshell#176>", line 1, in <module>
    num = int(input("Enter a number: "))
ValueError: invalid literal for int() with base 10: 'dasd'
```

Here you can see it's a `ValueError`, so the previous example becomes:

```
is_number = False
num = 0

while not is_number:
    is_number = True
    try:
        num = int(input("enter a number: "))
    except ValueError:
        print("I said a number!")
        is_number = False

if num%2 == 0:
    print("Your number is divisible by 2")
elif num%3 == 0:
    print("your number is divisible by 3")
elif num%5 == 0:
    print("your number is divisible by 5")
else:
    print("your number isn't divisible by 2,3 or 5")
```

Exercise 2

Try to fix the number-guessing game from the start of this section using a `try` statement to catch exceptions caused by the users entering bad data.

Making Code Reusable with Functions

We've already used quite a few functions. For example, `print()` and `input()`. These standard functions are built into Python, but you can also build your own to perform whatever you want to do. You did this in the previous chapter, so we'll just re-cap it here. Take a look at:

```
>>> def square(num):
    return num**2
>>> square(4)
16
```

This code defines a function called `square` and then uses it to calculate the square of 4. When you use it, you need to enter a single number enclosed in brackets after it—this is known as a *parameter*. When the function is run, the name that you've given the parameter (in this case num) takes the value of the parameter. Somewhere in the function there can also be a `return` statement that's used to send data back to the main program. If there's more than one `return` statement, Python will finish executing the function after the first `return` it reaches.

You can also create functions with more than one parameter. For example, the following program has a function that takes two parameters and returns the largest.

```
def biggest(a,b):
    if a>b:
        return a
    else:
        return b

print("The biggest of 2 and 3 is ", biggest(2,3))
print("The biggest of 10 and 5 is ", biggest(10,5))
```

So far, this all works well, but what about a function that changes the data? Take a look at the following program:

```
def add_one(num):
    num = num + 1
    return num

number_1 = 1
number_2 = add_one(number_1)

print("number_1: ", number_1)
print("number_2: ", number_2)
```

Before you run it, think about what you expect it to output. It's pretty clear that number_2 will be 2, but what should number_1 be? Should it be 1 because we set it to 1 in our main program, or should it be 2 because we passed it to add_one() and there it changed?

When you run it, you'll find that number_1 stays as 1. That's because in the line:

```
num = num + 1
```

you're effectively telling Python that you don't want num to have its old value (which was the same as number_1), but to give it a new value that's one larger.

However, *mutable* data types such as lists, sets, and objects can change. If we pass one of these to a function and change it, the original will change. Take a look at:

```
def add_item(list_1):
    list_1.append(1)
    return list_1


list_2 = [2,3,4]
list_3 = add_item(list_2)
print("list_2: ", list_2)
print("list_3: ", list_3)
```

If you run this, you'll get:

```
list_2:   [2, 3, 4, 1]
list_3:   [2, 3, 4, 1]
```

Usually, this shouldn't cause a problem, but occasionally you may come across a situation where you don't want this to happen. For these cases, you can use copy.deepcopy(), although first, you'll have to import copy. So, if you change the previous example to:

```
import copy
def add_item(list_1):
    list_1.append(1)
    return list_1


list_2 = [2,3,4]
list_3 = add_item(copy.deepcopy(list_2))
print("list_2: ", list_2)
print("list_3: ", list_3)
```

You'll get:

```
list_2:   [2, 3, 4]
list_3:   [2, 3, 4, 1]
```

Optional Parameters

Sometimes you may want to create a function that has parameters that are sometimes needed, and sometimes not. For example, you may want to create a function `increment()` that can take two numbers and add them. However, if only one parameter is given, the function just adds one to it. You do this by specifying a default value (in this case 1) for the parameter like so:

```python
def increment(num1=1, num2):
  return num2 + num1
```

The only thing you need to know about these is that the parameters that can be omitted must come after the ones that have to be there.

Bringing Everything Together

We've covered a lot of bits so far in this chapter, but it might not be completely clear how to bring them all together to create the programs you want. In this section, you'll see an example that uses most of what we've introduced so far to create a simple database of student results at a college.

It'll load some default data, and allow you to edit it. We'll use appropriate data types and structures to hold the various pieces of information, and functions to perform actions on that data. We'll even include a simple menu to let the user manipulate the data.

> **NOTE**   Most of the longer code examples in the book are available for download from the book's companion website at www.wiley.com/go/python-raspberrypi. To avoid potential typos, you can download and copy and paste the text into your IDE or code editor.

The code is as follows (you can also find it on the book's website as `chapter3-student-1.py`).

```python
students = [["Ben", {"Maths": 67, "English": 78, "Science": 72}],
            ["Mark", {"Maths": 56, "Art": 64, "History": 39,
             "Geography": 55}],
            ["Paul", {"English": 66, "History": 88}]]

grades = ((0, "FAIL"),(50, "D"),(60,"C"),(70, "B"), (80,"A"),
          (101, "CHEAT!"))

def print_report_card(report_student=None):
```

```
    for student in students:
        if (student[0] == report_student) or
            (report_student == None):
            print("Report card for student ", student[0])
            for subject, mark in student[1].items():
                for grade in grades:
                    if mark < grade[0]:
                        print(subject, " : ", prev_grade)
                        break
                    prev_grade = grade[1]

def add_student(student_name):
    global students
    for student in students:
        if student[0] == student_name:
            return "Student already in database"
    students.append([student_name, {}])
    return "Student added successfully"

def add_mark(student_name, subject, mark):
    global students
    for student in students:
        if student[0] == student_name:
            if subject in student[1].keys():
                print(student_name, " already has a mark for ",
                    subject)
                user_input = input("Overwrite Y/N? ")
                if user_input == "Y" or "y":
                    student[1][subject] = mark
                    return "Student's mark updated"
                else:
                    return "Student's mark not updated"
            else:
                student[1][subject] = mark
                return "Student's mark added"
    return "Student not found"

while True:
    print("Welcome to the Raspberry Pi student database")
    print("What can I help you with?")
    print("Enter 1 to view all report cards")
    print("Enter 2 to view the report card for a student")
    print("Enter 3 to add a student")
    print("Enter 4 to add a mark to a student")
```

```python
    print("Enter 5 to exit")

    try:
        user_choice = int(input("Choice: "))
    except ValueError:
        print("That's not a number I recognise")
        user_choice = 0

    if user_choice == 1:
        print_report_card()
    elif user_choice == 2:
        enter_student = input("Which student? ")
        print_report_card(enter_student)
    elif user_choice == 3:
        enter_student = input("Student name? ")
        print(add_student(enter_student))
    elif user_choice == 4:
        enter_student = input("Student name? ")
        enter_subject = input("Subject? ")
        num_error = True
        while num_error:
            num_error = False
            try:
                enter_mark = int(input("Mark? "))
            except ValueError:
                print("I don't recognise that as a number")
                num_error = True
        print(add_mark(enter_student, enter_subject, enter_mark))
    elif user_choice == 5:
        break
    else:
        print("Unknown choice")
    input("Press enter to continue")
print("Goodbye and thank you for using the Raspberry Pi"
    , "Student database")
```

The students' data structure is currently a list of lists with dictionaries. It could equally be a dictionary of dictionaries, or a list of lists containing lists. Try to alter the program to match each of these two scenarios. Which feels more natural?

Exercise 3
Could the data also be held in tuples? Why or why not? See the end of the chapter for the answer.

Building Objects with Classes

Classes allow you to link together data and functions into a single object. In fact, we used them in the previous chapter. Remember the lines:

```
window = turtle.Screen()
babbage = turtle.Turtle()
```

At the time we skipped over them quite briefly, but now we'll look at what they do. The statement `turtle.Turtle()` returns a new object made from the `Turtle` class that's in the `turtle` module. Likewise, `turtle.Screen()` returns an object made from the `Screen` class in the `turtle` module. Basically, classes are the blueprints from which you can create objects. These objects then hold data and have methods that you can call to manipulate that data. Methods are really just functions that are held inside classes.

You've already seen how objects can be useful. In the examples in the last chapter, you didn't have to worry about keeping track of any of the turtle data because it was all held in an object. You just stored the turtle object in a variable called `babbage` and whenever you called a method, it knew everything it needed to. This helped you keep the code clear and easy to use. For example, look at the following code:

```
babbage.forward(100)
```

This moved the turtle forwards and drew the result on the screen. It knew what colour to draw, where the turtle was starting from, and a whole myriad of other information that it needed to draw the line on the screen because it was all stored inside the object.

Let's take a look at what's in a class with a simple example:

```
class Person():
    def __init__(self, age, name):
        self.age = age
        self.name = name

    def birthday(self):
        self.age = self.age + 1

ben = Person(31, "Ben")
paul = Person(42, "Paul")
print(ben.name, ben.age)
print(paul.name, paul.age)
```

There are a few things to notice here. In Python, the normal style is to start all variable, function, and method names with lowercase letters. Classes are the exception, so the `Person` class starts with a capital P. Python won't give you any errors if you don't follow this, but the convention makes it easier to understand other people's code. You can see that methods are defined much like functions, except that the parameters always start with `self`. This brings in the local variables. In this example, these local variables are `self.age` and `self.name`. These are re-created for each instance of the class. In this example, we create two objects from the class `Person` (these are known as instances of the class). Each one of these has its own copy of `self.age` and `self.person`. We can access these from outside the object (as we have done in the `print` methods). They're known as the *attributes* of the class `Person`.

There are also two methods. `__init__` is a special method that every class has. It's called when an instance is created or "initiated". So, the line `ben = Person(31, "Ben")` creates a new object from the `Person` class and calls the `__init__` method with the parameters `(31, "Ben")`. This sets up the attributes. The second method, `birthday()`, shows how using classes means we don't have to keep track of the data outside of these classes. To give a `Person` object a birthday, just run (for example):

```
ben.birthday()
```

This increases their age by one.

Sometimes, you won't want to create a class from scratch, but build a new class that's built upon an existing one. For example, if we wanted to build a class that holds information about parents, they would also have ages, names, and birthdays, so it would be a waste if we had to rewrite this code just for the `Parent` class. Python allows us to inherit from other classes, such as in the following:

```
class Person():
    def __init__(self, age, name):
        self.age = age
        self.name = name

    def birthday(self):
        self.age = self.age + 1

class Parent(Person):
    def __init__(self, age, name):
        Person.__init__(self,age,name)
        self.children = []

    def add_child(self, child):
        self.children.append(child)

    def print_children(self):
        print("The children of ", self.name, " are:")
```

```
    for child in self.children:
        print(child.name)

john = Parent(60, "John")
ben = Person(32, "Ben")
print(john.name, john.age)
john.add_child(ben)
john.print_children()
```

Person is the superclass of Parent, and Parent is a subclass of Person. By adding a class name in the brackets after a class definition, it becomes a superclass of the one you're defining. You can call the __init__ method of the superclass, and automatically get access to all the attributes and methods of the superclass without having to rewrite the code for the class. This is called *inheritance* because the subclasses inherit the features of the superclass.

The big advantage of classes is they make it really easy to reuse code. As we saw in the previous chapter, it was simple to manipulate the turtle without worrying too much about how it actually did what it did. Because the turtle class encapsulated everything, you just had to know the methods and you could use it without any problems. Throughout this book, you'll see how using classes from outside modules makes it really easy to create quite complex programs without worrying about the technicalities of how these things work.

Take a look at the following code, which is a rewrite of the student database using classes to get a feel for how classes work (chapter3-student-2.py on the website).

```
student_data= [["Ben", {"Maths": 67, "English": 78,
                    "Science": 72}],
        ["Mark", {"Maths": 56, "Art": 64, "History": 39,
                    "Geography": 55}],
        ["Paul", {"English": 66, "History": 88}]]

grades = ((0, "FAIL"),(50, "D"),(60,"C"),(70, "B"), (80,"A"),
        (101, "CHEAT!"))

class Student():
    def __init__(self, name, marks):
        self.name = name
        self.marks = marks

    def print_report_card(self):
        print("Report card for student ", self.name)
        for subject, mark in self.marks.items():
            for i in grades:
```

```python
            if mark < i[0]:
                print(subject, " : ", prev_grade)
                break
            prev_grade = i[1]

    def add_mark(self, subject, mark):
        if subject in self.marks.keys():
            print(student_name, " already has a mark for ",
                subject)
            user_input = input("Overwrite Y/N? ")
            if user_input == "Y" or "y":
                self.marks[subject] = mark
                return "Student's mark updated"
            else:
                return "Student's mark not updated"
        else:
            self.marks[subject] = mark
            return "Student's mark added"

class Students():
    def __init__(self, all_students):
        self.students = []
        for student, mark in all_students:
            self.add_student(student, mark)

    def add_student(self,student_name, marks = {}):
        if self.exists(student_name):
            return "Student already in database"
        else:
            self.students.append(Student(student_name, marks))
            return "Student added"

    def print_report_cards(self, student_name = None):
        for student in self.students:
            if student_name == None or student.name:
                student.print_report_card()

    def exists(self, student_name):
        for student in self.students:
            if student_name == student.name:
                return True
        return False

    def add_mark(self, student_name, subject, mark):
        for student in self.students:
```

```
            if student_name == student.name:
                return student.add_mark(subject, mark)
        return "Student not found"

students = Students(student_data)
print(students.students)
while True:
    print("Welcome to the Raspberry Pi student database")
    print("What can I help you with?")
    print("Enter 1 to view all report cards")
    print("Enter 2 to view the report card for a student")
    print("Enter 3 to add a student")
    print("Enter 4 to add a mark to a student")
    print("Enter 5 to exit")

    try:
        user_choice = int(input("Choice: "))
    except ValueError:
        print("That's not a number I recognise")
        user_choice = 0

    if user_choice == 1:
        students.print_report_cards()
    elif user_choice == 2:
        enter_student = input("Which student? ")
        students.print_report_cards(enter_student)
    elif user_choice == 3:
        enter_student = input("Student name? ")
        print(students.add_student(enter_student))
    elif user_choice ==4:
        enter_student = input("Student name? ")
        enter_subject = input("Subject? ")
        num_error = True
        while num_error:
            num_error = False
            try:
                enter_mark = int(input("Mark? "))
            except ValueError:
                print("I don't recognise that as a number")
                num_error = True
        print(students.add_mark(enter_student, enter_subject,
                                enter_mark))
    elif user_choice == 5:
        break
    else:
```

```
        print("Unknown choice")
    input("Press enter to continue")

print("Goodbye and thank you for using the Raspberry"
      , "Pi Student database")
```

Getting Extra Features from Modules

You've seen `import` lines quite a few times by now, but we haven't really explained what they do. Actually, it's incredibly simple—`import` just brings Python code from another file into the current program. If you create a file called `module_example.py` that contains the following:

```
print("Hello World")
```

Save it in your home directory (that is, `/home/pi` for the default user). Now, you enter a Python interpreter session in IDLE 3 and enter the following:

```
>>> import module_example
Hello World
```

Of course, this is a fairly pointless module. Usually they contain functions or objects that can then be used. Change `module_example` to:

```
def hello():
   print ("Hello World")
```

You'll have to restart IDLE for it to pick this up. Once you've done so, you can run:

```
>>> import module_example
>>> module_example.hello()
```

The line `import module_example` brings all the functions and classes into your project and you can access them by prefixing them with the module name. Sometimes, though, you'll only want some of the module. You can import individual parts like this:

```
>>> from module_example import hello
```

Now you can just enter the following to run the function:

```
>>> hello()
```

Notice that you don't need to prefix it with the module name. This is because it's imported into the current namespace. When you do this, you need to make sure that it doesn't clash with any of the other functions or classes you're using. You can even bring everything from a particular module into the current namespace to make it easier to use:

```
>>> from module_example import *
```

With this, you obviously have to be very careful to avoid namespace clashes.

There are a number of advantages to creating modules rather than just putting everything in the same file. It means you can reuse code between projects (remember what we've said about code reuse?). It also means that big projects don't just live in one massive file that's hard to work with. You can also split the various modules up between different members of a group to make it easier to work as a team.

In the remaining chapters, much of what we'll do will revolve round particular modules that help you add really cool features to your Raspberry Pi projects.

Summary

We haven't covered absolutely everything that's in Python. To do that would require a much larger book, and we wouldn't have space to include all the fun stuff we're going to do in the next few chapters. However, we've shown you enough to get started, and hopefully enough to understand most Python programs you see. If you get stuck at any point, just flick back to this chapter, or take a look at the Python documentation (which really does cover everything, but can be a little hard to read). You should now know:

- Variables are places you can store values.
- Values have data types such as `int`, `float`, or `bool`.
- You can group values in lists, tuples, dictionaries, or sets to make them easier to access.
- `while` loops keep repeating until their condition is `False`.
- `for` loops operate on every item in a collection of data.
- Functions help you reuse code so you don't have to repeat it.
- Classes allow you to encapsulate data and methods to make them easier to use.
- There are hundreds of modules that you can import to add extra features to your project.
- You can also create your own modules. This helps split your programs up into manageable files.

Solutions to Exercises

Exercise 1

The variables are

- prompt_text holds "Enter a number: " which is a string.

- user_in holds whatever the user types and is a string.

- user_num holds the number version of whatever the user types, converted into an int.

- i holds the numbers 1 to 9 as int.

- even is a bool that holds True or False (depending on whether the user's number is even).

Exercise 2

```
import random

secret = int(random.uniform(0,10))
print("I'm thinking of a number between zero and ten."
      , "Can you guess what it is?")
guess = 11

while guess != secret:
    try:
        guess = int(input("Take a guess: "))
    except ValueError:
        print("A number! Guess a number!")

print("Well done!")
```

Exercise 3

Technically they could, but it would make the code needlessly complex because you can't change the values. Therefore, you'd have to create new tuples each time rather than simply adding to or amending the current one.

Chapter 4

Graphical Programming

IN THE LAST chapter, we dealt a lot with how to handle data, and how to process it. After all, manipulating data is the fundamental job of a computer. You saw how to build a simple text-driven menu to help control the program. However, such interfaces went out of style in the 1980s. They still have a use in some applications, but these days, most people want to use a mouse (or touch screen).

There are modules using three different graphical toolkits that you're likely to come across—Tk, GTK, and Qt. Tk is quite an old fashioned library that is still used, but lacks some modern features. GTK is a popular toolkit, and the one that LXDE (the default Raspbian desktop) is built in. Qt (sometimes pronounced cute) is a toolkit that was originally developed by Nokia for their ill-fated smartphones. Nokia has since sold it to Digia who continues to develop it. Both GTK and Qt are free to use, and to be honest, there's not much to choose between them. This chapter uses Qt because it's a bit more portable and it's a bit better supported.

You'll need to install the `pyside` module before you can start using it. In LXTerminal, enter the following:

```
sudo apt-get install python3-pyside
```

This may take a little while, so you might want to get a cup of tea.

Graphical User Interface (GUI) Programming

Throughout this book you're going to learn that you can create things in Python very easily if you let the right modules take care of the hard work. Graphical User Interface (GUI) programming is no different. All manner of useful widgets are available; all you have to do is pick which ones you want and add them to your project.

You can also use inheritance. In the last chapter, we introduced classes, and showed that you can create a new class that inherits all the features of a superclass. Here, you'll see how to use this to quickly create new classes that build upon the old ones.

Let's get straight into an example. In Chapter 2 you saw the turtle module, and even how to set it to listen for keypresses. This is a little better than basic text entry, but not by much, so in the first example here, you'll see how to create a simple GUI to control the turtle. Start with the following code (either enter it by hand, or find it in file `chapter4-turtle-start.py` on the website):

```python
import turtle
import sys
from PySide.QtCore import *
from PySide.QtGui import *

class TurtleControl(QWidget):
    def __init__(self, turtle):
        super(TurtleControl, self).__init__()
        self.turtle = turtle

        self.left_btn = QPushButton("Left", self)
        self.right_btn = QPushButton("Right", self)
        self.move_btn = QPushButton("Move", self)
        self.distance_spin = QSpinBox()

        self.controlsLayout = QGridLayout()
        self.controlsLayout.addWidget(self.left_btn, 0, 0)
        self.controlsLayout.addWidget(self.right_btn, 0, 1)
        self.controlsLayout.addWidget(self.distance_spin,1 , 0)
        self.controlsLayout.addWidget(self.move_btn,1 , 1)
        self.setLayout(self.controlsLayout)

        self.distance_spin.setRange(0, 100)
        self.distance_spin.setSingleStep(5)
        self.distance_spin.setValue(20)
```

```
#set up turtle
window = turtle.Screen()
babbage = turtle.Turtle()

# Create a Qt application
app = QApplication(sys.argv)
control_window = TurtleControl(babbage)
control_window.show()

# Enter Qt application main loop
app.exec_()
sys.exit()
```

You can run it now, but none of the buttons will do anything (you'll add that in a bit). First of all, let's take a look at what's going on here. The main part of the code is in the class TurtleControl, which inherits from Qwidget (most of the Qt classes start with the letter Q). By extending from this class, you get all the basic functionality you need. All that you have to do is change it from a generic widget into one that fits the specific needs of this program. In short, you just have to tell it what items you want where.

There are three buttons and a *spinbox* (allows you to enter a number and raise and lower it— take a look at the running program to see how a spinbox works).

In addition to the items that the user will see, there's also a layout that you add these to. Qt has a few different layouts (you'll see another one later), but this program uses the QGridLayout. The grid layout is great for simple control panels like this one. It works on the basis of dividing the window up into a grid, and you tell Qt where you want the item to go in the grid. If the user resizes the window, Qt dynamically resizes the grid to take advantage of the extra space, but still keeping everything in the right portion of the grid.

To display any of the widgets on in the window, you have to add them to the layout. These are the lines like this:

```
self.controlsLayout.addWidget(self.right_btn, 0, 1)
```

The 0 and 1 are the horizontal and vertical coordinates taken from the top-left corner (that is, upside down when compared to graph coordinates). This button, then, is on the top line, one column across from the left side.

When everything's added to the layout, you need to tell the window to use that layout. This is done with the line:

```
self.setLayout(self.controlsLayout)
```

There are also some settings for widgets that you can change to alter their behavior. In this case, the spinbox is adjusted with the following:

```
self.distance_spin.setRange(0, 100)
self.distance_spin.setSingleStep(5)
self.distance_spin.setValue(20)
```

This sets the minimum and maximum values, the amount each click moves it, and the initial value.

Hopefully, you'll recognise the turtle code from before. The last five lines just create the control window and execute it.

Adding Controls

All this code has created a nice looking control window, but it doesn't actually do anything. The next stage, then, is to tell Qt what you want the controls to do. This is done by connecting an event with an action. The events here will be button clicks, and actions will be the methods you want to run when that event happens.

To set this up, add the following code to the end of the __init__ method of the TurtleControl class:

```
    self.move_btn.clicked.connect(self.move_turtle)
    self.right_btn.clicked.connect(self.turn_turtle_right)
    self.left_btn.clicked.connect(self.turn_turtle_left)

def turn_turtle_left(self):
    self.turtle.left(45)

def turn_turtle_right(self):
    self.turtle.right(45)

def move_turtle(self):
    self.turtle.forward(self.distance_spin.value())
```

You'll notice that in each of the connect calls, the method in the parameter doesn't have any brackets after it like methods normally do. That is, it's this:

```
self.move_btn.clicked.connect(self.move_turtle)
```

Rather than this:

```
self.move_btn.clicked.connect(self.move_turtle())
```

This is because when you put the brackets after it, you're telling Python to run the method and send the result as a parameter, as so:

```
def move_turtle(self):
    self.turtle.forward(self.distance_spin.value())
```

However, when you don't put the brackets after the method, you're telling Python to send the method itself as the parameter. That's what you need to do here so Qt knows what to run when the event happens.

You'll find the complete code on the website as `chapter4-turtle.py`. You can see it running in Figure 4-1.

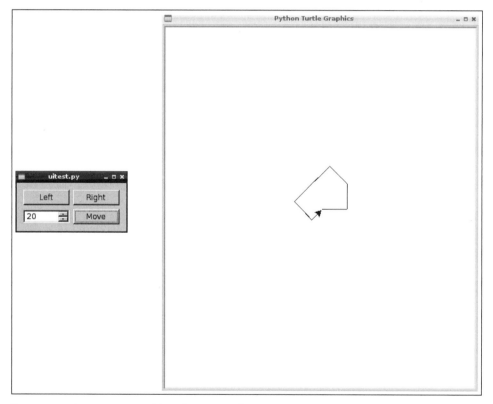

FIGURE 4-1: A mouse-powered interface to a turtle.

That's more or less all the basics of PySide and Qt. It doesn't get much more complex, but there are a huge number of widgets. We won't be able to demonstrate them all, but in the next example, we'll try to show you a large enough range that you get a feel for the toolkit and you should then be able to use the other widgets as you need them.

Test Your Knowledge

Exercise 1

Extend the turtle controller program so that you can change the colour of the turtle as well as move it. We'll give you a hint to get you started. If you change the set up turtle lines to:

```
#set up turtle
window = turtle.Screen()
babbage = turtle.Turtle()
window.colormode(255)
```

Then you'll be able to set the turtle's colour with red, green, and blue values between 1 and 255, such as:

```
turtle.color(100,0,0)
```

Another thing you may find useful are `QLablels`. They let you add pieces of text to the window, and are created like this:

```
self.red_label = QLabel("Red", self)
```

They might be useful for labeling spinboxes (nudge, nudge, wink, wink).

Creating a Web Browser

In the previous example, you saw how easy it was to link things together to create an interface. In this example, we'll use Qt's widgets to build our own web browser (which is really just a set of widgets linked together). You'll see that you don't really need any programming at all; it'll just be linking together different parts of Qt.

First of all you need to create a window for the browser. In the previous example, you created a widget that Qt put in a window for you. That's fine for simple tools, but as you build more powerful applications, it can help to create the window explicitly and add everything to that. By starting with a `QMainWindow`, you can add things like menus. However, that's jumping ahead, and there's quite a bit to add before menus.

The first and most important part of any web browser is the bit that actually shows the web page. You'll learn a bit more about what's actually involved in web pages in Chapter 7, but for the purposes of this chapter, all you need to know is that the QWebView widget can take care of all that for you.

In the previous example, you used a grid layout. This works well for adding a lot of controls to a window, but in this application, you're going to use a box layout. This is a little different. It's created using two different layouts: QVBoxLayout and QHBoxLayout. These are vertical and horizontal boxes, respectively. As you add items to one of these box layouts, they are placed next to each other horizontally or vertically. To create complex layouts, you just need to nest these layouts inside each other in the appropriate way. It can take a little while to get used to this way of laying out widgets on windows, but once you become familiar with it, it's incredibly powerful.

The web browser will have a typical web browser layout. That is, a bar of controls along the top, then most of the window will be taken up with the web page you're viewing. To create this interface, you'll need two layouts—a QHBoxLayout for the controls, and then a QVBoxLayout that'll take both the previous layout box and the QWebView widget. As you resize the window, Qt will adjust the layouts so that the widgets always make the best use of the space.

Hopefully, this will all become clear as you create the browser, so let's get started! The following code creates the window, and adds the appropriate layouts (the file is on the website as chapter4-web-browser-begin.py).

```python
import sys
from PySide.QtCore import *
from PySide.QtGui import *
from PySide.QtWebKit import *


class Browser(QWidget):

    def __init__(self):
        super(Browser, self).__init__()

        self.webview = QWebView(self)
        self.webview.load("http://www.google.com")
        self.setGeometry(0, 0, 800, 600)

        self.menu_bar = QHBoxLayout()
        self.main_layout = QVBoxLayout()
        self.main_layout.addLayout(self.menu_bar)
        self.main_layout.addWidget(self.webview)
```

```
        self.setLayout(self.main_layout)


class BrowserWindow(QMainWindow):
    def __init__(self):
        super(BrowserWindow, self).__init__()
        self.widget = Browser()
        self.setCentralWidget(self.widget)


# Create a Qt application
app = QApplication(sys.argv)
window = BrowserWindow()
window.show()

# Enter Qt application main loop
app.exec_()
sys.exit()
```

This is all the code you need for a really simple web browser. You can run it and it'll start with the Google home page, and you can navigate from there (see Figure 4-2). The code should look familiar to you. The only new pieces are the `QMainWindow` (which will allow you a bit more control later on), the `QWebView` (which, as you can see, is a really easy way to add web browsing), and the box layouts.

FIGURE 4-2: The basics of a web browser.

The box layouts are now fully set up; all you need to do is add items to Browser's self. menu_bar and they'll appear along the top of the screen.

The most basic controls for web browsing are back and forwards buttons. For this task, you can use QPushButtons in the same way you used them in the previous example. Update your code for the Browser class to the following by adding the lines in bold:

```
class Browser(QWidget):

    def __init__(self):
        super(Browser, self).__init__()

        self.webview = QWebView(self)
        self.webview.load("http://www.google.com")
        self.setGeometry(0, 0, 800, 600)

        self.back_btn = QPushButton("<", self)
        self.back_btn.clicked.connect(self.webview.back)
        self.back_btn.setMaximumSize(20,20)

        self.forward_btn = QPushButton(">", self)
        self.forward_btn.clicked.connect(self.webview.forward)
        self.forward_btn.setMaximumSize(20,20)

        self.menu_bar = QHBoxLayout()
        self.menu_bar.addWidget(self.back_btn)
        self.menu_bar.addWidget(self.forward_btn)
        self.main_layout = QVBoxLayout()
        self.main_layout.addLayout(self.menu_bar)
        self.main_layout.addWidget(self.webview)

        self.setLayout(self.main_layout)
```

You can now run the code, and you'll have a browser with a history that you can move back and forwards through. Here again, the QWebView did all of the hard work. It only required connecting the button clicks to the QWebView's forward and back methods.

> **NOTE**   We've mentioned this before, but it's worth mentioning again—when you're programming, there's no point in implementing new features when you can get the functionality from a module. A little time spent learning about a module can save you a lot of time later on.

Unlike the grid layout that you used previously, in box layout, Qt has more freedom to work out what size to draw particular widgets. Sometimes this is a good thing, but other times, you need to give it a bit of guidance. In a web browser, you want the buttons to take up as little space as possible, giving all the free screen area to the web page. To do this, we call the `setMaximumSize()` method on the widgets we add. In the case of the buttons, we make sure they get no bigger than 20×20.

The next feature of the web browser will be a text input where the users can type the address of a site they want to visit. There are a few different Qt widgets for text entry. The most common is `QTextEdit`. This allows the users to display and edit text. Actually, it does more than just straight text, and it can handle images, tables, headings, and other such things.

`QPlainTextEdit` is another common widget that works like `QTextEdit` except that it's designed for just plain text rather than rich text. Both of these are really powerful options that you'll probably use at some point in your programming career. However, they're a bit too much for an address bar since they're designed for multi-line text entry. For a single line of plain text entry (like a URL field), a `QLineEdit` is the best option.

You'll also need a Go button to tell the browser to load the page. To do all this, update the `Browser` class to the following (updates are in bold):

```
class Browser(QWidget):

    def __init__(self):
        super(Browser, self).__init__()

        self.webview = QWebView(self)
        self.webview.load("http://www.google.com")
        self.setGeometry(0, 0, 800, 600)

        self.back_btn = QPushButton("<", self)
        self.back_btn.clicked.connect(self.webview.back)
        self.back_btn.setMaximumSize(20,20)

        self.forward_btn = QPushButton(">", self)
        self.forward_btn.clicked.connect(self.webview.forward)
        self.forward_btn.setMaximumSize(20,20)
```

```
        self.url_entry = QLineEdit(self)
        self.url_entry.setMinimumSize(200,20)
        self.url_entry.setMaximumSize(300,20)

        self.go_btn = QPushButton("Go", self)
        self.go_btn.clicked.connect(self.go_btn_clicked)
        self.go_btn.setMaximumSize(20,20)

        self.menu_bar = QHBoxLayout()
        self.menu_bar.addWidget(self.back_btn)
        self.menu_bar.addWidget(self.forward_btn)
        self.menu_bar.addWidget(self.url_entry)
        self.menu_bar.addWidget(self.go_btn)
        self.menu_bar.addStretch()
        self.main_layout = QVBoxLayout()
        self.main_layout.addLayout(self.menu_bar)
        self.main_layout.addWidget(self.webview)

        self.setLayout(self.main_layout)

    def go_btn_clicked(self):
        self.webview.load(self.url_entry.text())
```

There are a few new bits here. With the URL entry bar, there's a call to the method `setMin` `imumSize()`. Like `setMaximumSize`, this gives Qt some extra information about how you want the window laid out. Another new piece to help Qt lay out the window properly is the `addStretch()` method call. This adds a pseudo-widget that just changes shape to fill up space. In this case, it takes up all the spare room on the right side of the menu bar so Qt pushes all the controls to the left.

You can run it now and try it out. The only thing to note is that it does need you to enter `http://` at the start of the web address. (The technical reason for this is because a URL or Universal Resource Locater requires this as it specifies the protocol. For example, `http://` `yoursite.com/document` could point to something different than `ftp://yoursite.` `com/document`. Most modern browsers allow you to omit this and just assume you mean `http`. However, when a module asks for a URL, it usually needs the protocol prefix.)

In this case, we've added a new method to `Browser` called `go_btn_clicked()` because this gives us a little more power than just connecting methods to events. In this case, it allows you to add a parameter to the call to `webview`'s `load` method with the parameter `self.url_entry.text()`, which just returns the text that the user typed.

At this point, you have what could realistically be called a web browser. There's nothing essential missing, although it's less powerful than mainstream browsers like Firefox, Chrome, or Midori. The next feature we decided to add is a bookmarks picker. We chose this partially because it's a useful feature, and partially because it gives us an excuse to show off another useful Qt widget, the QComboBox.

Combo box is an odd name for something you're almost certainly familiar with. They're boxes with a drop-down arrow that opens a set of choices that users can pick from. If that doesn't seem familiar now, it will be as soon as you see it.

Later on in the book we'll look at some ways you can store information between sessions, but to keep things simple, we won't let the user change or add to the bookmarks. After all, this is a chapter on user interfaces, and we want to stick to that topic.

Add the bold sections of the following to the Browser class (the non-bold sections will let you know where to add it):

```python
self.go_btn = QPushButton("Go", self)
self.go_btn.clicked.connect(self.go_btn_clicked)
self.go_btn.setMaximumSize(20,20)

self.favourites = QComboBox(self)
self.favourites.addItems(["http://www.google.com",
                    "http://www.raspberrypi.org",
                    "http://docs.python.org/3/"])
self.favourites.activated.connect(self.favourite_selected)
self.favourites.setMinimumSize(200,20)
self.favourites.setMaximumSize(300,20)

self.menu_bar = QHBoxLayout()
self.menu_bar.addWidget(self.back_btn)
self.menu_bar.addWidget(self.forward_btn)
self.menu_bar.addWidget(self.url_entry)
self.menu_bar.addWidget(self.go_btn)
self.menu_bar.addStretch()
self.menu_bar.addWidget(self.favourites)
self.main_layout = QVBoxLayout()
self.main_layout.addLayout(self.menu_bar)
self.main_layout.addWidget(self.webview)

self.setLayout(self.main_layout)

def go_btn_clicked(self):
```

```
    self.webview.load(self.url_entry.text())

def favourite_selected(self):
    self.webview.load(self.favourites.currentText())
```

This is all quite straightforward, and if you run the code, you'll see a QComboBox in action.

As with the URL entry, we just call self.webview.load, but this time with a parameter that grabs the currently selected text from the combo box.

There are only two controls left to add to the menu bar, so let's make them in one edit. The first is a search bar that lets users enter a search term and then press a button to run a Google search. The second is a zoom slider bar that lets the user zoom in and out of the page.

Update the Browser class with the bold text from the following:

```
self.favourites = QComboBox(self)
self.favourites.addItems(["http://www.google.com",
                          "http://www.raspberrypi.org",
                          "http://docs.python.org/3/"])
self.favourites.activated.connect(self.favourite_selected)
self.favourites.setMinimumSize(200,20)
self.favourites.setMaximumSize(300,20)

self.search_box = QLineEdit(self)
self.search_box.setMinimumSize(200,20)
self.search_box.setMaximumSize(300,20)

self.search_btn = QPushButton("Search", self)
self.search_btn.clicked.connect(self.search_btn_clicked)
self.search_btn.setMaximumSize(50,20)

self.zoom_slider = QSlider(Qt.Orientation(1),self)
self.zoom_slider.setRange(2, 50)
self.zoom_slider.setValue(10)
self.zoom_slider.valueChanged.connect(self.zoom_changed)

self.zoom_label = QLabel("Zoom:")

self.webview.loadStarted.connect(self.page_loading)

self.menu_bar = QHBoxLayout()
self.menu_bar.addWidget(self.back_btn)
```

```python
self.menu_bar.addWidget(self.forward_btn)
self.menu_bar.addWidget(self.url_entry)
self.menu_bar.addWidget(self.go_btn)
self.menu_bar.addStretch()
self.menu_bar.addWidget(self.favourites)
self.menu_bar.addStretch()
self.menu_bar.addWidget(self.search_box)
self.menu_bar.addWidget(self.search_btn)
self.menu_bar.addWidget(self.zoom_label)
self.menu_bar.addWidget(self.zoom_slider)
self.main_layout = QVBoxLayout()
self.main_layout.addLayout(self.menu_bar)
self.main_layout.addWidget(self.webview)

self.setLayout(self.main_layout)

def go_btn_clicked(self):
self.webview.load(self.url_entry.text())

def favourite_selected(self):
self.webview.load(self.favourites.currentText())

def zoom_changed(self):
self.webview.setZoomFactor(self.zoom_slider.value()/10)

def search_btn_clicked(self):
self.webview.load("https://www.google.com/search?q="
                  + self.search_box.text())

def page_loading(self):
self.url_entry.setText(self.webview.url().toString())
```

Whilst there are two controls, there are four widgets to make them happen. The search box has a QLineEntry and a QPushButton as well. Together, these work in a very similar way to the URL entry control that you added earlier, except that it adds https://www.google.com/search?q= to the start of whatever you enter. For example, if you search for Raspberries, it will go to the URL https://www.google.com/search?q=Raspberries and this tells Google to search for Raspberries. This has https:// at the start rather than http://. The s stands for secure, and if you use https:// then any data between your browser and the website is encrypted. However, not every website supports https. QWebView allows you to use either protocol as long as the server supports it.

The zoom slider is a QSlider, which is another type of control that you're probably familiar with. It takes a little more setting up, though, which is what the following lines do:

```
self.zoom_slider.setRange(2, 50)
self.zoom_slider.setValue(10)
```

The first sets the maximum and minimum values for the slider, and the second sets the initial value.

You connected the `valueChanged` action to the `zoom_changed()` method. Once again, this just links into one of `QWebView`'s methods and lets it do all the hard work. The only thing `zoom_changed()` does is divide the value of the slider by 10 to make the zoom a bit more manageable.

If you were looking closely, you'll have noticed that this actually does a little more than adding two extra controls. It also has these lines:

```
  self.webview.loadStarted.connect(self.page_loading)
. . .
def page_loading(self):
  self.url_entry.setText(self.webview.url().toString())
```

Which will make sure the URL entry box is always updated with the address of the current page.

Adding Window Menus

The main browser layout is finished, but there's still a bit more to add before the application's done. Remember that at the start we said that we extended a `QMainWindow` so that we could add menus? Well now's the time to do that.

The `Window` already has a menu; all you need to do is add things to it. These menu items are similar to widgets, except they're made from `QActions`.

To add a file menu with an entry to close the window, change the `BrowserWindow` class to the following:

```
class BrowserWindow(QMainWindow):
  def __init__(self):
    super(BrowserWindow, self).__init__()
    self.widget = Browser()
    self.setCentralWidget(self.widget)

    self.exitAction = QAction(QIcon('exit.png'), '&Exit', self)
    self.exitAction.setShortcut('Ctrl+Q')
```

```
self.exitAction.setStatusTip('Exit application')
self.exitAction.triggered.connect(self.close)

self.menu = self.menuBar()
self.fileMenu = self.menu.addMenu('&File')
self.fileMenu.addAction(self.exitAction)
```

There's one more menu entry to add, one to open a locally stored file. This is a bit different to everything in the web browser because it opens a new window. In the new window, the users will get to browse through their files and select the one they want to open. At this point, you might be thinking that it'll require quite a bit of work to create this new window, add a whole layout, and link up all the required widgets. However, this is another place where we can just let Qt do all the hard work for us. There are a range of Qt widgets known as *dialogs*. These are simple windows to perform common functions, and they can make your life a lot easier. To add an open file dialog to the web browser, update the following `BrowserWindow` class:

```
self.exitAction = QAction(QIcon('exit.png'), '&Exit', self)
self.exitAction.setShortcut('Ctrl+Q')
self.exitAction.setStatusTip('Exit application')
self.exitAction.triggered.connect(self.close)

self.openFile = QAction(QIcon('open.png'), 'Open', self)
self.openFile.setShortcut('Ctrl+O')
self.openFile.setStatusTip('Open new File')
self.openFile.triggered.connect(self.showDialog)

self.menu = self.menuBar()
self.fileMenu = self.menu.addMenu('&File')
self.fileMenu.addAction(self.openFile)
self.fileMenu.addAction(self.exitAction)

def showDialog(self):
    fname, _ = QFileDialog.getOpenFileName(self, 'Open file',
            '/home')
    self.widget.webview.load("file:///" + fname)
```

In this case, we don't have to create a new object, instead we can just call the `getOpenFile Name()` method from `QFileDialog`. This will open a new window with the title "Open File in the directory /home" (see Figure 4-3). Once the users pick the file they want, it will return two things: the filename and the filter. However, since the web browser doesn't need to know the filter, assigning it to _ just drops it.

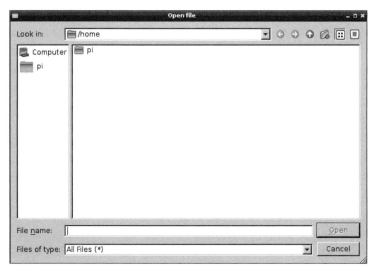

FIGURE 4-3: Opening a local file using `QFileDialog`.

The `QWebView` can open local files using the protocol `file:///` (note the three slashes), so you just need to prefix this on the filename before you can use it.

That brings us to the end of the web browser. If you haven't been following along, the complete code is on the website as `chapter4-web-browser-complete.py`. As with every application, there's still plenty we could add, but we've shown enough to introduce the `pyside` module and the Qt toolkit. It's a huge toolkit, so out of necessity, we've only been able to show you the basics. Everything is documented at `http://srinikom.github.io/pyside-docs/`.

Test Your Knowledge

Exercise 2
As you've seen, dialogs are great ways to add functionality to your programs quickly. In this exercise, go back to the turtle program and add a button that launches a `QColorDialog`, which sets the colour of the turtle.

Here are a few hints to help you out. `QColorDialog.getColor()` will return a value with the type `QColor`. To get the RGB values out of a variable that holds a `QColor`, use `variable_name.getRgb()[:3]`. You need the `[:3]` at the end because it returns a tuple with four values (the final one being the transparency, which you don't need in this case).

Summary

After consuming this chapter, you should know the following:

- PySide is a Python library that helps you write graphical user interfaces using the Qt toolkit.

- Qt contains a wide range of widgets that you can add to your projects to quickly create powerful interfaces.

- You can connect actions such as button presses, combo box changes, or slider movements to method calls.

- There are several ways you can lay out your Qt windows, including grid and box.

- If you build your interface on a class that extends QMainWindow, you can add menus.

- Qt includes a range of dialogs that are ready-made windows that you can add to your project.

Solutions to Exercises

Exercise 1

```
import turtle
import sys
from PySide.QtCore import *
from PySide.QtGui import *

class TurtleControl(QWidget):
    def __init__(self, turtle):
        super(TurtleControl, self).__init__()
        self.turtle = turtle

        self.left_btn = QPushButton("Left", self)
        self.right_btn = QPushButton("Right", self)
        self.move_btn = QPushButton("Move", self)
        self.distance_spin = QSpinBox()
        self.red_spin = QSpinBox()
        self.green_spin = QSpinBox()
        self.blue_spin = QSpinBox()
        self.red_label = QLabel("Red", self)
        self.green_label = QLabel("Green", self)
        self.blue_label = QLabel("Blue", self)
        self.colour_btn = QPushButton("Colour", self)
```

```python
        self.controlsLayout = QGridLayout()
        self.controlsLayout.addWidget(self.left_btn, 0, 0)
        self.controlsLayout.addWidget(self.right_btn, 0, 1)
        self.controlsLayout.addWidget(self.distance_spin, 1 , 0)
        self.controlsLayout.addWidget(self.move_btn, 1 , 1)
        self.controlsLayout.addWidget(self.red_spin, 2,1)
        self.controlsLayout.addWidget(self.green_spin, 3,1)
        self.controlsLayout.addWidget(self.blue_spin, 4,1)
        self.controlsLayout.addWidget(self.red_label, 2,0)
        self.controlsLayout.addWidget(self.green_label, 3,0)
        self.controlsLayout.addWidget(self.blue_label, 4,0)
        self.controlsLayout.addWidget(self.colour_btn, 5,0)
        self.setLayout(self.controlsLayout)

        self.distance_spin.setRange(0, 100)
        self.distance_spin.setSingleStep(5)
        self.distance_spin.setValue(20)

        for spinner in [self.red_spin, self.green_spin,
                        self.blue_spin]:
            spinner.setRange(0, 255)
            spinner.setSingleStep(5)
            spinner.setValue(150)

        self.move_btn.clicked.connect(self.move_turtle)
        self.right_btn.clicked.connect(self.turn_turtle_right)
        self.left_btn.clicked.connect(self.turn_turtle_left)
        self.colour_btn.clicked.connect(self.colour_turtle)

def turn_turtle_left(self):
    self.turtle.left(45)

def turn_turtle_right(self):
    self.turtle.right(45)

def move_turtle(self):
    self.turtle.forward(self.distance_spin.value())

def colour_turtle(self):
    self.turtle.color(self.red_spin.value(),
                self.green_spin.value(),
                self.blue_spin.value())
```

```
#set up turtle
window = turtle.Screen()
babbage = turtle.Turtle()
window.colormode(255)

# Create a Qt application
app = QApplication(sys.argv)
control_window = TurtleControl(babbage)
control_window.show()

# Enter Qt application main loop
app.exec_()
sys.exit()
```

Exercise 2

The following function will need to be connected to the clicked action of a button:

```
def colour_turtle(self):
    self.colour = QColorDialog.getColor()
    self.turtle.color(self.colour.getRgb()[:3])
```

Chapter 5
Creating Games

IN THE LAST chapter you built graphical software using a GUI toolkit. This made it really easy to add buttons, text boxes, and all sorts of widgets to our software, but there's another sort of graphical application that doesn't use any of these things: games. We still need to draw things on the screen, but instead of check boxes and menus, we want fireballs, heroes, pits of doom, and all manner of fantastical graphics. Clearly, PySide isn't up to the task, but there is another module that will do exactly what we want, PyGame.

Raspbian comes with PyGame installed, but only for Python 2. Since we're building with Python 3, we'll need to install it. In this case, you'll have to compile the module from scratch, but this is a good chance to learn the process. First you need to install all the packages that PyGame will need, so open LXTerminal, and use `apt-get` (the package manager) to install the dependencies like so:

```
sudo apt-get update
sudo apt-get install libsdl-dev libsdl-image1.2-dev \
   libsdl-mixer1.2-dev libsdl-ttf2.0-dev libsmpeg-dev \
   libportmidi-dev libavformat-dev libswscale-dev \
   mercurial python3-dev
```

You'll notice that a lot of this code ends in `-dev`. These are the development files. You need them when compiling software that uses those libraries.

The next step is to get a copy of the latest version of PyGame. Since we're using Python 3, we need to get the very latest version, so we'll grab it straight from the development platform with the following:

```
hg clone https://bitbucket.org/pygame/pygame
cd pygame
```

These two lines will download the current version of PyGame into a new directory called pygame, then move into it. Once it's there, you can build and install the module for Python 3 with:

```
python3 setup.py build
sudo python3 setup.py install
```

If everything's gone well, you'll now be able to use PyGame in Python 3. To test that it works, open up the Python Shell in IDLE, and enter:

```
>>> import pygame
```

If there are any errors, then something has gone wrong and you'll need to go back and repeat the steps before continuing with the chapter. Whilst you're in the shell, you can try out a few things to see how PyGame works.

```
>>> pygame.init()
>>> window = pygame.display.set_mode((500, 500))
>>> screen = pygame.display.get_surface()
>>> rect = pygame.Rect(100, 99, 98, 97)
>>> pygame.draw.rect(screen, (100, 100, 100), rect, 0)
>>> pygame.display.update()
```

You should see this open a new window and draw a grey rectangle. The first line just gets PyGame up and running. The second line opens a new window. The parameter - (500, 500) - is a tuple containing the width and height of the new window. Notice how there's two opening and closing brackets? One set denotes the parameter and the other, the tuple. The third line gets the surface that you can draw on and stores it in the variable screen.

There are two main PyGame classes that you'll be using: Rect and Sprite. The second one we'll look at later, but the first, Rect, is absolutely critical to the way PyGame works. In the fourth line, you create one of these rectangles, which has its top-left corner at coordinates 100, 99, and is 98 pixels wide by 97 tall. The one thing you need to know about PyGame coordinates is that they start from the top-left corner of the screen, so compared to normal graph coordinates, they're upside down.

Rectangles aren't always displayed on the screen (they serve a number of other useful purposes as you'll discover later), but this one will be drawn, and that's done in the next line. The parameter (100, 100, 100) holds the red, green, and blue colours (each one is from 0 to 255), and the

0 is the line thickness (0 means fill, 1 or higher means line thickness). If you were paying attention as you typed, you'd notice that the rectangle doesn't appear in the window. That's because you need to update the screen for any changes to take effect. This we do in the final line.

Try drawing a few other rectangles on the screen to get a feel for how all the different parameters affect the shape.

Building a Game

Those are the very basics of PyGame. Now onto the game you'll build, which is a simple platform game where you control a character who has to run and jump through a level to try and reach a goal. To make it a little tricky, we'll rain down fireballs that she has to dodge as she makes her way there, and if she falls off the platform, there'll be a burning pit of doom waiting to finish her off.

When programming, we don't usually start with the first line. Instead, we make a plan of how we think the program will work. This is like the skeleton of the program that we'll then flesh out. We do this by designing all the classes and their methods, but leaving the implementation blank. As we program, we add flesh to this design until, hopefully, we end up with a finished program. For our game, we have the following design (you can type it out, but it'll be easier to download it from the website as `chapter5-pygame-skell.py` and add to it as you go through the chapter):

```python
import pygame
import sys
from pygame.locals import *
from random import randint

class Player(pygame.sprite.Sprite):
    '''The class that holds the main player, and controls
    how they jump. nb. The player doesn't move left or right,
    the world moves around them'''

    def __init__(self, start_x, start_y, width, height):
        pass

    def move_y(self):
        '''this calculates the y-axis movement for the player
        in the current speed'''
        pass
```

```python
    def jump(self, speed):
        '''This sets the player to jump, but it only can if
        its feet are on the floor'''
        pass

class World():
    '''This will hold the platforms and the goal.
    nb. In this game, the world moves left and right rather
        than the player'''

    def __init__(self, level, block_size, colour_platform,
                 colour_goals):
        pass

    def move(self, dist):
        '''move the world dist pixels right (a negative dist
        means left)'''
        pass

    def collided_get_y(self, player_rect):
        '''get the y value of the platform the player is
        currently on'''
        pass

    def at_goal(self, player_rect):
        '''return True if the player is currently in contact
        with the goal. False otherwise'''
        pass

    def update(self, screen):
        '''draw all the rectangles onto the screen'''
        pass

class Doom():
    '''this class holds all the things that can kill the player'''

    def __init__(self, fireball_num, pit_depth, colour):
        pass

    def move(self, dist):
        '''move everything right dist pixels (negative dist
        means left)'''
        pass
```

```
    def update(self, screen):
        '''move fireballs down, and draw everything on
        the screen'''
        pass

    def collided(self, player_rect):
        '''check if the player is currently in contact with
        any of the doom.
        nb. shrink the rectangle for the fireballs to
        make it fairer'''
        pass

class Fireball(pygame.sprite.Sprite):
    '''this class holds the fireballs that fall from the sky'''

    def __init__(self):
        pass

    def reset(self):
        '''re-generate the fireball a random distance along
        the screen and give them a random speed'''
        pass

    def move_x(self, dist):
        '''move the fireballs dist pixels to the right
        (negative dist means left)'''
        pass

    def move_y(self):
        '''move the fireball the appropriate distance down
        the screen
        nb. fireballs don't accellerate with gravity, but
        have a random speed. if the fireball has reached the
        bottom of the screen, regenerate it'''
        pass

    def update(self, screen, colour):
        '''draw the fireball onto the screen'''
        pass

#options
#initialise pygame.mixer
#initialise pygame
```

```
#load level
#initialise variables
finished = False
#setup the background
while not finished:
    pass
    #blank screen
    #check events
    #check which keys are held
    #move the player with gravity
    #render the frame
    #update the display
    #check if the player is dead
    #check if the player has completed the level
    #set the speed
```

There are only a few pieces of actual code here, but it's enough for us to know what's going on. This is actually a legal Python program, so you can enter it and run it. It won't do anything except spin itself round in a loop until you hit Ctrl+C to stop it, but this gives you a base to work from. As we add pieces, we'll make sure it stays as a running program so you can constantly check how it's playing, and that it's working correctly. Notice the **pass** statement in every method. This statement does nothing, but Python complains if you have a method with no code in it, so this simple line is required for the code to run.

This is quite a good way to start when you write your own programs. Rather than trying to create the whole thing in one go, you can start by planning how everything will work, and then build up bit-by-bit until you have a fully working program. If needed, you can always change your plan, but it helps to know what you're working towards.

Initialising PyGame

We'll now add a couple of things to get it started. Add the following code to the file where the comments match.

```
#options
screen_x = 600
screen_y = 400
game_name = Awesome Raspberry Pi Platformer"

#initialise pygame
pygame.init()
window = pygame.display.set_mode((screen_x, screen_y))
pygame.display.set_caption(game_name)
screen = pygame.display.get_surface()
```

```
#initialise variables
clock = pygame.time.Clock()

    #check events
    for event in pygame.event.get():
        if event.type == QUIT:
            finished = True

    #set the speed
    clock.tick(20)
```

You should recognise the section under `initialise pygame` from earlier. The only change here is that we've taken the screen size out and stored it in two variables. This is so that you can easily change it later without having to try to remember what code does what. All the key options will be stored as global variables in the same place to allow you to tweak the way the game works.

The section under `#check events` just waits until the user clicks on the cross to close the window, then exits the loop. The two lines for the clock use PyGame's timer to moderate the speed the loop runs at. Since each turn of the loop will correspond to a singe frame of the game, we need to make sure it doesn't run too fast (otherwise, all the action would be over before the user had a chance to do anything). You could just tell Python to sleep for a certain amount of time like you did in the simple turtle game in Chapter 2, but this has the slight problem that you don't know how long the rest of the loop will take. If you run it on a slower computer, the game will run at a different speed to on a fast machine. `clock.tick(fps)` is the solution to this. It tries to hold the loop at `fps` loops per second by pausing the loop for the appropriate amount of time, taking into account how long the rest of the loop has taken to run. In the previous code, the final line will calculate how long to wait for so that the loop runs exactly 20 times a second.

Now, let's start building the classes, starting with the `Player` class. Add the following initialisation method to it:

```
def __init__(self, start_x, start_y, width, height):

    pygame.sprite.Sprite.__init__(self)
    self.image = pygame.transform.scale(
        pygame.image.load(player_image), (width, height))
    self.rect = self.image.get_rect()
    self.rect.x = start_x
    self.rect.y = start_y
    self.speed_y = 0
    self.base = pygame.Rect(start_x, start_y + height, width,2)
```

The key thing about `Player` is that it inherits from `pygame.sprite.Sprite`. This allows you to use it to draw an image, but first you have to set up two key variables: `self.image` and `self.rect`. Once these are set up, the parts it inherits from `pygame.sprite.Sprite` will allow you to draw it. Fairly obviously, `self.image` is the image that you want the sprite to have and `self.rect` is the rectangle that PyGame will draw it in. Once set up, you can then move and manipulate this rectangle just like any other, and PyGame will move the image round the screen for you. As you'll see later, you move rectangles round by updating their `x` and `y` attributes.

The penultimate local variable (`speed_y`) is used to keep track of the player's up and down speed as she jumps, whilst the final one (`base`) is a very short rectangle that represents the character's feet. You'll use this to check whether she's standing on a platform.

The player is now ready to draw on the screen, but first you'll need a bit more code. Add the following to the appropriate areas:

```
#options
player_spawn_x = 50
player_spawn_y = 200
player_image = "lidia.png"

#initialise variables
player = Player(player_spawn_x, player_spawn_y, 20, 30)
player_plain = pygame.sprite.RenderPlain(player)

#render the frame
player_plain.draw(screen)

#update the display
pygame.display.update()
```

In order to draw a sprite, you need to give it an image to draw. If you're artistic, you may want to create this yourself. However, there's a great collection of images you can use for games at `http://opengameart.org`. These are all free to download and use in your games, but some of them have licenses that say if you make a game with it, and you distribute that game to other people, you have to let them have the Python code so they can modify it, and build other games with your code if they want to. This concept is known as *open source* (see note). There are links on every file of `http://opengameart.org` that tell you exactly what license they're under. The important thing to realise is that you don't have to worry about it unless you distribute your game to other people. Not all of the files there will work well with PyGame. We recommend sticking with `.png` files for images. After a bit of searching, we like using `http://opengameart.org/sites/default/files/styles/medium/public/lidia.png` for our game's main character, but feel free to pick a different one (although you'll have to update the `player_image` variable). As the code is currently, it'll look for the `player_image` image file in the same directory it's being run from.

Open Source

Open source is a concept in which people share the programs they've written. Not just the executable files that can be run, but also the actual program code so that other people can modify it in whatever way they see fit. For example, the Linux operating system on the Raspberry Pi is open source, so are all of the tools that come standard, like the Midori web browser and even Python itself. Roughly speaking, there are two different types of open source—ones where you have to share any modifications you make, and ones where you don't. Creative Commons is a similar concept to open source, instead for works of art like pictures, sounds, and writing. When incorporating pieces of open source software or Creative Commons artwork into your programs, it's important that you understand what your responsibilities are. There will always be a link to the exact license that it's released under. In the case of Creative Commons, these are easy to read and understand. If you need to share your work in order to comply with a license (or if you want to make your work open source), the easiest way is to put it on an open source hosting website such as github.com, which will host it for free.

To draw a sprite, you also need to add it to a `RenderPlain`. This just creates the object that you draw on the screen. Here, the player object has its own `RenderPlain` object called `player_plain`.

You should now be able to run the code and it'll display the sprite at the coordinates `player_spawn_x`, `player_spawn_y`. Technically, it'll be redrawing it 20 times a second, but since it's always in the same place, you can't tell. It should look like Figure 5-1.

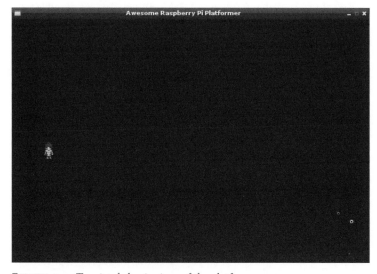

FIGURE 5-1: The simple beginnings of the platform game.

With the character drawn, the next task is to make her move. This is just some test code to make sure the animation is working properly. A little later you'll update this to let your character jump. Add the following method to the Player class:

```
def move_y(self):
    self.rect.y = self.rect.y + 1
```

This will just move the character slowly down. For this to do anything, though, we'll have to add the following to the appropriate places in our game loop:

```
#blank screen
screen.fill((0, 0, 0))

#move the player with gravity
player.move_y()
```

You can now run the code, and you'll see the player move down the window until she disappears off the bottom. We can't do much more with her until we've built a world for her to move round in.

Creating a World

We want to make it as easy as possible to extend this game and make it awesome, so we want it to be really easy to design new levels. We've done this by defining each level as a list of strings. Each string corresponds to a line on the screen, and each character in the string corresponds to a block on that line. A - means that there's a platform there, a G means there's a goal there (the place the player has to reach to finish the level), and anything else means it's blank. To create the basic level, then, add the following under #options:

```
level=[
 "                        ",
 "                        ",
 "                        ",
 "                        ",
 "                        ",
 "                        ",
 "                        ",
 "          ---          G",
 "    -- --    ---     ------",
 " -- -          -------     "]]
platform_colour = (100, 100, 100)
goal_colour = (0, 0, 255)
```

If you've entered it correctly, all the lines should be the same length. This is a really simple level, but it'll do for testing. The final two lines also set the colours for the platform and the goal, respectively. As we saw with the rectangle at the start of this chapter, these colours are in RGB values.

Now add the following code to the __init__ method of the World class to load this:

```python
def __init__(self, level, block_size,
        colour_platform,
        colour_goals):
    self.platforms = []
    self.goals = []
    self.posn_y = 0
    self.colour = colour_platform
    self.colour_goals = colour_goals
    self.block_size = block_size

    for line in level:
        self.posn_x = 0
        for block in line:
            if block == "-":
                self.platforms.append(pygame.Rect(
                    self.posn_x, self.posn_y,
                    block_size, block_size))
            if block == "G":
                self.goals.append(pygame.Rect(
                    self.posn_x, self.posn_y,
                    block_size, block_size))
            self.posn_x = self.posn_x + block_size
        self.posn_y = self.posn_y + block_size
```

The code is fairly simple; it just loops through every line, then every character in the line, and builds the appropriate rectangles when it finds the appropriate characters. Before you can use these blocks, you need to also add the update method to the World class, which will draw the blocks onto the screen:

```python
def update(self, screen):
        '''draw all the rectangles onto the screen'''

    for block in self.platforms:
        pygame.draw.rect(screen, self.colour, block, 0)
    for block in self.goals:
        pygame.draw.rect(screen, self.colour_goals, block, 0)
```

Now you just need to add the following code to create the objects and render them. As always, put them in the right place by looking at the comments.

```
#initialise variables
world = World(level, 30, platform_colour, goal_colour)

#render the frame
world.update(screen)
```

You can now run the game, but you still won't find much to play. The world will be drawn, but the character will slowly fall through the level, and continue falling until she disappears off the screen.

Detecting Collisions

Fortunately, it's really easy to get two game elements to interact using PyGame's Rect's colliderect() method. This is incredibly simple, and the format is

```
rect1.colliderect(rect2)
```

Where rect1 and rect2 are rectangles. This will return True if the two rectangles overlap, and False otherwise. You can use this to detect when the player is in contact with the world so she doesn't just fall through it. Start with the World class and add:

```
def collided_get_y(self, player_rect):
        '''get the y value of the platform the player is
        currently on'''
        return_y = -1
        for block in self.platforms:
            if block.colliderect(player_rect):
                return_y = block.y - block.height + 1
        return return_y
```

This doesn't just check if the player is in contact with any part of the world, but also returns the top of the rectangle that the player is touching, or -1 if the player isn't touching anything. The next step is to update the Player class to move or not, as appropriate

```
def move_y(self):
    '''this calculates the y-axis movement for the player
    in the current speed'''
    collided_y = world.collided_get_y(self.base)
```

```
if self.speed_y <= 0 or collided_y < 0:
    self.rect.y = self.rect.y + self.speed_y
    self.speed_y = self.speed_y + gravity
if collided_y > 0 and self.speed_y > 0:
    self.rect.y = collided_y
self.base.y = self.rect.y+self.rect.height
```

You'll also need to add one thing to help the player fall realistically:

```
#options
gravity = 1
```

You can now run this. The player will now fall until she rests on top of the platform, as shown in Figure 5-2.

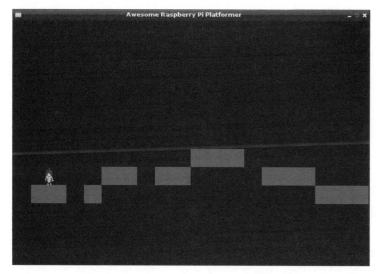

FIGURE 5-2: Our heroine can now stand atop the world we've created.

Let's take a look at move_y() to see why this happens. The code deals with two possibilities, and each one has its own if block. The first possibility is that the players are free to move up or down depending on their current speed and gravity. This is the case if they're not touching any part of the world (that is, collided_get_y returns -1). We also want the players to be able to jump up through platforms to get to higher ones, so if the players are currently moving upwards (that is, if self.speed_y <= 0), we treat the character as though she's not touching the world. If either of these conditions is true, then we run:

```
self.rect.y = self.rect.y + self.speed_y
self.speed_y = self.speed_y + gravity
```

This moves the character by a distance determined by the current speed, then updates the current speed by gravity (gravity is an acceleration, so this mimics the physics of the real world).

The second possibility (which is checked by the second `if` block) is that the players are currently in contact with a platform and they're not moving up. If this is the case, the program just adjusts the coordinates of the character so that she's correctly aligned with the world. This is because if the players fall at more than one pixel per frame, it's possible that they could be several pixels below the top of the platform before this is checked. Later on, you may notice that sometimes you can see the character going down then back up slightly as she lands from higher falls, but this mimics people recovering from a landing.

Moving Left and Right

You've almost got something that represents a game now. There's a player and a world, but the players still can't explore it. The next thing to add is movement. There'll be two kinds of movements. Firstly we'll allow the players to jump, but only if they're in contact with the floor, and secondly they'll be able to move left and right.

First add the `jump()` method to the `Player` class. Since you already have the character falling, jumping is simple. All you have to do is make sure she's on the ground, then set her moving upwards and let her fall on her own:

```
def jump(self, speed):
    if world.collided_get_y(self.base)>0:
        self.speed_y = speed
```

Now to move the player left and right. Actually, it's easier if the players stay still and the world moves left and right behind them. This gives the effect of moving without the problem of the character disappearing off the screen.

All you need to do is loop through every rectangle in the world (that is, both the platforms and the goal), and move them by a given offset. We could just update the rectangle's x and y attributes, but there are also two methods in the `Rect` class that you and use: `move(x-distance, y-distance)` and `move_ip(x-distance, y-distance)`. `move()` returns a new rectangle that is the same but offset by the given distances, whilst `move_ip()` changes the current rectangle by the distances (`ip` stands for in place). Since we don't want to keep creating new rectangles every time we move, we'll use `move_ip()`. The code is

```
def move(self, dist):
    for block in self.platforms + self.goals:
        block.move_ip(dist, 0)
```

The only thing left is to add code to the main loop to run the appropriate methods when keys are pressed. There are two ways of doing this in PyGame. The first way involves listening for keypress events and then taking action depending on which keypresses are detected. This is good if you only care about when keys are pressed. The second way is using `pygame.key.get_pressed()` to return a list with an entry for each key. The value of the item that corresponds to a key will be `True` if it's held down and `False` if it isn't. This second method works better if you want users to be able to hold down keys to keep moving. Since we do want users to be able to hold down keys, add the following to the appropriate part of the game loop:

```
#check which keys are held
    key_state = pygame.key.get_pressed()
    if key_state[K_LEFT]:
        world.move(2)
    elif key_state[K_RIGHT]:
        world.move(-2)
    if key_state[K_SPACE]:
        player.jump(jump_speed)
```

Note that `K_LEFT`, `K_RIGHT`, and `K_SPACE` are all constants that we imported with `pygame.locals`. There are also `K_a` to `K_z` for the letter keys.

Add the option for the speed of the jump (negative because the PyGame coordinate system is from the top-left):

```
#options
jump_speed = -10
```

If you run the code now, you'll have what could be called the basics of a platform game (see Figure 5-3). You can move the character about, and jump over gaps. However, two crucial parts are missing. Firstly, there's no way to complete the level, and secondly, there's nothing trying to stop you.

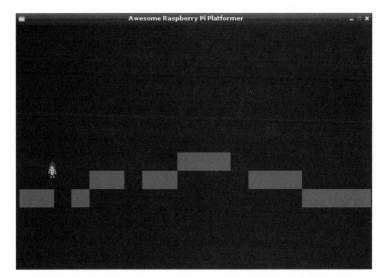

FIGURE 5-3: The basics of a platform game running on a Raspberry Pi with less than two hundred lines of Python.

Reaching the Goal

Let's deal with the first of these shortcomings first. Partly because it's easier and partly because you'll then have a game you can play-test. Since the code creates, displays, and moves the goal as appropriate, all we have to do is find out if the character's at the goal. This is done in two stages. First, add the following method to the `World` class:

```
def at_goal(self, player_rect):
    for block in self.goals:
        if block.colliderect(player_rect):
            return True
    return False
```

This works in exactly the same way as the `collide_get_y()` method that we created earlier, except that it only returns `True` or `False`. You then need to check this method in the game loop, so add:

```
#check if the player has completed the level
    if world.at_goal(player.rect):
        print("Winner!")
        finished = True
```

If you save and run the code now, you'll find that you can run and jump to the goal, then finish the level. You can even fall off the platform and disappear into the abyss never to be seen again, but it still doesn't have much of a challenge to it.

Making a Challenge

To add some game play, there'll be a class called Doom, which holds all the things that can kill the player. In this game, there are two challenges to avoid. Firstly, there's the burning pit of doom that covers the bottom of the screen. This will kill the players if they fall into it. Secondly, and more importantly from the perspective of the game play, there'll be fireballs that drop down from the sky. The players will have to dodge these as they make their way towards the goal.

Firstly, add the burning pit of doom. We'll draw this as a rectangle along the bottom of the screen. Add the following to the Doom class:

```
def __init__(self, fireball_num, pit_depth, colour):
    self.base = pygame.Rect(0, screen_y-pit_depth,
                screen_x, pit_depth)
    self.colour = colour

def collided(self, player_rect):
    return self.base.colliderect(player_rect)

def update(self, screen):
    '''move fireballs down, and draw everything on the screen'''
    pygame.draw.rect(screen, self.colour, self.base, 0)
```

Also add the following to the appropriate parts of the options, variables, and game loop:

```
#options
doom_colour = (255, 0, 0)
#initialise variables
doom = Doom(0, 10, doom_colour)
    #render the frame
    doom.update(screen)
    #check if the player is dead
    if doom.collided(player.rect):
        print("You Lose!")
        finished = True
```

This should all be fairly self explanatory. Notice that you don't need to move the burning pit of doom rectangle, as it should always cover the bottom of the screen. The call to the update() method is to move the fireballs, so let's look at them now.

We'll add the whole class in one go here:

```python
class Fireball(pygame.sprite.Sprite):
    '''this class holds the fireballs that fall from the sky'''
    def __init__(self):
        pygame.sprite.Sprite.__init__(self)
        self.image = pygame.transform.scale(
                    pygame.image.load(fireball_image),
                    (fireball_size, fireball_size))
        self.rect = self.image.get_rect()
        self.reset()

    def reset(self):
        self.y = 0
        self.speed_y = randint(fireball_low_speed,
                    fireball_high_speed)
        self.x = randint(0,screen_x)
        self.rect.topleft = self.x, self.y

    def move_x(self, dist):
        self.rect.move_ip(dist, 0)
        if self.rect.x < -50 or self.rect.x > screen_x:
            self.reset()

    def move_y(self):
        self.rect.move_ip(0, self.speed_y)
        if self.rect.y > screen_y:
            self.reset()
```

As you can see, this class extends the Sprite class in the same way that the Player class does. The move_x() method works in a similar way to the equivalent method in World, except that here it has to move only a single fireball because we will have one of these fireball objects for each fireball.

To keep up the challenge, the fireballs should constantly fall from the sky. There are a few ways of achieving this, but we've chosen to create a fixed number of fireballs and simply reset them whenever they go off the screen. This reset() method places the fireballs at a random position along the top of the screen and gives them a random velocity.

The randint(a, b) method returns a random integer between a and b, inclusive (that is, including the values of a and b). The screen_x variable makes sure it's on the screen, and two global variables (fireball_low_speed and fireball_high_speed) set the range of speeds a fireball can move at. These numbers are pixels per frame. You don't need a collide method here because you'll deal with that in the Doom class.

Now, update the Doom class to:

```python
class Doom():
    '''this class holds all the things that can kill the player'''
    def __init__(self, fireball_num, pit_depth, colour):
        self.base = pygame.Rect(0, screen_y-pit_depth,
                    screen_x, pit_depth)
        self.colour = colour
        self.fireballs = []
        for i in range(0,fireball_num):
            self.fireballs.append(Fireball())
        self.fireball_plain = pygame.sprite.RenderPlain(
                            self.fireballs)

    def move(self, dist):
        for fireball in self.fireballs:
            fireball.move_x(dist)

    def update(self, screen):
        for fireball in self.fireballs:
            fireball.move_y()
        self.fireball_plain.draw(screen)
        pygame.draw.rect(screen, self.colour, self.base, 0)

    def collided(self, player_rect):
        for fireball in self.fireballs:
            if fireball.rect.colliderect(player_rect):
                hit_box = fireball.rect.inflate(
                            -int(fireball_size/2),
                            -int(fireball_size/2))
                if hit_box.colliderect(player_rect):
                    return True
        return self.base.colliderect(player_rect)
```

As you can see, this creates a list of fireballs and adds them to `fireball_plain`. This is a `RenderPlain` that works in the same way as `player_plain`, and allows you to draw the fireballs on the screen. Notice that there are global variables for the number and size of fireballs. Changing these has a dramatic effect on how the game plays, and in many ways, they're the key variables for changing difficulty.

The `collided()` method is a little different to the previous ones we've done so far. It compares the player to a rectangle half the size of the fireball rectangle. This is because neither the player nor the fireball are perfect rectangles, and the two bounding rectangles can collide even if the actual sprites are some distance apart. This is extremely frustrating for the person playing the game. The method we've used isn't perfect, but it errs towards the player not dying. In other words, it may be possible for the player to skim a fireball and get away with it, but if this collide method returns `True` then there's definitely a collision.

> **NOTE** It is actually possible to do perfect sprite collision in PyGame using `pygame.sprite.collide_mask(sprite1, sprite2)`. However, this uses significantly more computing power, and is a bit overkill for this task.

With these two classes added, you just need the following code to get it all working:

```
#options
fireball_size = 30
fireball_number = 10
fireball_low_speed = 3
fireball_high_speed = 7
fireball_image = "flame.png"
```

Change the initialisation of Doom to include fireballs:

```
doom = Doom(fireball_number, 10, doom_colour)
```

You'll also need to add lines to the keypress section to make the fireballs move with the background (the lines in bold are the ones you need to add):

```
#check which keys are held
  key_state = pygame.key.get_pressed()
  if key_state[K_LEFT]:
      world.move(2)
      doom.move(2)
  elif key_state[K_RIGHT]:
      world.move(-2)
      doom.move(-2)
```

Again, we're using a sprite that we got from `http://opengameart.org`. In this case it's the one from `http://opengameart.org/sites/default/files/flame.png`. Feel free to pick another or draw your own. For this to work, the file has to be downloaded and saved in the same directory you're running the game from. Alternatively, you can give the sprites an absolute path. For example, if you're saving everything in the directory `/home/pi/my_game/`, you could change the line:

```
fireball_image = "flame.png"
```

to

```
fireball_image = "/home/pi/my_game/flame.png"
```

That way it would work wherever you ran the game from. Now save and run, and the game should look like Figure 5-4.

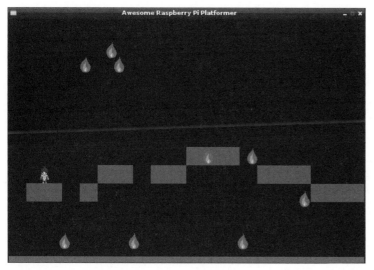

FIGURE 5-4: It's a little rough round the edges, but it's a working platform game.

Making It Your Own

The mechanics of the game are now in place. Players have to move through the world, dodge the fireballs, and get to the goal. There's still a little polish left to add, but the basics are there. Now's a great time to start making it your own. After all, this isn't a chapter about how to copy code until you have a game; this is a chapter about building your own game. By now you should know enough about what the various bits do to start customising it. The options section is the best place to start.

Depending on your monitor, you may want to change the size of the window. If you think it's a bit too easy, add some more fireballs, or make them larger. Perhaps you want to jump higher, or run faster. All of these should be pretty easy. In fact, you should have learned enough in earlier chapters to now make a simple game menu that you can add to the start of the game. You could make it a simple text-based menu that goes just before #initialise pygame, and lets you set the level of difficulty. At harder levels you could ... actually, we'll let you work that out for yourself. If you're feeling ambitious, you could make this menu graphical rather than text-based.

Adding Sound

Hopefully, you now have your own customised version of our game, but don't worry if you don't. The rest of this chapter will still work and you can go back and add your own tweaks later.

Now it's time to add a bit of flare. These are things that don't affect the mechanics of the game, but make it more enjoyable to play. The first is a sound effect, and the second is a background.

Before we can add sounds, we need to initialise the mixer. This basically just gets the sound infrastructure set up and ready to play. It's done with the following code:

```
#initialise pygame.mixer
pygame.mixer.pre_init(44100, -16, 8, 2048)
pygame.mixer.init()
```

This allows us to play up to eight sounds at once, although at first, we'll just add a jumping sound effect. Again, we've gone to http://opengameart.org. This time the file is http://opengameart.org/sites/default/files/qubodup-cfork-ccby3-jump.ogg, so again you'll need to download this or a corresponding file. We'll add this file to the options with:

```
#options
jump_sound = "qubodup-cfork-ccby3-jump.ogg"
```

> **NOTE** MP3 sound files will sometimes work, but can be a little persnickety. They have also been known to crash PyGame games, so it's best to stick with OGG files if you can.

Then we need to update the Player class to play the noise at the appropriate time. Add the following to the end of the __init__() method:

```
self.sound = pygame.mixer.Sound(jump_sound)
```

You'll also need to change the `jump()` method so that it is

```
def jump(self, speed):
    if world.collided_get_y(self.base)>0:
        self.speed_y = speed
        self.sound.play()
```

That's all you need to add a bit of sound to the game. You should now find it quite easy to add more effects, like one that plays when players reach the goal, or one that plays when they die. You could also add some background music. However, remember that most music you buy is copyrighted. You can include it in a game you make for yourself without any problems, but if you want to distribute your game, you could get into trouble. Instead, take a look at http://freemusicarchive.org. Like http://opengameart.org, this site contains a wide range of files that you can download and include in your own games. There's a wide range of styles, so you'll almost certainly find something you like. Many of these are also licensed so that if you distribute your game, you also have to distribute the source code.

Adding Scenery

The second nicety we'll add to the game is a background. Of course, you'll need a background image to do this, and we've gone for the file `background.png` that's in http://opengameart.org/sites/default/files/background.zip. This gives a nice, countryside backdrop, but you could alter the feel of the game by going for something darker and moodier. You'll need to add the following to the options to bring in the file:

```
#options
background_image = "background.png"
```

Before, when using images, you extended the `Sprite` class to create a new class (such as `Player` and `Fireball`) to draw them. However, since you don't need to manipulate the rectangle for this, or do any collisions, you can simply load it as an image. This is done with the following code:

```
#set up the background
background = pygame.transform.scale(pygame.image.load(
            background_image), (screen_x, screen_y)).convert()
bg_1_x = -100
bg_2_x = screen_x - 100
```

The first line loads the image and scales it to the screen size. It also runs `convert()` on it. This converts the image from a PNG to a PyGame surface. This makes it render on the screen much faster, which is especially important for an image of this size. You could have done this with the other images you've used, but then you'd lose the transparent sections round the images, making them purely rectangular. The second and third lines set up the variables that hold the `x` positions of the image. There are two of these because we'll draw the image twice to create a constantly looping background that the players can never move off the end of.

To move the background, update the appropriate section of the game loop to:

```
#check which keys are held
  key_state = pygame.key.get_pressed()
  if key_state[K_LEFT]:
    world.move(2)
    doom.move(2)
bg_1_x = bg_1_x + 1
    bg_2_x = bg_2_x + 1
    if bg_1_x < screen_x:
        bg_1_x = -screen_x
    if bg_2_x < screen_x:
        bg_2_x = -screen_x
  elif key_state[K_RIGHT]:
    world.move(-2)
    doom.move(-2)
    bg_1_x = bg_1_x - 1
    bg_2_x = bg_2_x - 1
    if bg_1_x > -screen_x:
        bg_1_x = screen_x
    if bg_2_x > -screen_x:
        bg_2_x = screen_x
```

There's quite a bit going on here. Firstly, did you notice that we move the background by less than we move the world or the doom? This is called *parallax scrolling*. It creates the appearance of depth by moving objects farther behind at different speeds. It's like when you look out of the window of a moving vehicle and the objects close to you appear to be moving faster than those farther away. It's not exactly advanced 3D graphics, but it helps create a sense of depth. If you want to take things further, you can add layers of backgrounds here. For example, you could draw some trees that move only a bit slower than the platforms, then some hills that move bit slower than the trees, and finally a sun that moves really slowly. As with the sounds, you can take this as far as you want to go.

The second thing that's going on in the code is the `if` blocks that move the background. Whenever the image moves so it's off one side of the screen, the program moves it back to the other side of the screen. This creates the infinitely scrolling background that constantly loops between the two background images. The only thing left to do is draw the image on the screen:

```
#render the frame
screen.blit(background, (bg_1_x, 0))
screen.blit(background, (bg_2_x, 0))
```

These have to be the first lines under `#render the frame` because otherwise they'll be drawn over the top of the other parts. Figure 5-5 shows the final game.

FIGURE 5-5: The game with all the elements.

Adding the Finishing Touches

This, in essence, is the game fully complete. However, there is one more bit we'll add to make it easier to use. So far, we've been using a level that's hard coded into the game. However, it would be much better if we could set it up so that the users can specify a file to load, and the program would pull the level out of the text in that file. Since the levels are defined by text, this should be quite easy.

Running `python3 chapter5-platformer.py` (or whatever you've called the file) will run the default level that's inside the main game file, but `python3 chapter5-platformer.py mylevel` will run the game with the level specified in the file `mylevel`. To do this, we need to use `sys.argv`. This is in the `sys` module, and it's a list containing all the arguments that get passed to Python. `sys.argv[0]` will be the name of the script we're running, so the argument that contains the filename (if it exists) will be `sys.argv[1]`. All we have to do, then, is add the following to our program:

```
#load level
if len(sys.argv) > 1:
    with open(sys.argv[1]) as f:
        level = f.readlines()
```

The specified file will be read in the same way as the array we've been using up until now. That is, a - is a platform and a G is a goal, and multiple lines define the multiple levels of the game.

NOTE   If you haven't been following along, you can download the entire game from the website as `chapter5-platformer.py`, although we strongly encourage you to work through this chapter as it'll help you understand much more about what's going on.

Taking the Game to the Next Level

We could go on and on and add more and more to the game. However, we'll end the tutorial here. Not because the game's finished, but because you should now know enough to finish it by yourself. We're not going to dictate to you what the game should have—it's your game, add what you want. However, we will give you some ideas for how to move on:

- If you haven't already tried tweaking the options, try that now.

- Creating new levels is a great way to make the game feel like it's your own.

- The artwork we've used is only a suggestion. See what you can find online, or try making some of your own.

- Add sprites to the items that are currently just rectangles, like the platform and the burning pit of doom.

- Build up levels into worlds. Each world could have a different theme, and different artwork to match the theme.

- Add things that players can collect. These could be coins that count towards the score, or power-ups that allow the players to run faster or jump higher.

- Add more things that could kill the players. This could be, for example, something that constantly moves right so the players have to keep moving in order to avoid it, something that comes for the players and they have to kill by jumping on, or something that shoots up from below.

- Score each level on completion. You could do this with timing, or objects that the players collect, or something else.

- Animate the sprites. Many of the images on `http://opengameart.org` have a range of poses to allow you to animate objects by constantly scrolling between a set of images.

- It could speed up if you hold the arrow key down rather than just always moving at a constant speed, or there could be some Run button that enables the players to move faster.

These are just a few ideas to get you started. It's not intended to be a complete list of everything you can do with the game, so get your creative juices flowing and see what you can come up with. If it gets good, you could submit it to the Raspberry Pi store and let other people play it. Just remember the licenses of any images or sounds you've used.

Realistic Game Physics

PyGame is a great module for creating simple games. As you've seen, it's really easy to draw objects on the screen and move them round. However, sometimes you need a bit more power. In the previous example, the character fell as though affected by gravity, but the rest of the physics were a bit off. If you need objects that can interact with each other in more realistic ways, such as bouncing of each other, you'll need to use a physics library.

PyMunk is one such module that allows you to create more life-like games. Using it, you can create a space and add objects, then let PyMunk work out how they'll interact.

You can download PyMunk from `http://code.google.com/p/pymunk/downloads/list` (you'll need the source release). Once it has downloaded, you can unzip it and move into the new directory with the following (use LXTerminal rather than Python to run these commands):

```
unzip pymunk-4.0.0.zip
cd pymunk-4.0.0
```

Unfortunately, there is a slight error in the build file that stops it building correctly on the Raspberry Pi. In order to install it, you need to open `setup.py` with a text editor (such as LeafPad) and find the lines:

```
elif arch == 32 and platform.system() == 'Linux':
  compiler_preargs += ['-m32', '-O3']]
```

Make sure it's the line with `arch == 32`, not 64. Delete `'-m32'` from the second line so that it reads:

```
compiler_preargs += ['-O3']]
```

Then save the file. Now you'll be able to install PyMunk with:

```
python3 setup.py build_chipmunk
python3 setup.py build
python3 setup.py install
```

Again, these both have to be entered in LXTerminal in the PyMunk directory. This may take a while, but once it's complete, you can check that it worked by opening Python and entering the following:

```
>>> import pymunk
```

Hopefully, you won't get any errors.

The following example is on the website at `chapter5-pymunk.py`:

```python
import pygame, pymunk
from pygame.locals import *
from pygame.color import *
from pymunk import Vec2d
import math, sys, random

def to_pygame(position):
    return int(position.x), int(-position.y+screen_y)

def line_to_pygame(line):
    body = line.body
    point_1 = body.position + line.a.rotated(body.angle)
    point_2 = body.position + line.b.rotated(body.angle)
    return to_pygame(point_1), to_pygame(point_2)

###options####
screen_x = 600
screen_y = 400
num_balls = 10
```

```
pygame.init()
screen = pygame.display.set_mode((screen_x, screen_y))
clock = pygame.time.Clock()
running = True

space = pymunk.Space()
space.gravity = (0.0, -200.0)

#create the base segment
base = pymunk.Segment(pymunk.Body(),(0, 50), (screen_x, 0), 0)
base.elasticity = 0.90
space.add(base)

#create the spinner
spinner_points = [(0, 0), (100, -50), (-100, -50)]
spinner_body = pymunk.Body(100000, 100000)
spinner_body.position = 300, 200
spinner_shape = pymunk.Poly(spinner_body, spinner_points)
spinner_shape.elasticity = 0.5
spinner_joint_body = pymunk.Body()
spinner_joint_body.position = spinner_body.position
joint = pymunk.PinJoint(spinner_body, spinner_joint_body, (0, 0),
                        (0, 0))
space.add(joint, spinner_body, spinner_shape)

#create the balls
balls = []
for i in range(1, num_balls):
    ball_x = int(screen_x/2)
    radius = random.randint(7, 20)
    inertia = pymunk.moment_for_circle(radius, 0, radius, (0, 0))
    body = pymunk.Body(radius, inertia)
    body.position = ball_x, screen_y
    shape = pymunk.Circle(body, radius, (0, 0))
    shape.elasticity = 0.99
    space.add(body, shape)
    balls.append(shape)

while running:
    for event in pygame.event.get():
        if event.type == QUIT:
            running = False
```

```
    screen.fill((0, 0, 0))
#draw the ball
    for ball in balls:
        pygame.draw.circle(screen,(100, 100, 100), to_pygame(ball.
  body.position), int(ball.radius), 0)

#draw the spinner
    points = spinner_shape.get_vertices()
    points.append(points[0])
    pygame_points = []
    for point in points:
        x,y = to_pygame(point)
        pygame_points.append((x, y))
    color = THECOLORS["red"]
    pygame.draw.lines(screen, color, False, pygame_points)

#draw the line
    pygame.draw.lines(screen, THECOLORS["lightgray"], False,
                       line_to_pygame(base))

    space.step(1.0/50.0)
    pygame.display.flip()
    clock.tick(50)
```

As you can see, this code uses PyGame to handle the drawing of the graphics and PyMunk to work out how they move.

PyMunk works with spaces like the one set up in the following lines:

```
space = pymunk.Space()
space.gravity = (0.0, -200.0)
```

This creates a new object from the `Space` class and sets its gravity. We can then create objects and add them to the space. This example uses circles, segments (that is, lines), and a polygon that's defined by a series of points. (Note, however, that on the Raspberry Pi, there's a bug that means you can only add a single segment to a space.) There's also a pin joint which, roughly speaking, makes the shape behave as though a single pin has been attached at that position, allowing it to pivot round, but not fall, due to gravity.

In the main loop, we call `space.step(1.0/50.0)`, which tells PyMunk to move all the objects in the space by 1/50th of a second.

The one slightly confusing thing about using PyGame with PyMunk is that they use different coordinate systems. As you saw before, PyGame has the point 0, 0 in the top-left corner, but Pymunk has it in the bottom-left. This means that to draw objects in the right place, you need to calculate the new y value. This is the purpose of the function to_pygame(position).

As well as defining the position of the various objects, in PyMunk you can also define the various physical properties they have, such as elasticity and inertia. By tweaking these properties, you can define how your world interacts.

If you run the code, you'll see that PyMunk has done all the difficult tasks of working out the movement, such as handling collisions and calculating how the balls bounce off the floor and each other. The results are in Figure 5-6. However, it comes at a price—this takes much more processing power than our previous game. Whilst the Raspberry Pi can handle simple physics simulations, you need to use them sparingly; otherwise, they'll run too slowly. Using the raspi-config tool, you can overclock your Raspberry Pi, which will help simulations run faster.

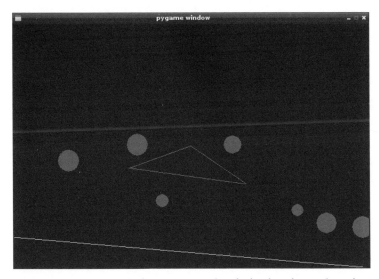

FIGURE 5-6: The PyMunk physics engine takes the hard work out of simulating real-world interactions.

Raspberry Pis will, by default, run at 700MHz. This means they can execute instructions at a rate of 700,000,000 per second. For tasks that require a lot of computing power, you can overclock the CPU using the raspi-config tool. It can go up to 1,000MHz (or 1GHz if you prefer). However, not all Raspberry Pis will work well when overclocked, and they can become unstable. If your Pi starts freezing, try reducing the overclocking.

TIP

We've only touched on the basics here, but hopefully it's enough to get you started. There are some samples in the PyMunk ZIP file that you downloaded earlier. Not all of them run well under Python 3, but they should give you more of a taste of what's going on. There is also some slightly outdated but otherwise good documentation at `http://pymunk.googlecode.com/svn/tags/pymunk-2.0.0/docs/api/index.html`.

Summary

After reading this chapter, you should know the following:

- PyGame is a module to help you create games in Python.

- Classes that extend `Pygame.sprite.Sprite` can draw images on the screen.

- Sprites are drawn inside a class's `self.rect` rectangle.

- You can also use this rectangle to detect collisions between objects.

- Parallax scrolling can be used to create a sense of depth with 2D graphics.

- PyGame can also handle audio.

- For more realistic physics, you can use a physics engine like PyMunk, but it will slow down the execution.

Chapter 6

Creating Graphics with OpenGL

THERE'S NO DENYING that 3D graphics look cool. The sense of depth they create uses more than 2D graphics, and allows you as a programmer to create richer worlds. However, this comes at a cost. Firstly, they take much more computing power to render than 2D graphics, and secondly they are significantly more complex to program.

You often find graphics cards (sometimes known as a Graphics Processing Units, or GPUs) on normal PCs. These provide additional processing power that the computer can use to render complex 3D scenes. Basically, these add a lot of processors that can handle floating-point maths very quickly. A quick look at a Raspberry Pi will tell you that there's no space to add a GPU because it doesn't have the same layout as a PC. Instead of a motherboard with a processor, memory, and expansion slots, everything is enclosed on a System on a Chip (SoC). This is the largest square chip in the middle of the Pi. If you look carefully at it from the side, you'll see that it's made up of two layers. The top layer is the RAM, and the bottom layer does the processing.

The bottom layer isn't just a CPU (Central Processing Unit), though. In fact, the CPU is only a small part of it. It also contains a GPU that's far more powerful than the CPU. When you run normal programs, the GPU sits idly by while the CPU does all the work. When working with 3D graphics, though, the CPU can't handle it by itself, so you have to off-load some of the work to the GPU. In this chapter, we'll look at how to use OpenGL (the GL stands for Graphics Library) to create 3D scenes using the GPU.

We may as well be honest with you from the start: this is the most complex chapter in the book. There's no way around that. Using OpenGL requires some maths, a new programming language, and a host of new concepts. We'll take it slowly though, and explain everything as we go along. However, if you're just looking for a way to easily draw cubes in a 3D world, you can skip ahead to Chapter 8.

Getting Modules

There are two modules you'll need: PyGame and RPiGL. If you haven't already installed PyGame, follow the instructions in Chapter 4. RPiGL is available from `https://github.com/stephanh42/rpigl`. Use the Download Zip button to get a zip, then unzip and install it with the following (in LXTerminal).

```
unzip rpigl-master.zip
cd rpigl-master
python3 setup.py build
sudo python3 setup.py install
```

If this works, you'll now be able to run the demo programs, so try running the following:

```
cd demos
python3 bumpedspere.py
```

You should see a bumpy sphere spinning round (yes, there does appear to be a typo in the filename). If you get any errors, you'll need to fix them before moving on.

Creating a Spinning Cube

A spinning cube is the standard graphic for all new 3D programmers to try. It's simple enough to be easily understood, yet covers all of the basics, and it doesn't require vast amounts of data to build the 3D model.

> **NOTE** Recall that the book's companion website is at `www.wiley.com/go/python-raspberrypi`. To avoid potential typos, you can download and copy and paste the text into your IDE or code editor.

The full code is on the website as `chapter6-spinning-cube.py`. We'll go through it in stages, as there's quite a lot going on.

First of all, you need to set up the data:

```
vertices = [(0.0,0.0,0.0), (0.5,0.0,0.0), (0.5,0.5,0.0),
            (0.0, 0.5,0.0), 0.0,0.0,-0.5), (0.5,0.0,-0.5),
            (0.5,0.5,-0.5), (0.0, 0.5,-0.5)]


indices_face_1 = (0, 1, 2, 0, 3)
```

The list `vertices` holds a list of all the corners of the cube we'll draw. You're actually going to draw a bit more than just a spinning cube. There'll be four of the six faces of a spinning cube, the edges of a static cube, and some points. Doing this, you'll learn the different ways of drawing things on the screen.

The tuple `indices_face_1` holds a list of the points that you'll use for drawing the particular item on the screen (the number is the index of the list `vertices`). Here there are the indices (the plural of index) for one of the faces of the cube, but there are more in the actual code. You'll use these later to draw multiple items from the same pool of vertices.

The next bit is to set up OpenGL (note that if you're following along with the downloaded file, we're not going through it in order).

```
self.vertex_shader = glesutils.VertexShader(vertex_glsl)
self.fragment_shader = glesutils.FragmentShader(
                        fragment_glsl)

self.program1 = glesutils.Program(self.vertex_shader,
                                   self.fragment_shader)
self.program1.use()

glClearDepthf(1.0)
glDepthFunc(GL_LESS)
glEnable(GL_DEPTH_TEST)

glClearColor(0.5, 0.5, 0.5, 1)
```

Earlier, we said that the GPU is an extra processing unit that you can use to perform some of the maths needed for 3D graphics. In order to use it, we need to create a program for it, and this has to have source code. These programs are built of two parts, the vertex shader and the fragment shader. The variables `vertex_glsl` and `fragment_glsl` contain the code for this program-within-a-program (we'll look at them in detail later). In order to use them, you have to convert them into shader objects, then combine these shader objects into a program that you can run. You can have more than one OpenGL program within your Python program, and you switch between them using the `use()` method. Here, there is just one program, so there's just one `use()` call at the start.

The final four lines set up OpenGL. Firstly, there are three lines that set it to clear at a depth of 1.0, then the final line blanks the screen out to a mid grey. The four values of OpenGL colours are Red, Blue, Green, and Alpha (transparency). Each takes values in the range of 0 to 1.

The next task is to load the data into the GPU.

```
self.verteces_buffer = array_spec.create_buffer(
                        vertex_attrib=vertices)

self.elements_face_1 = glesutils.ElementBuffer(
                        indices_face_1)
```

The main program is running on the CPU and the 3D modeling is taking place on the GPU. These are very close together on the Raspberry Pi, but it still takes a bit of time to transfer data between the two. Because of this, it's best to load as much information as possible into the GPU before you start running it. This is what buffers are for. Here you use two types of buffers to hold the vertex and index information. Once the program is running, you only need to send the identity of the buffer you're using. In this particular example, there are only a few items in each buffer, so it might not make too much difference. However, if you're loading complex 3D models, these could each hold huge amounts of information, and the lag in transferring them each time could be significant.

Vectors and Matrices

In the 3D worlds you create, every point is defined by a set of coordinates (x, y, z). The x is the horizontal position, y is vertical, and z is depth. In mathematical terms, this set of numbers is called a *vector*. Every point on an object is known as a vertex, and every vertex has a vector that describes its position. In order to move objects around this 3D world, you need to manipulate these vectors. For example, you may want to zoom in on an object, which would mean moving every vector by a scaling factor. Or if you want to spin an object, you would need to move every vertex's vector accordingly.

This is done by vector-matrix algebra. In short, for every transition you want to make, you create a matrix (a square grid of numbers). You then multiply the vector by this matrix and you get a new vector.

Don't be confused by the word *multiply*; it's not like normal multiplication. The exact maths of what's going on is a little complex, and since OpenGL handles it all for you, you don't need to worry about it. All you need to know at this stage is that to move an object around, you create a matrix and multiply the vertices's vectors by the appropriate matrix. If you want to go beyond what we do in this chapter, it will be useful to learn more about what's going on, and there are plenty of resources, both online and in print, that can help you.

The following bit of code creates two matrices that show off the basics of how to do this. `transforms.compose()` is used to combine many matrices into a single one.

```
self.outer_matrix = transforms.compose(
        transforms.rotation_degrees(20, "z"),
        transforms.rotation_degrees(20, "y"),
        transforms.rotation_degrees(20, "x"),
        transforms.scaling(1.2))

self.points_matrix = transforms.compose(
        transforms.stretching(0.1, 1, 1.5),
        transforms.translation(-0.5, -0.5, -0.5))
```

transforms.rotation_degrees(), transforms.scaling(), and transforms.
stretching() each return a matrix that will perform the specified action when multiplied
by a vector.

Before going on and drawing anything on the screen, let's now take a step backwards and
look at the code we loaded into the GPU in the vertex and fragment shaders:

```
array_spec = glesutils.ArraySpec("vertex_attrib:3f")

vertex_glsl = array_spec.glsl() + """
uniform mat4 transform_matrix;
void main(void) {
  gl_Position = transform_matrix * vec4(vertex_attrib, 1.0);
  gl_PointSize = 2.0;
}
"""

fragment_glsl = """
uniform vec4 color;
void main(void) {
  gl_FragColor = color;
}
"""
```

This creates two strings, vertex_glsl and fragment_glsl, that contain code. However,
as you've probably noticed, it's not Python code. Programs for the GPU have to be written in
a special language called GLSL (Graphics Library Shader Language). It's similar to C (which is
a programming language that you can write for the main CPU). The main differences with
GLSL are

- Every statement has to end with a semicolon.
- The indent level doesn't matter, but code blocks are enclosed between curly braces.

■ Variables have a type associated with them and can only hold data of that type.

There are also differences in the keywords and functions. Since this is all new, we'll go through it line-by-line.

```
array_spec = glesutils.ArraySpec("vertex_attrib:3f")
```

This creates a new `ArraySpec` object (which you'll need elsewhere). The parameter tells it that you'll pass the attribute `vertex_attrib`, which will be a series of three-dimensional float (i.e., `3f`) vectors.

```
vertex_glsl = array_spec.glsl() + """
```

This creates the variable name and assigns the string to it. `array_spec.glsl()` just returns the code to properly create the attributes in `array_spec` (`vertex_attrib`). The three quotation marks tell Python that you're starting a multi-line string.

```
uniform mat4 transform_matrix;
```

This creates a new uniform variable called `transform_matrix` that's a four by four matrix. The `uniform` keyword means that it can be set from the Python code.

```
void main(void) {
```

This creates the `main` function, which will be run every time the program is run. The first `void` means it doesn't return anything, and the second means it doesn't take any parameters. Note the curly brace, which means you're starting the code block.

```
gl_Position = transform_matrix * vec4(vertex_attrib, 1.0);
```

The indent here isn't necessary (as it would be in Python), but is included because it makes the code easier to read. This is where you multiply the vector that describes the position of the vertex by the matrix that describes the transform. Notice that these are both four-dimensional. For now, don't worry about the last value and set it as 1.0.

Every vertex shader must set `gl_Position` as it's the variable that draws the vertex on the screen. Once it's set, OpenGL takes care of the rest.

```
gl_PointSize = 2.0;
}
"""
```

`gl_PointSize` simply sets the size of points you draw on the screen (we'll cover points, lines, and triangles in a bit). The curly brace then finishes the `main` function, and the three quote marks end the string.

The vertex shader is called once for each vertex, while the fragment shader is called once for every point on the model. Therefore, the fragment shader is run far more times than the vertex shader, and you'll usually find that they're far simpler because of this. In this case, it's just four lines:

```
fragment_glsl = """
uniform vec4 color;
void main(void) {
  gl_FragColor = color;
}
"""
```

Just as the vertex shaders always set `gl_Position`, fragment shaders always set `gl_FragColor`. This is a 4D vector that is the colour for that position.

With all this now in place, the only thing left to do is to place the items into the 3D world:

```
#Draw outer lines
self.program1.uniform.transform_matrix.value =
                              self.outer_matrix
self.program1.uniform.color.value = (1, 1, 1, 1)
self.verteces_buffer.draw(elements=self.elements_outer,
                     mode=GL_LINE_STRIP)
#Draw points
self.program1.uniform.transform_matrix.value =
                              self.points_matrix
self.program1.uniform.color.value = (0, 0, 0, 1)
self.verteces_buffer.draw(elements=self.elements_points,
                     mode=GL_POINTS)

#Draw spinning cube
rotation_matrix =
       transforms.compose(
       transforms.rotation_degrees(self.angle, "z"),
       transforms.rotation_degrees(self.angle, "y"),
       transforms.rotation_degrees(self.angle, "x")))

self.program1.uniform.transform_matrix.value =
                           rotation_matrix
```

```
self.program1.uniform.color.value = (1, 0, 0, 1)
self.verteces_buffer.draw(elements=self.elements_face_1,
                          mode=GL_TRIANGLE_STRIP)
```

There are three different sets of draw functions, but they all follow the same format. Firstly, they set the `transform_matrix` variable in the vertex shader with the attribute `self.program1.uniform.transform_matrix.value`. Then they use a similar line to set the colour variable in the fragment shader. Finally, they draw the points into the world with a call to `self.verteces_buffer.draw()`. This takes two parameters. Firstly, it takes the `elements`, which is simply the element buffer that contains the right indices of points, and secondly it takes a `mode`, which tells OpenGL what these vertices mean. The three here are `GL_POINTS`, `GL_LINE_STRIP`, and `GL_TRIANGLE_STRIP`.

`GL_POINTS` should be pretty obvious. It simply draws a point for every vertex. `GL_LINE_STRIP` draws a continuous line and each vertex is a point on the line. There is also a mode called `GL_LINES`, which draws separate lines for every pair of vertices.

`GL_TRIANGLE_STRIP` draws a continuous chain of triangles. In this case we're using five vertices to define a square. Actually, that's not quite true: we're using four vertices, but one of them is used twice. With triangle strips, the first three points have to make a triangle, then the third, fourth, and fifth, then the fifth, sixth, and seventh, then the seventh, eighth, and ninth, and so on. In each case, the last two points of the previous triangle make the first two points of the current triangle. In this way you can map out any surface.

There is also `GL_TRIANGLES`, which draws a triangle every three points and `GL_TRIANGLE_FAN`, where every point shares a single point and they're fanned out a bit like the petals on a flower.

Bringing It All Together

The full code is as follows (remember, it's on the website as `chapter6-spinning-cube.py`):

```
import pygame
from rpigl import glesutils, transforms
from rpigl.gles2 import *

vertices = [(0.0,0.0,0.0), (0.5,0.0,0.0), (0.5,0.5,0.0),
            (0.0, 0.5,0.0),
            (0.0,0.0,-0.5), (0.5,0.0,-0.5), (0.5,0.5,-0.5),
            (0.0, 0.5,-0.5)]

indices_face_1 = (0, 1, 2, 0, 3)
indices_face_2 = (4, 5, 6, 4, 7)
indices_face_3 = (1, 5, 6, 1, 2)
```

```python
indices_face_4 = (0, 4, 7, 0 ,3)
indices_outer = (0, 1, 2, 3, 0, 4, 5, 1, 5, 6, 2, 6, 7, 3, 7, 4)
indices_points = (0, 1, 2, 3)

array_spec = glesutils.ArraySpec("vertex_attrib:3f")

vertex_glsl = array_spec.glsl() + """
uniform mat4 transform_matrix;
void main(void) {
  gl_Position = transform_matrix * vec4(vertex_attrib, 1.0);
  gl_PointSize = 2.0;
}
"""

fragment_glsl = """
uniform vec4 color;
void main(void) {
  gl_FragColor = color;
}
"""

class MyWindow(glesutils.GameWindow):

    def init(self):

        self.angle = 10

        self.vertex_shader = glesutils.VertexShader(vertex_glsl)
        self.fragment_shader =
                    glesutils.FragmentShader(fragment_glsl)

        self.program1 = glesutils.Program(self.vertex_shader,
                                        self.fragment_shader)
        self.program1.use()

        glClearDepthf(1.0)
        glDepthFunc(GL_LESS)
        glEnable(GL_DEPTH_TEST)

        glClearColor(0.5, 0.5, 0.5, 1)

        self.program1.uniform.light_dir.value = ((0, 1, -1))
```

```
        self.verteces_buffer =
                array_spec.create_buffer(vertex_attrib=vertices)
        self.elements_face_1 =
                glesutils.ElementBuffer(indices_face_1)
        self.elements_face_2 =
                glesutils.ElementBuffer(indices_face_2)
        self.elements_face_3 =
                glesutils.ElementBuffer(indices_face_3)
        self.elements_face_4 =
                glesutils.ElementBuffer(indices_face_4)

        self.elements_outer =
                glesutils.ElementBuffer(indices_outer)
        self.elements_points =
                glesutils.ElementBuffer(indices_points)

        self.outer_matrix =
                transforms.compose(
                transforms.rotation_degrees(20, "z"),
                transforms.rotation_degrees(20, "y"),
                transforms.rotation_degrees(20, "x"),
                transforms.scaling(1.2))

        self.points_matrix =
                transforms.compose(
                transforms.stretching(0.1, 1, 1.5),
                transforms.translation(-0.5, -0.5, -0.5))

    def on_frame(self, time):
        self.angle = self.angle + time*0.02
        self.redraw()

    def draw(self):
        #Draw outer lines
        self.program1.uniform.transform_matrix.value =
                                self.outer_matrix
        self.program1.uniform.color.value = (1, 1, 1, 1)
        self.verteces_buffer.draw(elements=self.elements_outer,
                                mode=GL_LINE_STRIP)

        #Draw points
        self.program1.uniform.transform_matrix.value =
                                self.points_matrix
        self.program1.uniform.color.value = (0, 0, 0, 1)
        self.verteces_buffer.draw(elements=self.elements_points,
                                mode=GL_POINTS)
```

```
#Draw spinning cube
        rotation_matrix = transforms.compose
                (transforms.rotation_degrees(self.angle, "z"),
                 transforms.rotation_degrees(self.angle, "y"),
                 transforms.rotation_degrees(self.angle, "x"))

        self.program1.uniform.transform_matrix.value =
                                rotation_matrix
        self.program1.uniform.color.value = (1, 0, 0, 1)
        self.verteces_buffer.draw(elements=self.elements_face_1,
                                mode=GL_TRIANGLE_STRIP)
        self.program1.uniform.color.value = (0, 1, 0, 1)
        self.verteces_buffer.draw(elements=self.elements_face_2,
                                mode=GL_TRIANGLE_STRIP)
        self.program1.uniform.color.value = (0, 0, 1, 1)
        self.verteces_buffer.draw(elements=self.elements_face_3,
                                mode=GL_TRIANGLE_STRIP)
        self.program1.uniform.color.value = (0, 1, 1, 1)
        self.verteces_buffer.draw(elements=self.elements_face_4,
                                mode=GL_TRIANGLE_STRIP)


MyWindow(200, 200, pygame.RESIZABLE).run()
```

The result should be a 3D rendering like the one shown in Figure 6-1.

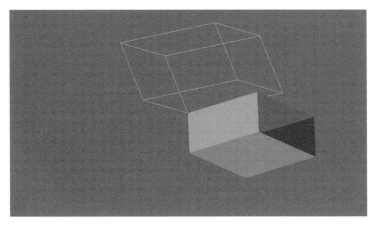

FIGURE 6-1: This demonstrates the basic technique from which most 3D graphics are built.

Let There Be Light

When you run the previous example, you should see four sides of a cube spinning round as well as a few lines and some dots. However, you may notice that there's something missing: light. All the faces are the same brightness regardless of which way they're facing. In the real world, this rarely happens. Instead, you usually have one or more sources of light that illuminate the objects differently, depending on which way they're facing.

Some versions of OpenGL can handle this automatically. However OpenGL ES, the version on the Raspberry Pi (and most mobile devices) doesn't, so you have to calculate the lighting yourself.

The following example will create a spinning cube that is lit from a point light source. You'll see the various parts of the cube get brighter and dimmer as they move. There are two things that you use to calculate the brightness of a particular point—the distance of the point on the cube from the source of light, and the angle of the face compared to the light.

Calculating the Distance of the Point from the Light Source

Let's look at the first of these. Each face on the cube is displayed by hundreds of pixels on the screen. The value of each of these pixels is calculated by the fragment shader. In order to calculate the colour of the pixel, the fragment shader needs to know how bright to make the pixel. This is done with the following code:

```
fragment_glsl = """
uniform vec4 color;

varying float brightness;

void main(void) {
  gl_FragColor = brightness*color;
}
"""
```

As you can see, this uses two variables, `color` and `brightness`. `brightness` is a `float` that can be used to alter the value that `gl_FragColor` gets set to. You'll notice that they're different data types, but that isn't a problem. When you multiply a vector by a floating-point, you simply multiply every part of the vector by the number. For example, if you had the colour (0.8,0.8, 0.8) (which would be a light grey), and you multiplied it by 0.5, the resulting colour would be (0.4,0.4, 0.4) (a mid-grey).

`brightness`, then, should vary between 0 for no light and 1 for fully lit.

The two variables are declared differently. `color` is created with the keyword `uniform`, and `brightness` is set with `varying`. `uniform` variables are set in the main Python code (as you saw in the previous example). `varying` variables, however, are set in the vertex shader as shown here:

```
vertex_glsl = array_spec.glsl() + """

...

varying float brightness;

void main(void) {
  ...6;
  float distance = length(vec4(light_position, 1.0) - gl_Position);
  brightness = 1.0/(distance * distance);
}
"""
```

This is missing the code to calculate the angles and position (which we'll look at later), but has everything to calculate how the brightness dims due to distance. The `length()` function returns the length of a vector (which can be calculated using the Pythagorean theorem). In this case, it's used to calculate the distance between the vertex and the light source.

As an object moves away from a light source, it gets dimmer. However, this doesn't happen linearly. If you move an object twice as far away, it doesn't get half as bright, it gets a quarter as bright. The relationship between the distance from a light source and brightness follows an inverse square. This is calculated in the final line.

This code, though, only calculates the brightness for the vertices. For the program to run properly, it needs to know what the brightness is for every point on the face. Fortunately, OpenGL takes care of this for you. Whenever you use the `varying` keyword to create a variable, it will interpolate the values passed to the fragment shader. This means that it will vary the value of `brightness` depending on the distance of the point it's rendering to the three vertices to create a smooth blend of brightness.

Calculating Reflecting Angles

The second aspect of brightness is the angle between the face and the source of light. To calculate this angle, you need a normal. A *normal* is a vector that sticks out of a face at 90 degrees.

Vectors can be used to describe positions, but they can also be used to describe lines. For example, the vector (1,1,1) could describe the point at those coordinates, or it could describe a line that's the same length and direction as the line from (0,0,0) to (1,1,1), but at any point in the 3D world. The vectors for vertices are position vectors, where as the vectors for normals are line vectors like this.

The normal is a vector to describe what direction the object is facing. Take for example the first face of the cube with vertices at (0.0,0.0,0.0), (0.5,0.0,0.0), (0.5,0.5,0.0), (0.0, 0.5,0.0).

These vertices are all flat on the z-axis, so the normal is (0,0,1.0). If you drew a line from (0,0,0) to (0,0,1), it would be at 90 degrees to this face. Normals also always have a length of 1.

To calculate the brightness, then, you need to calculate the difference between this angle and the light from the light source. If they're exactly in line then the face should be fully lit, and if they're 90 degrees or more, the face shouldn't be lit at all. However, just as with the distance, there isn't a linear relationship between the two; instead the brightness varies in a sine curve. The sine function, however, would be the wrong way around, so you need to calculate the cosine.

For this, you need to reach into the trigonometric toolbox. There's a function called the *dot product* that takes two vectors, and returns a number such that:

```
dot(A,B) = length(A) * length(B) * cosine(A,B)
```

Calculating the dot product is far quicker than calculating the cosine, so we can use this as a mathematical shortcut. It becomes simpler if both vectors have a length of 1. Then the dot product simply returns the cosine.

Normals always have a length of 1 so you can safely ignore that. There is also a function in GLSL called `normalize()` that takes any vector and returns one that's in the same direction but that has a length of 1. You can calculate the cosine of the two vectors with:

```
cosine = dot(surface_normal, normalize(gl_Position -
                                       light_position)
```

However, most of the time there isn't just one light source. There's loads of light reflected off walls and other objects. Calculating all of this is phenomenally complicated, and the easiest thing to do is set an ambient light value. This is simply the amount of light that's everywhere regardless of which direction the object's facing. You can calculate the ambient with:

```
brightness = max(cosine, ambient_light)
```

All of this is then combined to make the vertex shader in the following code:

```
vertex_glsl = array_spec.glsl() + """
uniform mat4 transform_matrix;
uniform vec3 light_position;
uniform float ambient_light;
uniform vec3 face_normal;

varying float brightness;
```

```
void main(void) {
  gl_Position = transform_matrix * vec4(vertex_attrib, 1.0);
  vec4 spun_face_normal = normalize(transform_matrix *
                                  vec4(face_normal, 1.0));
  float distance = length(vec4(light_position, 1.0) - gl_Position);
  vec4 light_direction = normalize(vec4(light_position, 1.0) -
                                  gl_Position);
  float light_amount_angle = max(dot(spun_face_normal,
                                  light_direction), ambient_light);

  float light_distance_drop = 1.0/(distance * distance);
  brightness = light_amount_angle * light_distance_drop;
}
"""
```

Note that this doesn't run the dot product on the original surface normal, but on the surface normal that's been transformed in the same way as the cube has. In this example, the transform_matrix won't scale or stretch the normal so technically, it doesn't need to be normalised. However, we've included this to make the code more useful in other programs.

The rest of the code is then basically the same as in the previous examples. There aren't the points or lines, and there are all six faces of the cube. This is on the website as chapter6-lighting.py.

```
import pygame
from rpigl import glesutils, transforms
from rpigl.gles2 import *

vertices = [(0.0,0.0,0.0), (0.5,0.0,0.0), x/4984720?c=pledges
            (0.5,0.5,0.0), (0.0, 0.5,0.0),
            (0.0,0.0,-0.5), (0.5,0.0,-0.5),
            (0.5,0.5,-0.5), (0.0, 0.5,-0.5)]

faces = [{"vertex_index":(0, 1, 2, 0, 3), "normal":(0,0,1),
          "colour":(1, 0, 0, 1)},
         {"vertex_index":(4, 5, 6, 4, 7), "normal":(0,0,-1),
          "colour":(0, 1, 0, 1)},
         {"vertex_index":(1, 5, 6, 1, 2), "normal":(1,0,0),
          "colour":(0, 0, 1, 1)},
         {"vertex_index":(0, 4, 7, 0 ,3), "normal":(-1,0,0),
          "colour":(1, 0, 1, 1)},
         {"vertex_index":(3, 2, 6, 3, 7), "normal":(0,1,0),
          "colour":(1, 1, 0, 1)},
         {"vertex_index":(0, 1, 5, 0, 4), "normal":(0,-1,0),
          "colour":(0, 1, 1, 1)}]
```

```python
array_spec = glesutils.ArraySpec("vertex_attrib:3f")

vertex_glsl = array_spec.glsl() + """
uniform mat4 transform_matrix;
uniform vec3 light_position;
uniform float ambient_light;
uniform vec3 face_normal;

varying float brightness;

void main(void) {
  gl_Position = transform_matrix * vec4(vertex_attrib, 1.0);
  vec4 spun_face_normal = normalize(transform_matrix *
                                    vec4(face_normal, 1.0));
  float distance = length(vec4(light_position, 1.0) - gl_Position);
  vec4 light_direction = normalize(vec4(light_position, 1.0) -
                                   gl_Position);
  float light_amount_angle = max(dot(spun_face_normal,
                                 light_direction), ambient_light);
  float light_distance_drop = 1.0/(distance * distance);
  brightness = light_amount_angle * light_distance_drop;
  gl_PointSize = 2.0;
}
"""

fragment_glsl = """
uniform vec4 color;

varying float brightness;

void main(void) {
  gl_FragColor = brightness*color;
}
"""


class MyWindow(glesutils.GameWindow):

    def init(self):

        self.angle = 10
        self.framerate = 20

        self.vertex_shader = glesutils.VertexShader(vertex_glsl)
        self.fragment_shader =
                    glesutils.FragmentShader(fragment_glsl)
```

```python
        self.program1 = glesutils.Program(self.vertex_shader,
                                          self.fragment_shader)
        self.program1.use()

        glClearDepthf(1.0)
        glDepthFunc(GL_LESS)
        glEnable(GL_DEPTH_TEST)
        glFrontFace(GL_CW)

        glClearColor(0.5, 0.5, 0.5, 1)

        self.program1.uniform.light_dir.value = ((0, 1, -1))

        self.verteces_buffer = \
                array_spec.create_buffer(vertex_attrib=vertices)
        for face in faces:
            face["element_buffer"] = \
                glesutils.ElementBuffer(face["vertex_index"])

        self.outer_matrix = transforms.compose(
                transforms.rotation_degrees(20, "z"),
                transforms.rotation_degrees(20, "y"),
                transforms.rotation_degrees(20, "x"),
                transforms.scaling(1.2))

        self.points_matrix = transforms.compose(
                        transforms.stretching(0.1, 1, 1.5),
                        transforms.translation(-0.5, -0.5, -0.5))

    def on_frame(self, time):
        self.angle = self.angle + time*0.02
        self.redraw()

    def draw(self):
        self.program1.uniform.light_position.value = (0,0,-1)
        self.program1.uniform.ambient_light.value = 0.3

        rotation_matrix = transforms.compose(
                transforms.rotation_degrees(self.angle, "z"),
                transforms.rotation_degrees(self.angle, "y"),
                transforms.rotation_degrees(self.angle, "x"))

        self.program1.uniform.transform_matrix.value = \
                                        rotation_matrix
```

```
    for face in faces:
        self.program1.uniform.color.value = face["colour"]
        self.program1.uniform.face_normal.value =
                                        face["normal"]

    self.verteces_buffer.draw(elements=face["element_buffer"],
                    mode=GL_TRIANGLE_STRIP)

MyWindow(200, 200, pygame.RESIZABLE).run()
```

The result is shown in Figure 6-2.

FIGURE 6-2: The light adds a sense of realism that isn't in the first program.

Making the Screen Dance

So far, you've seen how to draw cubes on the screen and light them, but not anything more than that. In the next project, you'll see how to create a 3D model that moves to music. Most computer music players have similar features that visualise the sound and provide a bit of video entertainment for the listener.

Since this is a chapter about 3D graphics and not audio processing, we'll make things simple for ourselves by only working with WAV files. This means we can use the `wave` Python module to extract the sound data from the file. If your music collection is stored as MP3 files, you'll need to convert one or more of them to WAV before continuing. You can do this with the `mpg123` command-line tool in LXTerminal. First you'll need to install it with:

```
sudo apt-get install mpg123
```

Then you can convert the files with:

```
mpg123 -w output-filename.wav input-filename.mp3
```

If you don't have any suitable music, you can download some legally from http://free musicarchive.org/.

The first step is to play the music. You do this in exactly the same way as you did the sounds in the previous chapter, using a PyGame mixer. This plays the sound through the Pi's audio channel, but it doesn't provide you with the sound data needed to manipulate the 3D graphics. For this we'll use a second module, wave.

The following code can be used to import music from the file test.wav.

```
print("opening file")
sound_file = wave.open("test.wav",';rb')

print("getting parameters")
(channels, sample_size, frame_rate, frames, compression_type,
  compression_name) = sound_file.getparams()

print("Number of channels: ", channels)
print("Sample size: ", sample_size)
print("Frame rate: ", frame_rate)
print("Number of Frames: ", frames)
print("Compression type: ", compression_type)
print("Compression name: ", compression_name)

print("readframes")
data = sound_file.readframes(channels*sample_size*frames)
print(len(data))
```

This creates the variable data, which contains the sound as a list of bytes. The sound, though, will be encoded in two-byte blocks. To read the value of a single block, you have to combine them using the from_byte() method of the int class.

```
sound_data = int.from_bytes(data[i:i+1],
                            byteorder='little', signed=True)
```

The data is stored in frames. Each frame is one of these two-byte blocks, and the value of each can vary between –32768 and 32767. For each point in time there are two frames if the sound file is in stereo. Typically, there are 44,100 of these frames every second (this is the number held in the frame_rate variable).

There are a number of ways that you could display this data. The only real requirement is that the output move in some entertaining way when the sound is playing. We're going to use two things. A set of 3D bars along the bottom of the screen that will plot out how the volume is changing, and a set of points (or stars if you're feeling poetic) that will flash to the music. Just to add some flair, we'll also make the whole visualisation spin around on the vertical axis, and blend the colour from blue at the bottom to red at the top.

Building the 3D Model

There are numerous ways we could model the data, but we're going to use the vertex data of a single cube and manipulate it with a transformation matrix for each bar on the chart. The stars will simply be a group of randomly positioned points. Let's deal with the blocks first.

Every block has the same set of vertices and indices. The difference between them is the size (which will simply be a stretching matrix), and the position (which will be a translation matrix). There will also be a couple more matrices that will be the same for every block: one to spin them around (which will change every frame), and one to zoom in and out (which will be set at the start).

You'll need to combine all these matrices. You could use the Python method `transforms.compose()` to do this. However, this needs to chunk through quite a bit of data every frame, and we mentioned at the start that the GPU is more powerful than the CPU. Therefore, it's more efficient to let the GPU handle all the matrix operations.

The shaders, then, are

```
vertex_glsl = array_spec.glsl() + """
uniform mat4 position_matrix;
uniform mat4 eye_matrix;
uniform mat4 scaling_matrix;
uniform mat4 sound_matrix;
uniform float point_size;

varying float red;

void main(void) {
  gl_Position = eye_matrix * position_matrix * scaling_matrix *
                sound_matrix * vec4(vertex_attrib, 1.0);

  red = (gl_Position[1]+0.9)/2.0;

  gl_PointSize = point_size;
}
"""
```

```
fragment_glsl = """
uniform vec4 color;
varying float red;

void main(void) {
  gl_FragColor = vec4(red, 0.0, (1.0-red)/5.0, 1.0);
}
"""
```

These are pretty similar to the ones you've seen before. It's worth noting that matrix multiplication isn't commutative. This is a fancy way of saying that the order in which you multiply the matrices does matter. It won't always make a difference, but does sometimes. In this example, it's important to make sure the `eye_matrix` (which should spin the entire scene) comes before the `position_matrix` (which puts the individual bars in the right place). If they are the other way round then the individual bars will spin on the spot rather than the scene spinning as a whole. This isn't necessarily a problem, we just felt it looked better like this. Getting the matrices in the right order is simply a case of thinking about which order you want the transformations to take place in (or, failing that, trial and error).

You'll notice that there is a `varying` variable named `red`. This takes the vertical aspect of the `gl_Position` vector (which is y, or 1) and transforms it into a value for the colour.

You may also note that the size of the points is set by a uniform variable. This will be dealt with a little later.

Calculating the Sound Level

Every time a new frame is displayed, the program will calculate the current sound level and set one of the bars to that sound level. It'll cycle through the bars in order so together they show how the sound level has changed over the past 20 screen draws.

In order to do this, you need to be able to calculate the sound level. This can be done using the `on_frame()` method.

```
 scale_factor = 0

 if frame_position + 1000 < len(data):
     for i in range(1,500):
         scale_factor1 = scale_factor +
                 int.from_bytes(data[frame_position+2*i:
                 frame_position+(2*i)+1],
                 byteorder='little', signed=True)**2
```

```
scale_factor1 = scale_factor1 / 500

self.sound_matrix[self.counter%20] =
          transforms.stretching(1.0,scale_factor1,1.0)

self.program1.uniform.point_size.value =
          float(scale_factor1/4)

    self.counter = self.counter+1
```

For any position in the sound (which is calculated by seeing how much time has passed since the track started playing), this checks the sound level for the next 500 frames and sums their squares. Squaring the sound level does two things. Firstly it makes sure all the values are positive since the square of a negative number is always positive. Secondly, it makes the blocks jump up far more with each increase in music, and this looks better onscreen. The point of this is to make something that looks pretty, not something that produces a scientifically correct graph, so manipulations like this are perfectly acceptable.

The reason it adds together 500 frames is simply because the more frames it adds together the more accurate it is, but also the slower it is. We found this to be a good compromise between performance (which corresponds to the frame rate of the display) and ability to accurately model the music. If you wish to make this perfectly correct, you'll need to introduce some timing functions like you saw in the previous chapter.

You'll notice that it also sets the size for the stars. The amount we shrunk the scaling factor by (500 for the bars and 4 for the stars) was determined by seeing what looked good, not by calculation.

The full code of the visualiser is as follows (it's on the website as `chapter6-music.py`).

```
import pygame
from rpigl import glesutils, transforms
from rpigl.gles2 import *
import random
import wave
import time

vertices = [(0.0,0.0,0.0), (0.5,0.0,0.0),
            (0.5,0.5,0.0), (0.0, 0.5,0.0),
            (0.0,0.0,-0.5), (0.5,0.0,-0.5),
            (0.5,0.5,-0.5), (0.0, 0.5,-0.5)]

indices_outer = (0, 1, 2, 3, 0, 4, 5, 1, 5, 6, 2, 6, 7, 3, 7, 4)
```

```python
vertices_points = []
indices_points = []

for i in range(0,100):
    vertices_points.append(((20 * random.random())-10,
                (20 * random.random()), (20 * random.random())-10))
    indices_points.append(i)

array_spec = glesutils.ArraySpec("vertex_attrib:3f")

vertex_glsl = array_spec.glsl() + """
uniform mat4 position_matrix;
uniform mat4 eye_matrix;
uniform mat4 scaling_matrix;
uniform mat4 sound_matrix;
uniform float point_size;

varying float red;

void main(void) {
  gl_Position = eye_matrix * position_matrix * scaling_matrix *
  sound_matrix * vec4(vertex_attrib, 1.0);
  red = (gl_Position[1]+0.9)/2.0;
  gl_PointSize = point_size;
}
"""

fragment_glsl = """
uniform vec4 color;
varying float red;

void main(void) {
  gl_FragColor = vec4(red, 0.0, (1.0-red)/5.0, 1.0);
}
"""

class MyWindow(glesutils.GameWindow):

    def init(self):
        self.angle_x = 5
        self.angle_y = 10
        self.angle_z = 5
        self.counter = 0
```

```
self.vertex_shader = glesutils.VertexShader(vertex_glsl)
self.fragment_shader = glesutils.FragmentShader(
                       fragment_glsl)

self.program1 = glesutils.Program(self.vertex_shader,
                                  self.fragment_shader)
self.program1.use()

glClearDepthf(1.0)
glDepthFunc(GL_LESS)
glEnable(GL_DEPTH_TEST)

glClearColor(0.0, 0.0, 0.0, 1)

self.program1.uniform.light_dir.value = ((0, 1, -1))

self.verteces_buffer = array_spec.create_buffer(
                       vertex_attrib=vertices)
self.points_buffer = array_spec.create_buffer(
                     vertex_attrib=vertices_points)

self.elements_outer = glesutils.ElementBuffer(
                      indices_outer)
self.elements_points = glesutils.ElementBuffer(
                       indices_points)

self.blank_matrix = transforms.translation(0.0, 0.0, 0.0)

self.position_matrix = []
for i in range(0,20):

self.position_matrix.append(transforms.translation(((i/10)-0.95,
                                                    0.0, 0.0))
self.sound_matrix = []
for i in range(0,20):

    self.sound_matrix.append(transforms.translation(
                             0.0, 0.0, 0.0))

self.program1.uniform.scaling_matrix.value =
                              transforms.scaling(0.1)
```

```python
    self.program1.uniform.eye_matrix.value =
            transforms.compose(
            transforms.rotation_degrees(self.angle_z, "z"),
            transforms.rotation_degrees(self.angle_x, "y"),
            transforms.rotation_degrees(self.angle_x, "x"),
            transforms.translation(0.0, -0.9, 0.0))
    self.counter = 0

def on_frame(self, ftime):
    global start_time
    global data

    self.angle_y = self.angle_y + .5

    self.program1.uniform.eye_matrix.value =
            transforms.compose(
            transforms.rotation_degrees(self.angle_z, "z"),
            transforms.rotation_degrees(self.angle_y, "y"),
            transforms.rotation_degrees(self.angle_x, "x"),
            transforms.translation(0.0, -0.9, 0.0))

    frame_position = int((pygame.time.get_ticks() -
                        start_time) * 44.1 * 4)

    scale_factor = 0

    if frame_position + 1000 < len(data):
        for i in range(1,500):
            scale_factor1 = scale_factor +
                    int.from_bytes(data[frame_position+2*i:
                    frame_position+(2*i)+1],
                    byteorder='little', signed=True)**2

        scale_factor1 = scale_factor1 / 500

        self.sound_matrix[self.counter%20] =
                transforms.stretching(1.0,scale_factor1,1.0)

        self.program1.uniform.point_size.value =
                float(scale_factor1/4)

        self.counter = self.counter+1

    self.redraw()
```

```python
    def draw(self):
        self.program1.uniform.color.value = (1, 1, 1, 1)
        for i in range(0,20):
            self.program1.uniform.position_matrix.value =
                                    self.position_matrix[i]
            self.program1.uniform.sound_matrix.value =
                                    self.sound_matrix[i]
            self.verteces_buffer.draw(elements=self.elements_outer,
                                    mode=GL_LINE_STRIP)
            self.counter = self.counter +1

        self.program1.uniform.position_matrix.value =
                                        self.blank_matrix
        self.program1.uniform.sound_matrix.value =
                                        self.blank_matrix
        self.points_buffer.draw(mode=GL_POINTS)

print("starting pygame mixer")
pygame.mixer.pre_init(44100, -16, 2, 2048)
pygame.mixer.init()

music = pygame.mixer.Sound("tell.wav")

print("opening file")
sound_file = wave.open("test.wav",'rb')

print("getting parameters")
(channels, sample_size, frame_rate, frames, compression_type,
  compression_name) = sound_file.getparams()

print("Number of channels: ", channels)
print("Sample size: ", sample_size)
print("Frame rate: ", frame_rate)
print("Number of Frames: ", frames)
print("Compression type: ", compression_type)
print("Compression name: ", compression_name)

print("readframes")
data = sound_file.readframes(4*frames)
print(len(data))

print("starting audio")
music.play()
```

```
start_time = pygame.time.get_ticks()

print("start time: ", time.clock())

MyWindow(200, 200, pygame.RESIZABLE).run()
```

The result, which has a surprisingly '80s feel to it, is shown in Figure 6-3.

FIGURE 6-3: This looks much better when it's moving. But don't take our word for it. Run the code and see for yourself.

Taking Things Further

Consider these ideas for taking the project to the next level:

- Make the stars a constant size, but make them change in brightness. You could use a separate OpenGL program to do this, although it's not essential.

- You could add lighting, although for it to make sense, you'd need to replace the lines with triangle strips.

- Experiment with the number of bars and stars. You should be able to make this easily configurable.

- Make the graph show the frequency breakdown rather than the volume over time. To do this, you'll need to calculate the Fourier Transform of the music using the SciPi module. Note that this is quite a challenging and maths-y option for interested readers.

- Create a better interface for selecting which songs to play. This could be command-line, text-based, or graphical depending on your preferences. There are examples of all three elsewhere in the book.

- Change the visualisation. Falling or swirling stars are one option. You could also investigate zooming in and out as well as rotating. The colour blend doesn't have to stay constant either. Be creative; the 3D world is there for you to mold into your imagination.

Adding Some Texture

We said at the start that this would be the most complex chapter in the book. Even though it has been, it's done little more than introduce OpenGL. There is much more that we haven't covered. If you've found it interesting and want to explore further, one of the most interesting things to look into are textures. These allow you to add more detail to your 3D models. There are a couple of examples that come with RPiGL to get you started. You can find them in the demos subfolder of the Python module that you downloaded at the start.

The first is icosa.py, and it takes a map of the world and projects it onto a spinning sphere. It takes the image from world_cube_net.png and loads it using the method glesutils. Texture.from_surface(), and then it uses bind() to make it available to the shaders.

The second is bumpedspere.py, and this works a little differently. Remember how you used the normal to calculate the amount of light reflected? Well, you can use this to make a smooth surface appear to have a texture. If you vary the normal so that it's not exactly perpendicular to the surface, it will vary the amount of light on it as though the surface is slightly bumped. This is really an optical illusion as there's no way that such a surface could exist in real life, but the effect is a surface that appears to have small bumps on it without the need for a vast web of triangles.

> **TIP** There is loads of really useful information on OpenGL in print and on the Internet. However, you need to remember that not all versions of OpenGL work the same. The version of the Raspberry Pi is OpenGL ES 2.0, so you need to make sure that whatever you're trying works with this version.

Summary

After reading this chapter, you should understand the following a bit better:

- OpenGL provides a powerful way of creating and manipulating 3D graphics.

- However, with that power comes complexity.

- Coordinates are stored as vectors, and you can manipulate them by multiplying the vector by a transform matrix.

- If there are many transforms, then you can chain these multiplications together. However, the order in which you do this is important.

- OpenGL runs as a separate program that is comprised of two shaders—the vertex shader and the attribute shader.

- These shaders aren't written in Python but in the GL Shader Language or GLSL, which is similar to C.

- In GLSL, every line has to end with a semicolon, and code blocks are enclosed in curly braces.

- In GLSL `uniform` variables are set by the program and are constant for the entire `draw()` method call. `varying` vectors are set in the vertex shader and are interpolated for points on the surface.

- OpenGL ES doesn't include any lighting, so you have to calculate it yourself using both the distance from the light and the cosine of the normal and the light direction.

- Textures can be used to add detail to your objects.

Chapter 7
Networked Python

THE WORLD TODAY is more connected than it's ever been, and almost everything that you do on computers has some form of online component. The Raspberry Pi is no different. As long as you have a Model B, or a wireless USB dongle, getting your Pi connected to the Internet is trivial. There's the Midori browser you can use to surf the web, and mail clients are available. These are good for consuming content—getting information off the web and using services that other people have created. The power of the Raspberry Pi, however, lies in creating things. With a few lines of Python, you can grab information off the web or use your Raspberry Pi to serve up content and services to the world. Read on to find out how.

Understanding Hosts, Ports, and Sockets

To communicate with another computer, you need to know where to send data to. It might be that you're just sending information to another computer in the same room, or you might be sending it halfway round the world. Regardless, you need to specify an address. The standard way of locating computers is by Internet Protocol (IP) address. There are two types of IP address, version 4 and version 6. At the time of writing, version 4 (IPv4) is almost universally used, so you'll read only about it. IPv6 addresses work in the same basic way, so you shouldn't have any difficulty using these should they become mainstream any time soon.

Locating Computers with IP Addresses

IPv4 addresses contain four numbers separated by dots. To determine your Raspberry Pi's IP addresses (it has more than one), open a terminal (not a Python session, but an LXTerminal session). And run `ifconfig`. This should output something like the following:

```
eth0   Link encap:Ethernet   HWaddr b8:27:eb:f3:d5:23
       inet addr:192.168.0.13  Bcast:192.168.0.255
           Mask:255.255.255.0
       UP BROADCAST RUNNING MULTICAST  MTU:1500  Metric:1
       RX packets:87523 errors:0 dropped:0 overruns:0 frame:0
       TX packets:59811 errors:0 dropped:0 overruns:0 carrier:0
       collisions:0 txqueuelen:1000
       RX bytes:97997131 (93.4 MiB)  TX bytes:12573160 (11.9 MiB)

lo     Link encap:Local Loopback
       inet addr:127.0.0.1  Mask:255.0.0.0
       UP LOOPBACK RUNNING  MTU:16436  Metric:1
       RX packets:0 errors:0 dropped:0 overruns:0 frame:0
       TX packets:0 errors:0 dropped:0 overruns:0 carrier:0
       collisions:0 txqueuelen:0
       RX bytes:0 (0.0 B)  TX bytes:0 (0.0 B)
```

This shows that there are two network interfaces: `eth0` and `lo`. `eth0` is the wired network connection, and `lo` is the loopback connection that just loops back to the same machine. In the previous example, the Ethernet connection has an IP address of `192.168.0.13`, while the loop back is `127.0.0.1` (this is always the same).

As well as by IP addresses, we can also locate computers by hostname (such as `www.google.com`, or *localhost*). These are a convenient shorthand for IP addresses. When you use one of these, you computer connects to a name server and asks what IP address that hostname corresponds to, then connects to the returned IP address. Localhost is a slightly unusual case as it always corresponds to `127.0.0.1` and is therefore the local machine.

If you think of the IP addresses (or hostnames) as similar to building addresses in the real world, then within each building, you still have to address it to the right person. In a computer network, this is done with *ports*. If you have a piece of software that serves information, it will listen on a particular port. Clients can then connect to a particular port, and get that information. Some ports are used for particular services. For example, web servers generally listen on port 80, whereas SSH connections go over port 22.

In Python, *sockets* are objects that connect to a particular port on a particular host, or listen for a connection coming into a particular port. Once they're connected, you can send and receive data through the socket. That sounds a bit complicated, but it's actually quite simple in practice. The easiest way to understand it is with an example.

Building a Chat Server

Unlike most of the programs in this book, this program has two parts that need to be run at the same time: a client and a server. The server just sits and waits for a connection to come in, while the client establishes a connection. Here's the code for the server:

```
import socket

comms_socket = socket.socket()
comms_socket.bind(('localhost', 50000))
comms_socket.listen(10)
connection, address = comms_socket.accept()

while True:
    print(connection.recv(4096).decode("UTF-8"))
    send_data = input("Reply: ")
    connection.send(bytes(send_data, "UTF-8"))
```

You can see that this gets most of its functionality from the socket module. With a server socket, you first need to bind it to a port on the host. (Any of the ports above 50,000 should be free for temporary use. Actually, you can use pretty much any one that's not currently in use, but it's best to avoid the ones below 100 unless you're sure they're not being used.) `listen()` then sets it to wait for a connection. When a connection comes in, it moves onto the following line:

```
connection, address = comms_socket.accept()
```

This sets up a new socket (stored in the variable `connection`), which is connected to the client. You can now send and receive data over this new connection using the `send()` and `recv()` methods. These take streams of bytes not strings, so you have to convert back and forward between the bytes and UTF-8 (universal character set Transformation Format; it's 8-bit) encoding that you use to display the information.

Here's the code for the client:

```
import socket

comms_socket = socket.socket()
comms_socket.connect(('localhost', 50000))
```

```
while True:
    send_data = input("message: ")
    comms_socket.send(bytes(send_data, "UTF-8"))
    print(comms_socket.recv(4096).decode("UTF-8"))
```

You can see that this time, instead of binding the socket to a host and port, the code connects to them. This time, the code doesn't create a new socket, but sends and receives on the original one.

Other than this, the two programs are very similar. To run a chat, you'll need two Python sessions, and the easiest way to open two is with two LXTerminal windows. In the first window, type `python3 server.py` (if you've called the server `server.py`), and in the second, type `python3 client.py`.

You'll be able to pass messages back and forth between the two programs. Of course, these aren't very networked. In fact, they're running on the same machine. There are places where it's useful to run networking between two programs on the same machine, but generally with networking, you want to send data between two computers.

This code has all the basics needed to communicate between machines, but it just needs a bit of a menu to help users connect to the place they want to go. It'd also be easier if there was a single program that could handle both the client and server sides. An improved version of the chat program with these properties is as follows (you can find it on the website as `chapter7-chat.py`):

```
import socket

def server():
    global port
    host = "localhost"

    comms_socket = socket.socket()
    comms_socket.bind((host, port))

    print("Waiting for a chat at ", host, " on port ", port)

    comms_socket.listen(10)
    send_data = ""

    while True:
        connection, address = comms_socket.accept()
        print("opening chat with ", address)
        while send_data != "EXIT":
```

```python
        print(connection.recv(4096).decode("UTF-8"))
        send_data = input("Reply: ")
        connection.send(bytes(send_data, "UTF-8"))
    send_data = ""
    connection.close()

def client():
    global port
    host = input("Enter the host you want to communicate" +
                 " with(leave blank for localhost) ")
    if host == "":
        host = "localhost"

    comms_socket = socket.socket()

    print("Starting a chat with ", host, " on port ", port)
    comms_socket.connect((host, port))
    while True:
        send_data = input("message: ")
        comms_socket.send(bytes(send_data, "UTF-8"))
        print(comms_socket.recv(4096).decode("UTF-8"))

port = int(input("Enter the port you want to communicate on" +
                 " (0 for default)"))
if port == 0:
    port = 50000
while True:
    print("Your options are:")
    print("1 - wait for a chat")
    print("2 - initiate a chat")
    print("3 - exit")

    option = int(input("option :"))

    if option == 1:
        server()
    elif option == 2:
        client()
    elif option == 3:
        break
    else:
        print("I don't recognise that option")
```

You should recognise the networking code in this, and the rest you should be fairly familiar with. In order to communicate between two computers, you need to agree on a port, set one to listen for a connection, then connect from the other.

This approach does have a few problems. Firstly, the two chatters have to alternate messages, and secondly you can only communicate with people on your local network. Actually, this second problem depends on how your local network is set up. Remember that we said IP addresses were a little like building addresses? In many ways they are, and local area networks (LANs) are like towns. In the same way you can have two different buildings with the address "1 The High Street," as long as they are in different towns, you can have two different computers with the IP address `192.168.1.2` as long as they are on different LANs. There are three IP address blocks reserved just for local networks:

- 10.0.0.0 – 10.255.255.255

- 172.16.0.0 – 172.31.255.255

- 192.168.0.0 – 192.168.255.255

Any IPv4 address that falls within these is a local-only address (this means you can only communicate with other computers on your local network), whereas ones that fall outside of it are public (which means any computer on the Internet can send data to them).

It is sometimes possible to connect to a local IP address from outside on the Internet. Whether this is possible depends on your Internet provider and router (look for the port-forwarding settings). However, there are too many different setups for us to be able to provide much guidance here.

Tweeting to the World

Instead of doing battle with your ISP and router, there are a number of other ways to get around these two problems. By far, the easiest is to use another service to handle the messages for you. Twitter is just such a service; it handles text-message passing between one computer and the world.

Each Twitter user can send *tweets* of up to 140 characters long. If any of these tweets mention another Twitter user (all usernames start with an @), then the tweet will show up in their connections page. If you don't already have a Twitter account, you'll need one for this section. Even if you do have one, it's probably a good idea to get a new one so that you can try things out without sending test messages to all your followers. It's free and quite simple to get an account. Just head to `www.twitter.com` and follow the instructions. You'll also get a tour of the site, so it should all make a bit more sense after setting up an account.

Twitter is normally used by people sending messages via the website, but that's not the only way of doing it. They also have an Application Programming Interface (API) that allows you to send and receive messages from programs rather than from the web interface.

There's a Twitter module that makes accessing the Twitter API simple. It's not included in Raspbian by default, so you'll need to download it from `https://github.com/sixohsix/` `twitter/tree/master` (use the Download Zip button on the bottom right). Once you have it, open an LXTerminal session, then unzip and install the module with:

```
unzip twitter-master.zip
cd twitter-master
python3 setup.py build
sudo python3 setup.py install
```

You're now almost ready to go, but as well as needing a Twitter username, you also need to register your application with Twitter to get the appropriate credentials for your application.

Once you've logged in to Twitter, go to `http://dev.twitter.com`, and select My applications from the user menu in the top-right corner. In the new screen, press Create An Application. On this form, you'll have to enter details of your program.

- The name has to be unique on Twitter, so `test-app` won't work. Be a little creative, or just mash a few keys to come up with something that hasn't been done before.

- The description can be anything as long as it's over 10 characters.

- The website doesn't have to be a website at all, it just has to look like one. We entered `http://none.example.com`.

- The callback URL can be left blank.

Other than that, you just have to agree to the Rules of the Road and enter the captcha.

The applications page has a series of tabs. You need to change one of the default settings, so go to the Settings tab, and switch Application Type from Read Only to Read and Write. This will allow you to post statuses as well as read information. Once this is done, press Update This Twitter Application's Settings.

Now you need to create an access token, so switch back to the Details tab, and click Create My Access Token. Once this is done, it'll take Twitter a few moments to update itself, and you may have to refresh the page for the section Your Access Token to appear. Once it refreshes, you're all set up and ready to go. You just need to get four pieces of information from the details page on this website: Access Token, Access Token Secret, Consumer Key, and Consumer Secret. These are all random strings that you'll need to copy and paste into the following example (see chapter7-twitter.py on the website):

```python
import twitter

def print_tweets(tweets):
    for tweet in tweets:
        print('text: ', tweet['text'])
        print('from: ', tweet['user']['screen_name'])

twitter_user = twitter.Twitter(
    auth=twitter.OAuth("ACCESS-TOKEN","ACCESS-TOKEN-SECRET",
                       "CONSUMER-KEY","CONSUMER-SECRET"))

status = twitter_user.statuses

home = status.home_timeline()
print("home")
print_tweets(home)

mentions = status.mentions_timeline()
print("mentions")
print_tweets(mentions)

search_string = input("Enter text to search for,  " +
                      "or press enter to skip: ")
if search_string != "":
    search = twitter_user.search.tweets(q=search_string)
    print("search")
    print_tweets(search['statuses'])

tweet = input("Enter tweet, or press enter to exit: ")

if tweet != "":
    twitter_user.statuses.update(status=tweet)
```

This little Twitter client isn't the most user-friendly one available. In fact, it's hard to imagine that anyone would use it over the website. However, it does have many of the different ways of interacting with Twitter that you may want to include in any applications you create. It should be fairly easy to adapt this code to your needs.

Weather Forecasts with JSON

In the previous example, the Twitter module provided all the basic functionality, but there won't always be modules you can use. Sometimes you'll have to write your own code to interact with web services. Fortunately there is a standard format for sending data back and forth than makes it easy to incorporate web services into your projects. JavaScript Object Notation, more commonly called JSON, is that standard. Originally, it was designed to work with JavaScript, which is a programming language mainly used on web pages, but it also works well with Python.

OpenWeatherMap.org is a website that provides free access to weather forecasts that you can include in your software. It also happens to use JSON. To get a feel for what a JSON document looks like, point your web browser to http://api.openweathermap.org/data/2.5/forecast/daily?cnt=7&units=meteric&mode=json&q=London. This is will return a seven-day forecast for London. It's not particularly easy to read, but you should notice that it looks like a Python dictionary that contains (amongst other things) a list of more dictionaries. Python can pull that information from the Internet using the urllib.request module in the following code:

```
import urllib.request

url = http://api.openweathermap.org/data/2.5/forecast/" +
      "daily?cnt=7&units=meteric&mode=json&q=London"
req = urllib.request.Request(url)
print(urllib.request.urlopen(req).read())
```

This will grab the information from OpenWeatherMap.org and print it on the screen. However, the data is in a string. You can't simply access various parts of it as though they are dictionaries and lists even though they look like them. You could build a function to read through the string and split it up, but fortunately you don't have to. The json module can load it and return a dictionary that contains the various parts of it. For example:

```
import urllib.request, json

url = http://api.openweathermap.org/data/2.5/forecast/
      "daily?cnt=7&units=meteric&mode=json&q=London"
req = urllib.request.Request(url)
forecast_string = urllib.request.urlopen(req).read()
forecast_dict = json.loads(forecast_string.decode("UTF-8"))

print(forecast_dict)
```

You can now get any information you want out of the `forecast_dict` data structure. In the following example, we've built a simple weather forecast program that prints out a seven-day forecast for a given city (see `chapter7-weather.py` on the website):

```python
import urllib.request,json

city = input("Enter City: ")

def getForecast(city) :
    url = http://api.openweathermap.org/data/2.5/forecast/ +
        "daily?cnt=7&units=meteric&mode=json&q="
    url = url + city
    req = urllib.request.Request(url)
    response=urllib.request.urlopen(req)
    return json.loads(response.read().decode("UTF-8"))

forecast = getForecast(city)

print("Forecast for ", city, forecast['city']['country'])

day_num=1
for day in forecast['list']:
    print("Day : ", day_num)
    print(day['weather'][0]['description'])
    print("Cloud Cover : ", day['clouds'])
    print("Temp Min : ", round(day['temp']['min']-273.15, 1),
        "degrees C")
    print("Temp Max : ", round(day['temp']['max']-273.15, 1),
        "degrees C")
    print("Humidity : ", day['humidity'], "%")
    print("Wind Speed : ", day['speed'], "m/s")
    print()
    day_num = day_num+1
```

Note that the metric unit for temperature is Kelvin. To convert Kelvin to Celsius, simply subtract 273.15. This example uses only some of the data that the API returned. Take a look at the forecast data structure to see what else is in there that might be useful to print out.

Using this same basic method, you should be able to work with any web APIs that support JSON. There's a list of popular services at www.programmableweb.com/apis/directory/1?sort=mashups, where you should find a way to get almost any information your applications need off the web.

Testing Your Knowledge

So far, you've seen how to query an API to get information out of it. Now it's time to test whether you've fully understood what's been going on. Have a go at the exercise that follows, and then refer back to the previous examples for anything you're unsure of.

Exercise 1

You can get the current weather for a city (such as London) using the URL `http://api.openweathermap.org/data/2.5/weather?q=London`. Use this URL to create a program that tweets the current weather for a location. See the end of the chapter for an example solution to this exercise.

Getting On the Web

So far you've seen how to pass data back and forwards between two computers, and how to send and receive data to and from an online API. The obvious omission in all this is websites. These are, after all, the most popular way of viewing information online. In this section, you'll learn how to use your Raspberry Pi to host a web page.

There are two parts to the web: HTTP and HTML. The former is Hypertext Transfer Protocol (the method that web browsers and websites use to communicate), while the latter is Hypertext Markup Language (the language that web pages are written in). Hypertext is just a fancy name for any text with links embedded in it. There are modules that'll handle HTTP, but you will need to learn a little HTML for this to work.

Modern HTML is a complex language that can be used to create powerful applications with all sorts of animations and interactions. However, the basics of the language are quite simple. Every web page is a separate HTML file, and every HTML file has two parts, the head and the body. The head contains various pieces of information about the page, while the body contains what's displayed on the screen. HTML uses tags to describe the different parts of the document. Almost all tags come in pairs with an opening tag (such as `<h1>`, which denotes a main heading) and a closing tag (such as `</h1>`). Tags are always enclosed in triangular brackets, and closing brackets start with a forward slash. The following example uses most of the basic tags (see `chapter7-htmleg1.html` on the website):

```
<!DOCTYPE html>
<head>
An example HTML file</title>
</head>
<body>
<h1>An h1 heading</h1>
```

```
<h2>An h2 heading</h2>
<p>
A paragraph of text with a <a href=http://www.raspberrypi.org";link
  <to the Raspberry Pi websites</a>
</p>
<p>
Another paragraph
</p>
</body>
```

There is much more to HTML than this, but since this is a book about Python rather than HTML, we won't go into more detail. This is more or less what you need for this chapter. If you're interested in learning more, there are loads of great resources for taking things further. http://w3schools.org is a good place to start.

Once you've saved that file, you can just open it on your computer, and it should open in a browser. This is fine for checking your pages, but it's no good for sharing your creation with the world. To do that you need the aforementioned HTTP. In Python, it's really easy to whip up a quick HTTP server. For example:

```
import  http.server, os

os.chdir("/home/pi")
httpd = http.server.HTTPServer(('127.0.0.1', 8000),
        http.server.SimpleHTTPRequestHandler)
httpd.serve_forever()
```

This will start a web server running on your Pi with the root in your home directory. It'll run on port 8000. If you were paying close attention earlier, you'll remember that 80 is the default port for web servers. We're using 8000 here just in case you're running something else with a web server, but you can change it to 80 if you prefer.

Once you have the code running, you can point your Pi's web browser to http://localhost:8000/. Localhost always points back to the machine it's running on (it's linked to the IP address 127.0.0.1), and :8000 means use port 8000 rather than the default port 80. You should see a rather underwhelming list of files here.

HTTP works with directories and files in exactly the same way your computer does. It starts from a root directory. In the case of this example, that root directory is /home/pi. In your web browser, you can either specify a directory (which ends with a /) or a filename. If you enter a directory, the web server first checks to see if there is a file called index.html. If there is, it displays that instead of the directory contents. Change the name of your HTML file to `index.html`, then point your browser to `http://localhost:8000` again. This time you should see the file displayed.

Making Your Website Dynamic

The `http.server` module is great for quickly whipping up a server to share information, but it's not very good at serving up information that changes. It does have some ways of adding a more interactive experience, but there's a better alternative. The `tornado` module is designed to serve up content that's created on the fly rather than content that's stored in files. This makes it far more suitable for projects that need this extra versatility.

Unlike the previous example, which worked with the operating system's file structure, Tornado creates its own virtual structure, and instead of HTML files, you create classes that output the appropriate HTML. First you need to install it by opening the LXTerminal and entering the following:

```
sudo apt-get install python3-tornado
```

Take a look at the following simple example. It just creates a website with `"Hello World!"` on it.

```
import tornado.ioloop
import tornado.web

class MainHandler(tornado.web.RequestHandler):
    def get(self):
        self.write("<!DOCTYPE html><head><title>" +
                   "Hello world</title></head>" +
                   "<body>Hello World</body>")

if __name__ == "__main__":
    application = tornado.web.Application([
        (r"/", MainHandler),
    ],)
    application.listen(8888)
    tornado.ioloop.IOLoop.instance().start()
```

There are two parts to this example. In the first part, we define the class that creates the web page, while the second part (which starts with the line `if __name__ == "__main__":`) defines and starts the web server. The main part of this is:

```
application = tornado.web.Application([
        (r"/", MainHandler),
    ],)
```

This creates a new Tornado web application and sets the options for it. The main options are a list of tuples that define which class handles which pages. In this example, there's only one page, the root, or / and it's handled by the class `MainHandler`. There are other options that can be added here, which will be used in future examples. The final two lines just tell it to listen on port 8888 (so you can run it at the same time as the `http.server` server on port 8000), and set it running. With this running, you can point your web browser to `http://localhost:8888` to see it work.

All the handler classes have to extend `tornado.web.RequestHandler`, which provides all the basic functionality. All you need to add is a `get` method that calls `self.write()` (or as you'll see later, `self.render()`); the superclass handles everything else.

It might seem a little strange to define a class, but not create any objects from it. This is because Tornado uses the class and handles the object creation for you.

You can use Tornado like this to serve up static content, but it's not very good. For starters, all the HTML is inside the Python code, so it's a bit messy. The real advantage of Tornado is when you start creating dynamic pages that can change. The next example will generate a specific greeting for the users. You can use the same file as the previous example, but create a new class with the following code:

```
class HelloHandler(tornado.web.RequestHandler):
    def get(self, name):
        self.write("<!DOCTYPE html><head>
                    <title>Hello world</title></head>" +
                    "<body>Hello " + name + "</body>")
```

Then alter the bottom section of the code to bring it in (changes are shown in bold):

```
if __name__ == "__main__":
    application = tornado.web.Application([
        (r"/", MainHandler),
        (r"/hello/(.*)", HelloHandler),
    ],)
    application.listen(8888)
    tornado.ioloop.IOLoop.instance().start()
```

With these changes made and saved, run the code again. Point your browser to `http://localhost:8888/hello/Ben` or `http://localhost:8888/hello/Alex`, or use your own name.

Using Templates

Being able to modify the HTML code like this obviously lets you create far more powerful websites than you could before. However, this still means including the HTML in the Python, which isn't pleasant. The solution to this is to use templates. These are HTML documents with bits of Python in them that Tornado uses to build the final page. A template for the `HelloHandler` would be

```
<!DOCTYPE html>
<head>
<title>Hello</title>
</head>
<body>
Hello {{ name }}
</body>
```

As you can see, the Python variable to print goes inside double curly braces. Save this as `hello-template.html` in your home directory (`/home/pi`), and then update the `HelloHandler` class to be

```
class HelloHandler(tornado.web.RequestHandler):
    def get(self, name_in):
        self.name=name_in
        self.render("/home/ben/hello-template.html",
                    name=self.name)
```

Then rerun the program. You should get the same response, but you should also be able to see that this code is far cleaner and easier to maintain.

Sending Data Back with Forms

You've probably noticed, though, that not many websites get you to enter information through web addresses. This method is often done for page IDs (as you saw with the weather API).

HTTP has a method for sending back to the server: POST requests. So far, Tornado has only been serving GET requests (hence the method name). POST allows you to send more complex information back using HTML forms. Create a new HTML file with the following code:

```
<!DOCTYPE html>
<head>
<title>User Information</title>
</head>
<body>
```

```
<h1>User Information</h1>
<form action="/hello/" method="post">
Enter your name: <input type="text" name="name">
<input type="submit" value="Sign in">'
</form>
</body>
```

Save it in your home directory as `user-info.html`. Now change the `HelloHandler` class to the following (changes are shown in bold):

```
class HelloHandler(tornado.web.RequestHandler):
    def get(self):
        self.render("/home/ben/user-info.html")

    def post(self):
        self.render("hello-template.html", name = self.get_
                    argument("name"))
```

The final code block also needs to be updated to reflect the new changes:

```
if __name__ == "__main__":
    application = tornado.web.Application([
        (r"/", MainHandler),
        (r"/hello/", HelloHandler),
    ],)
    application.listen(8888)
    tornado.ioloop.IOLoop.instance().start()
```

Now run this, and again point your browser to `http://localhost:8888/hello/`. Roughly the same thing happens as before, but now you enter your name in the textbox.

The reason this works is the first time you go to `http://localhost:8888/hello/`, your browser sends a GET request, so Tornado renders `user-template.html`. When you click Sign In, your browser sends a POST request because the form has the action `/hello/` (if an address doesn't have a server name, the browser sends it to the same server) and the method POST. This time Tornado renders `hello-template.html`. `self.get_argument()` then grabs the data the user entered. `name` corresponds to the name you gave the text input in `user-info.html`.

As well as variables, you can also put certain pieces of Python code inside a template. This code is enclosed between {% and %}. The most common pieces are

```
{% set my_var = 0 %}
{% for x in y %} ... {% end %}
```

As you can see, this is a little different from regular Python. You need the word set before a variable assignment, and rather than using indenting (which doesn't work with HTML), code blocks are finished with {% end %}.

As an example, you could change hello-template.html to the following:

```
<!DOCTYPE html>
<head>
<title>Hello</title>
</head>
<body>
{% set char_number = 0 %}
{% for letter in name %}
{{ letter }} <br>
{% set char_number = char_number + 1 %}
{% end %}
{{ name }} has {{char_number}} characters
</body>
```

This not hugely useful code, but it does a bit more than the previous template. It displays each letter of the name on a different line (
 is the HTML tag for a line break), and it also counts the number of letters.

Exercise 2

Create a new web app into which the users can enter a city, and then get a web page displaying a seven-day weather forecast (with data taken from openweathermap.org). An example solution is at the end of the chapter.

Keeping Things Secure

As you develop more and more powerful web applications with Tornado, sooner or later security becomes important. Even if you're only running it on a local network, you may have things that you don't want unauthorised people messing with. The final example in this chapter is a web app that provides some information about the Raspberry Pi.

This web app uses cookies for the login system. *Cookies* are bits of information that the web app stores in the browser. They can be used for a wide variety of reasons, but here we'll use them to track which sessions are logged in. If the users successfully log in, we set a secure cookie with their usernames. When they log out, we clear it. When they try to view the web app, the program checks if they have the cookie set, and if they don't, it redirects them to the login page. All the files for this are on the web page as `chapter7-tornado.zip`.

```python
import tornado.ioloop
import tornado.web

users = {"ben": "mypassword"}

class SysStatusHandler(tornado.web.RequestHandler):
  def get(self):
    if not self.get_secure_cookie("user"):
      self.redirect("/login")
      return
    if self.get_argument("type") == "processes":
      com = [["pstree"],["top", "-bn1"]]
    elif self.get_argument("type") == "system":
      com = [["uname", "-a"],["uptime"]]
    elif self.get_argument("type") == "syslog":
      com = [["tail", "-n100", "/var/log/syslog"]]
    elif self.get_argument("type") == "storage":
      com =  [["df", "-h"], ["free"]]
    elif self.get_argument("type") == "network":
      com =  [["ifconfig"]]
    else:
      com = [["df", "-h"], ["free"], ["uname", "-a"], ["who"],
             ["uptime"], ["tail', "/var/log/syslog"],["pstree"],
             ["top", "-bn1"]]
    self.render("sysstatus-template.html", commands=com)

class LoginHandler(tornado.web.RequestHandler):
  def get(self):
    self.render("login-template.html")

  def post(self):
    print(self.get_argument("name"))
    print(self.get_argument("password"))
    if self.get_argument("name") in users.keys() and users[self.
  get_argument("name")] == self.get_argument("password"):
      self.set_secure_cookie("user", self.get_argument("name"))
      self.redirect("/sysstatus?type=system")
    else:
      self.render("login-fail.html")
```

```
class LogoutHandler(tornado.web.RequestHandler):
  def get(self):
    self.clear_cookie("user")
    self.render("logout-template.html")

if __name__ == "__main__":
  application = tornado.web.Application([
  (r"/login", LoginHandler),
  (r"/sysstatus", SysStatusHandler),
  (r"/logout", LogoutHandler),
  ], cookie_secret="put your own random text here')
  application.listen(8888)
  tornado.ioloop.IOLoop.instance().start()
```

As you can see, the handler that does most of the work (SysStatusHandler) takes a page argument called type, which can take the following values—processes, system, syslog, storage, network, or all. It then sends a list of lists that corresponds to various Linux system commands in the template.

In HTTP GET requests, arguments are sent after a question mark in the URL, so http://localhost:8888/sysstatus?type=network sends the argument type with the value network to the sysstatus page.

The template that does the hard work is sysstatus-template.html:

```
<!DOCTYPE html>
<head><title>Raspberry Pi System Status Checker</title></head>
<body><h1>Raspberry Pi System Status Checker</h1>
<a href="sysstatus?type=processes">Processes</a>
<a href="sysstatus?type=system">System</a>
<a href="sysstatus?type=syslog">System Log</a>
<a href="sysstatus?type=storage">Storage</a>
<a href="sysstatus?type=network">Network</a>
<a href="sysstatus?type=all">Display all</a>
<a href="logout">Logout</a>

{% import subprocess %}
{% for command in commands %}

<h2> Command: {{command[0]}} </h2>
<h2> Output: </h2>
<pre>
{% for line in subprocess.check_output(command).splitlines() %}
{{line}}
```

```
{% end %}
</pre>
{% end %}

</body>
```

subprocess is a Python module that lets you run commands on the underlying operating system. In the case of the Raspberry Pi, that's Linux. It takes a list as its input with the first item in the list being the command to run. Any subsequent items are the arguments passed to it. So, the list ["df", '-h"] runs the command df -h, which outputs the current disks on the system and information about where they're mounted and how much free space they have. You can try it out in LXTerminal. In fact, you can try out all of the commands used here in LXTerminal.

The <pre> tags are for pre-formatted text. That is, it makes HTML respect the tabs and new-lines in the text rather than just garbling it all together.

The other templates are straightforward. Here's login-fail.html:

```
<!DOCTYPE html>
<html>
<head>
<title>Login Fail</title>
</head>
<body>
Your login has failed. Please click <a href="login">here</a>
to try again.
</body>
```

Here's login-template.html:

```
<!DOCTYPE html>
<head>
<title>Raspberry Pi System Status Login Form</title>
</head>
<body>
<p>
Please enter your login information</p>
<form action="/login" method="post">
Username: <input type="text" name="name">
<br>
```

```
Password: <input type="password" name="password">
<br>
<input type="submit" value="Sign in">
</form>
</body>
```

Finally, here's `logout-template.html`:

```
<!DOCTYPE html>
<html>
<head>
<title>Login Fail</title>
</head>
<body>
You have logged out. Please click <a href="login">here</a>
if you wish to log in again.
</body>
```

The login method we've created here does provide some security, but it is far from completely secure. If you create a web app that handles sensitive information, or allows the users some control over the Raspberry Pi, and it's on a network where you don't trust all the users, you need to properly investigate web security. It's far too big a subject for us to cover here, but a good place to start is the Open Web Application Security Project (see `www.owasp.org`).

Summary

After reading this chapter, you should understand the following a bit better:

- Data can be sent back and forwards between two computers using the host and port number.

- Hosts can be defined by either IP addresses or hostnames.

- To connect to another computer, you need to use sockets, which allow you to send data.

- APIs are interfaces programmers can use to access web servers and their data.

- The Twitter API has a module that lets you easily retrieve and manipulate information from `twitter.com`.

- APIs use a universal data format called JSON to make it easier to parse and share data between programs.

- Web pages are written in HTML and served using HTTP.

- `http.server` allows you to create a really simple web server.

- You can use Tornado to create more complex web applications.

- Tornado templates make it easy to render complex, dynamic information in HTML.

- The server can receive information from users using HTML forms and POST requests.

- Cookies allow you to store information, such as usernames, on the client's browser.

Solutions to Exercises

Exercise 1

Here is an example program that tweets the weather to a particular location.

```
import twitter, urllib.request, json

twitter_user = twitter.Twitter(
    auth=twitter.OAuth("1824182228-
  lHOzvEpNA31LTiUCHkLSiqqW5Pbe7BvJKvKT2H6",

  "AwYIcpfRFUt6F4hMoGfqMGINDiUrW49R1mjVqY6Bts",
                      "xStMTHb0HQZaEFLi2bsWA",

  "YgFhiCpvlqLLe5Is5dRAZWNzlT84KnyZCMKfXIwN8"))

city = input("Which city? ")
url = "http://api.openweathermap.org/data/2.5/weather?q<="
url = url+city
req = urllib.request.Request(url)
forecast_string = urllib.request.urlopen(req).read()
forecast_dict = json.loads(forecast_string.decode("UTF-8"))

tweet_text = city + " weather is ' +
  forecast_dict['weather'][0]['description']

twitter_user.statuses.update(status=tweet_text)
```

Exercise 2

There are many ways of doing this, but we used three files. Firstly, a template called `city-info.html` contains the following:

```html
<!DOCTYPE html>
<head>
<title>Weather</title>
</head>
<body>
<h1>Which City?</h1>
<form action="/weather/" method="post">
Enter a city: <input type="text" name="city">
<input type="submit" value="Submit">
</form>
</body>
```

Another template called `weather-template` contains:

```html
<!DOCTYPE html>
<head>
<title>Weather</title>
</head>
<body>
{% set day_num = 0 %}
{% for day in forecast %}
<h2>Day : {{str(day_num)}} </h2>
<h3>{{day['weather'][0]['description']}} </h3>
Cloud Cover :  {{str(day['clouds'])}} <br>
Temp Min : {{str(round(day['temp']['min']-273.15, 1))}}
degrees C<br>
Temp Max : {{ str(round(day['temp']['max']-273.15, 1))}}
degrees C<br>
Humidity : {{str(day['humidity'])}} %<br>
Wind Speed : {{str(day['speed'])}}m/s<br>
{% set day_num = day_num + 1 %}
{% end %}
</body>
```

Finally, the Python file contains:

```python
import tornado.ioloop
import tornado.web
```

```python
import subprocess
import urllib.request,json

class WeatherHandler(tornado.web.RequestHandler):
    def get(self):
        self.render("/home/ben/city-info.html")

    def post(self):
        url = "http://api.openweathermap.org/data/2.5/forecast/"
                daily?cnt=7&units=meteric&mode=json&q="
                + self.get_argument("city")
        req = urllib.request.Request(url)
        response = urllib.request.urlopen(req)
        self.forecast = json.loads(response.read().decode("UTF-8"))
        self.render("weather-template.html",
                    forec   ast = self.forecast['list'])

if __name__ == "__main__":
    application = tornado.web.Application([
        (r"/weather/", WeatherHandler),
    ],)

    application.listen(8888)
    tornado.ioloop.IOLoop.instance().start()
```

Chapter 8
Minecraft

FOR THE UNINITIATED, Minecraft is a game of survival where your character can build things and acquire materials by mining the world around him. It's set in a world of blocks, and each of these blocks can be destroyed to reveal hidden treasures. Figure 8-1 shows a typical Minecraft world.

That's a pretty inadequate description, but it should give you an idea of what's going on. There's a full version that you can play on most computers, and there's a special version unique to the Raspberry Pi. The special thing about the Pi version is that you can control the game through Python. Not only can you move your player, but you can also manipulate the entire world around you.

FIGURE 8-1: The 3D blocks have become emblematic of this game.

Exploring Minecraft

That's enough trying to explain it, though. Minecraft is one of those things that you really have to see to understand. First of all, you'll need to download the software from `http://pi.minecraft.net`.

You should end up with a file called `minecraft-pi-0.1.1.tar.gz`. You can extract this archive through the terminal with this command:

```
tar zxvf  minecraft-pi-0.1.1.tar.gz
```

Then, you can start the game with this command:

```
mcpi/minecraft-pi
```

> **NOTE**   When you're playing Minecraft, it will capture the mouse and keyboard. If you need to switch back to a non-Minecraft window, just press Alt+Tab, and it will release control.

Controlling Your Minecraft World

The first thing to do is start a new game and get a feeling for moving about in the world (use the mouse to change the direction you're facing, the left mouse button to attach something, and the w, a, s, and d keys to move around). You can build things by changing the tool you're using (pressing one of the number keys will select from the items displayed at the bottom of the screen), and then pressing the right mouse button to use it. These are just the very basic Minecraft controls, but they should be enough to give you a feel for how to work in the world.

To control the world, you need to use the Python API. This is included in the archive you downloaded earlier, but that version doesn't support Python 3. Instead, you need to download `chapter8-minecraft-api.tar.gz` from the book's website.

> **NOTE**   The longer code examples and other appropriate APIs and downloads in the book are from the book's companion website at `www.wiley.com/go/python-raspberrypi`.

Once you have the new API, you need to extract it using the terminal command:

```
tar zxvf chapter8-minecraft.tar.gz
```

You'll need to change the directory using the terminal command cd into the new folder. Then you should create the programs for this chapter in that folder so they can pick up the Python APIs:

```
cd mcpi
```

The programs you write won't run Minecraft themselves, but instead connect to an instance of Minecraft that's currently running on the Pi.

With that in mind, start a new Python interpreter. Remember that it has to be in the chapter8-minecraft directory, and the easiest way to do this is open an LXTerminal session, navigate to chapter8-minecraft (use the previous cd line), and then enter python3.

The following code will connect to the currently running instance of Minecraft:

```
>>> import minecraft
>>> mc = minecraft.Minecraft.create()
```

You now have a Minecraft object called mc that you can manipulate. This object holds a player object that you can move around. For example, try the following:

```
>>> mc.player.setPos(10,10,10)
```

You should find that the player moves. Your player will move to these coordinates (10,10,10), but since worlds are randomly generated, this may be in the air, in which case your player will fall until he reaches the floor. Alternatively, he may end up underwater, or underground. Try changing the coordinates to find him a spot of land. The first and last coordinates are the player's position on the ground (x and z), while the middle one (y) is his vertical position.

Creating Minecraft Worlds in Python

Once you've found a good position for your player, you can alter the world around him using the setBlock(x,y,z,type) method. x, y, and z are the world coordinates and they are in the same format as for the player. type is the typeID of the block. Every different type of block has a typeID, which you'll need to use whenever you manipulate the world.

So, for example, if your player is at (10, 15, 22), you can create a mushroom next to her with the following:

```
>>> mc.setBlock(11,15,22, 40)
```

See Table 8-1 for a list of useful block types.

Table 8-1   Some Useful Type IDs

ID	Block Type	ID	Block Type
0	Air	1	Stone
2	Grass	3	Dirt
4	Cobble Stone	5	Wooden Plank
6	Sapline	8	Water (will flow)
10	Lava (will flow)	18	Leaves
22	Lapis Lazuli	40	Mushroom
41	Gold Block	246	Glowing Obsidian

Building Worlds

So far, you've been working with whatever world Minecraft created for you. However, if you're going to create any sort of reusable program, you need to be able to know where everything is located at the start. To do this, you need to set the world to be how you want it. The following script sets a 200 by 200 square in the centre of the world to be smooth grass (type 2), with air above it (type 0).

```
import minecraft
mc = minecraft.Minecraft.create()
mc.setBlocks(-100,-1, -100, 100, 0, 100, 2)
mc.setBlocks(-100, 1, -100, 100, 100, 100, 0)
```

This uses the method setBlocks(x1, y1, z1, x2, y2, z2, type), which sets every block between (x1,y1,z1) and (x2,y2,z2) to be of the appropriate type.

Drawing Pictures

Now you know how to set blocks, you can start doing something useful with them. Were this a full version of Minecraft, you could use this to build some form of ultimate fortress to shelter your character. However, the version of Minecraft on the Pi isn't the full version. Instead, you can use this version for more aesthetic reasons, such as drawing pictures with blocks. The following code does just that (it's on the website as chapter8-art.py):

```
import minecraft
import sys

mc = minecraft.Minecraft.create()

height = 10
start_x = 0
start_y = 0
```

```
canvas = "horizontal"

r = 246
g = 18
b = 22

picture = [["R", "R", "R"],
           ["G", "G", "G"],
           ["B", "B", "B"]]


if len(sys.argv) > 1:
    with open(sys.argv[1]) as f:
        picture = f.readlines()

pic_x = start_x
for line in picture:
    pic_y = start_y
    for block in line:

        if canvas == "horizontal":
            x = pic_y
            y = height
            z = pic_x
        else:
            x = height
            y = pic_y
            z = pic_x

        if block == "R":
            mc.setBlock(x,y,z,r)
        if block == "G":
            mc.setBlock(x,y,z,g)
        if block == "B":
            mc.setBlock(x,y,z,b)

        pic_y = pic_y + 1
    pic_x = pic_x + 1
```

This works in a similar way to the level-loading code from Chapter 4. It uses `sys.argv` to check if the user has specified a filename at the command line. If she has, it uses the text from that file to make a picture; otherwise, it uses the default, which draws three lines.

There are then two `for` loops that iterate through every line, and every character in that line. If the loop encounters an R, G, or B it draws a red, green, or blue block, respectively.

However, you don't have complete artistic control over the world. You can only create one of the predetermined block types, and not all of them will hover in the air. This example uses block type 246 (glowing obsidian) for red, type 18 (leaves) for green, and type 22 (lapis lazuli) for blue. Of course, you are free to change these to others if you want to create a different look.

The code for the coordinates is a little convoluted because it has two modes—vertical and horizontal—where it draws the picture in different orientations. Because of this, it has to manage two sets of coordinates: 2D ones for the picture and 3D ones for the Minecraft world. The `if` block translates between the two depending on which orientation is selected.

Notice that the program ignores any character that isn't an R, G, or B, so you can include them in your picture, but they will be represented as space. For example, the following text will create a smiley face (see Figure 8-2):

```
- - - - - - -
-G---G-
-G---G-
---B---
-R---R-
--RRR--
```

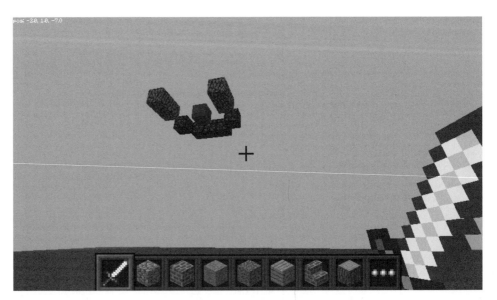

FIGURE 8-2: Smiling faces are just the start. You can use this method to draw whatever you want in the Minecraft world.

Taking Things Further

There are loads of ways you could expand this world. The simplest way is to expand the pallet from three colours up to as many as you have characters and block types for. A more complicated way of expanding this world would be to create 3D drawings. This will require you to change the file structure somehow. We recommend doing it as a series of 2D images with a specific line between them. So, for example, a smiley face two blocks thick would be:

```
-------
-G---G-
-G-B-G-
---B---
-R---R-
--RRR--
*
-------
-------
-G---G-
---B---
-R---R-
--RRR--
```

You could also use a similar file structure to define an animation, with each separate block being a separate frame.

Making the Game Snake

A key use of any 3D graphical environment is to make games. Minecraft itself is obviously a game, and you can also use it as a games engine to build more games. In this section, you see how to make the classic game Snake.

If you're unfamiliar with the game, you control a snake that moves around and eats apples. Every time it eats an apple, it grows one square longer. If it hits either itself or the walls of the level, it dies. The aim of the game is to get as long a snake as possible. It was one of the most popular games on mobile phones before the iPhone came along.

Remember that most of the longer code examples in the book are available for download from the book's companion website at www.wiley.com/go/python-raspberrypi. To avoid potential typos, you can download and copy and paste the text into your IDE or code editor. The code for the following example is chapter8-snake.py.

Code for the game is as follows (you can find it on the website as `chapter8-snake.py`).

```python
import minecraft
import pygame
import sys
import time
import random

from pygame.locals import *

mc = minecraft.Minecraft.create()
pygame.init()

#blank world
print("Resetting world")
mc.setBlocks(-100,-1,-100, 100, 0, 100, 2)
mc.setBlocks(-100,1,-100, 100, 100, 100, 0)
mc.player.setPos(0,2,0)

# create control window
display = pygame.display.set_mode((200,200))

#draw maze
print("drawing maze")
height = 10

start_x = 0
start_z = 0

difficulty = 0.5
apple_freq = 2

picture = [["R", "R", "R", "R", "R", "R", "R", "R", "R"],
           ["R", "-", "-", "-", "-", "-", "-", "-", "R"],
           ["R", "-", "-", "-", "-", "-", "-", "-", "R"],
           ["R", "-", "-", "-", "-", "-", "-", "-", "R"],
           ["R", "-", "-", "-", "-", "-", "-", "-", "R"],
           ["R", "-", "-", "-", "-", "-", "-", "-", "R"],
           ["R", "-", "-", "-", "-", "-", "-", "-", "R"],
           ["R", "-", "-", "-", "-", "-", "-", "-", "R"],
           ["R", "-", "-", "-", "-", "-", "-", "-", "R"],
           ["R", "-", "-", "-", "-", "-", "-", "-", "R"],
           ["R", "-", "-", "-", "-", "-", "-", "-", "R"],
```

```
             ["R", "-", "-", "-", "-", "-", "-", "-", "R"],
             ["R", "-", "-", "-", "-", "-", "-", "-", "R"],
             ["R", "-", "-", "-", "-", "-", "-", "-", "R"],
             ["R", "-", "-", "-", "-", "-", "-", "-", "R"],
             ["R", "R", "R", "R", "R", "R", "R", "R", "R"]]

if len(sys.argv) > 1:
    with open(sys.argv[1]) as f:
        picture = f.readlines()

posn_z = start_z
for line in picture:
    posn_x = start_x
    for block in line:
        x = height
        y = posn_x
        z = posn_z

        if block == "R":
            mc.setBlock(x,y,z,246)

        posn_x = posn_x + 1
    posn_z = posn_z + 1


snake = [(int((posn_z - start_z)/2),int((posn_x - start_x)/2))]
movement = [-1,0]

finished = False

grow_in = []
apple_in = apple_freq

while not finished:
    for event in pygame.event.get():
        if event.type == QUIT:
            finished = True

    key_state = pygame.key.get_pressed()
    if key_state[K_LEFT]:
        movement = [-1,0]
    if key_state[K_RIGHT]:
        movement = [1,0]
```

```python
    if key_state[K_UP]:
        movement = [0,1]
    if key_state[K_DOWN]:
        movement = [0,-1]

    next_position = (height, snake[0][1] + movement[1],
                    snake[0][0] + movement[0])
    next_block = mc.getBlock(next_position[0],
                            next_position[1], next_position[2])

    if next_block == 246 or next_block == 22:
        finished = True

    if next_block == 18:
        grow_in.append(len(snake))
        apple_in = apple_freq

    snake.insert(0, (next_position[2], next_position[1]))
    for block in snake:
        mc.setBlock(height, block[1], block[0], 22)

    if 0 not in grow_in:
        remove_block = snake.pop()
        mc.setBlock(height, remove_block[1], remove_block[0], 0)

    grow_in2 = []
    for number in grow_in:
        if number > -1:
            grow_in2.append(number - 1)
    grow_in = grow_in2

    if apple_in == 0:
        apple_y = random.randint(1,int(posn_x - start_x)-1)
        apple_x = random.randint(1,int(posn_z - start_z)-1)
        while mc.getBlock(height, apple_y, apple_x) != 0:
            apple_x = random.randint(1,int(posn_z - start_z)-1)
            apple_y = random.randint(1,int(posn_x - start_x)-1)
        mc.setBlock(height, apple_y, apple_x, 18)

    apple_in = apple_in - 1

    time.sleep(difficulty)

mc.postToChat("Game Over")
```

There are two Minecraft methods that you haven't seen before: `getBlock()` and `postTo-Chat()`. Both of these methods are fairly self-explanatory. The first returns the type of block at a particular location, and the second displays text on the player's screen.

You should recognise the first part of the code because it's almost the same as the code you saw previously to draw pictures. It's slightly simplified because here you need only one colour block for the maze that the snake moves through (we picked red, but you can substitute this for whatever you like).

The second part of the code (which includes the `while` loop and the five lines above it) contains the mechanics of the game. The snake is stored as a list of tuples. Each tuple contains the 2D coordinates for that section of the snake. These are then transformed into 3D coordinates and drawn on the screen.

Moving the Snake

The movement of the snake is done in two parts. Firstly, a new block is added to the start. This new block is calculated by adding the movement variable to the coordinate of the front of the snake. Secondly, the last position of the snake is removed from the list using `pop()`, which both takes it out of the list and returns it. The tile at this coordinate is set to 0 (air).

The key control is the same as you saw in Chapter 4. It uses PyGame. The only slight complication is that for this to work, there has to be a PyGame window, which must have focus in order to capture the keypresses. You should see a blank 200 by 200 window open when you run the program, and you'll need to click on it in order to be able to control the snake.

Growing the Snake

Perhaps the most complicated part of the code is the part that controls how the snake grows when it eats apples. This is because the snake doesn't get longer as soon as it eats the apple; instead, it gets longer when its whole body has passed through the block the apple was in.

To control this process, you use a list called `grow_in`. Every time the snake eats an apple, the length of the snake is added to the list. Each time the main loop is executed, every number in this list is reduced by one and negative numbers are discarded. This means that when the whole snake has passed through the apple, there will be a 0 in this list. The final portion of the snake is removed only when there isn't a 0 in the list. All this is done in the following section:

```
if 0 not in grow_in:
        remove_block = snake.pop()
        mc.setBlock(height, remove_block[1], remove_block[0], 0)

    grow_in2 = []
    for number in grow_in:
```

```
    if number > -1:
        grow_in2.append(number - 1)
grow_in = grow_in2
```

Adding the Apples

The only other part left to do is to add the apples. A new apple appears exactly `apple_freq` loops after the snake ate the previous one. They're created at random locations inside the level with this code:

```
if apple_in == 0:
    apple_y = random.randint(1,int(posn_x - start_x)-1)
    apple_x = random.randint(1,int(posn_z - start_z)-1)
    while mc.getBlock(height, apple_y, apple_x) != 0:
        apple_x = random.randint(1,int(posn_z - start_z)-1)
        apple_y = random.randint(1,int(posn_x - start_x)-1)
    mc.setBlock(height, apple_y, apple_x, 18)
```

This generates random positions, and then checks that there isn't already something in that position (if there is, it generates a new random position). The variable `apple_in` simply counts the number of loops since the previous apple was eaten.

Take a look at Figure 8-3 to see how it looks, or just run it for yourself.

FIGURE 8-3: You can make the game harder or easier by altering the map for the level. Just make sure there aren't any gaps that the snake can escape out of; otherwise, the snake can rampage unchecked through the Minecraft world.

Taking Things Further

As with the game from Chapter 4, this one isn't really complete yet, and we'll leave that up to you. Some ways it could be finished include:

- *Some more graphics.* For example, add an explosion when the snake dies, or add a countdown to the start. You could make the snake more graphically appealing, such as by using alternating blocks along its length.

- *A score.* This could be the length of the snake.

- *A method to change the difficulty (use the `time.sleep()` on the loop).* This could have a link into the score. It could even get faster as the snake gets longer.

- *Surprises.* For example, once you get past a certain length, the snake could change colour.

- *Bonuses.* These could appear on the map for a short period of time, and if the snake gets to them, the player gets bonus points.

- *More levels.* The maps could be different sizes, or they could have extra walls inside them to make it harder.

You don't have to limit yourself to just improvements to Snake. You could use these same methods to make entirely new games. For example, the same basic mechanics could be used for games like Tron. (This game is inspired by the film. Install it with `sudo apt-get xtron` to find out more).

You could even build it into a platformer like the one in Chapter 4, or … well, you could do anything. You're limited only by your imagination.

Summary

After reading this chapter, you should understand the following a bit better:

- Minecraft is a survival game set in a 3D world of blocks.

- There's a special version of Minecraft for the Raspberry Pi and it allows you to control the world from Python.

- You can move the player using `player.setPos(x,y,z)`.

- `setBlock()` and `setBlocks()` can be used to manipulate the world.

Chapter 9
Multimedia

IN THE PAST eight chapters, you've seen loads of ways of processing data, and getting it out of the Pi. However, so far you haven't seen many ways of getting data *into* the Pi. There's been some key and button pressing, and a bit with the mouse, but that's about it. In this chapter, we're going to change that. There are two additional sensors you can give your Pi to allow it to interact with the world in a far more natural way—microphones and cameras. We'll look at each in turn and see how you can use them in your Python programs.

Using PyAudio to Get Sound into Your Computer

There are all manner of things you can do once you have sound in the computer, but they all start with the same process of getting sound in. The module PyAudio is the best one for quickly and simply getting audio into the computer. Once you've captured the audio, you can do whatever you want with it, but if you want to use it in other programs, you'll need some format that other software understands. WAV is a simple lossless format that's great for simple audio data (although it can produce huge files if you're recording a lot of data).

You'll also need a USB microphone to get the sound. The jack port of the Pi is only for sound output.

As always, the first thing you'll need to do is install the modules with the following terminal command:

```
sudo apt-get install libportaudio0 libportaudio2 libportaudiocpp0
  \portaudio19-dev python3-setuptools python3-pip
sudo pip-3.2 install pyaudio
```

Now let's save some sound! The code for this is as follows (you can find it on the website as `chapter9-record.py`):

```python
import pyaudio
import wave

def record_sound(seconds, chunk_size, sample_rate, filename,
                 channels, format_type):
    p = pyaudio.PyAudio()

    stream = p.open(format=format_type,
        channels=channels,
        rate=sample_rate,
        input=True,
        frames_per_buffer=chunk_size)

    print("Speak now")

    frames = []

    for i in range(0, int(sample_rate / chunk_size * seconds)):
        data = stream.read(chunk_size)
        frames.append(data)
        if i%int(sample_rate/chunk_size) == 0:
            print(seconds - round(i/(sample_rate/chunk_size)),
                  "seconds remaining")

    print("Finished")

    stream.stop_stream()
    stream.close()
    p.terminate()

    wf = wave.open("filename", 'wb')
    wf.setnchannels(channels)
    wf.setsampwidth(p.get_sample_size(format_type))
    wf.setframerate(sample_rate)
    wf.writeframes(b''.join(frames))
    wf.close()

chunk_size = 1024
sample_rate = 44100
seconds = 15
filename = "output.wav"
channels = 1
format_type = pyaudio.paInt16
```

```
record_sound(seconds, chunk_size, sample_rate, filename, channels,
             format_type)
```

As you can see, there are a number of properties that you can alter to influence the recording. Some of these control how the data is captured and stored (for example, `chunk_size` and `sample_rate`), while others are more high level (like the number of seconds that you record for, or the number of channels you use). For now, just stick with these defaults unless you have a good reason to change them. Some of them are limited by the hardware, and PyAudio will throw an exception if you try to change them.

Recording the Sound

The `record_sound()` function does all of the hard work (it could be inline code rather than a function and it would work fine, but we make it a function here so that it is easier to include in other programs). The first and second lines create a new PyAudio object and then use it to open a stream. You get the audio data from this stream.

The main work of recording the sound is then done by the `for` loop:

```
for i in range(0, int(sample_rate / chunk_size * seconds)):
    data = stream.read(chunk_size)
    frames.append(data)
```

All this does is bring in the data in correctly sized chunks and save it into a list. Each of the chunks is a `bytes` data type, but you don't need to worry about that.

Now that you have the audio data as a string of bytes, you need to do something with it. The simplest thing is to store it as a WAV file using the `wave` module, and that's what the second half of the function does.

If you run the program, you'll first notice a string of errors. Don't worry about this; it's just PyAudio's way of letting you know everything that's going on. (They're thrown as PyAudio detects the audio hardware on the device. As long as there aren't any Python exceptions, everything's going fine.)

Then you'll have a file called `output.wav` in the directory you ran it from. This is a 15-second recording that you can play back with any audio software.

Speaking to Your Pi

There are all manner of things you can do with the audio you've recorded, but one of the coolest that doesn't require any musical talent is voice control. To do this, you need some way of processing the sound to extract its contents, and this is a surprisingly hard task.

Unfortunately, there aren't any modules that can make this process easy. However, as you saw in Chapter 7, Python modules aren't the only way of getting extra functionality for your program. Web services are another great source of features that you can easily plug into your software.

Google has an excellent speech-to-text web service that we can utilise here. It does have a couple of limitations, though. Firstly, the speech sections are limited to a maximum of 15 seconds, and secondly the audio clips have to be uploaded in FLAC format with a sample rate of 16,000.

The first rule shouldn't cause too many problems for voice control systems (although it rules out dictation software). However, the second restriction is a little awkward since there isn't a standard FLAC module for Python. There are a couple of options, but none of them is particularly suitable for our purposes. Here, we can turn to yet another source of extra features (that you'll learn more about next chapter) from the Linux command line. This allows you to run regular Linux programs and control them from inside your Python code.

The code to convert the speech to text (once it's FLAC-encoded; see later) is the following:

```
def google_speech_recognition(filename):
    global url

    audio = open(filename,'rb').read()
    http_header={'Content-Type': 'audio/x-flac; rate=16000'}
    request = urllib.request.Request(url, data=audio,
                                     headers=http_header)

    response = urllib.request.urlopen(request)
    out = response.read()
    json_data = json.loads(out.decode("utf-8"))

    return json_data
```

This should be fairly familiar to you if you've read Chapter 7, so we won't go over everything again. The only new things here are the extra parameters on the call to `urllib.request.Request()`. The `data` parameter, fairly obviously, sends the data, which in this case is the audio file, and the `headers` parameter sends HTTP headers. These headers tell the web server about who is requesting the data, and what, if any, data they are sending. In this case, we're telling the server that we're sending FLAC-encoded audio with a sample rate of 16,000.

This doesn't return the actual text, but returns JSON-encoded data that includes the text and the confidence that the text is right (with different accents and bits of slang, this is never going to be completely perfect). You can add a print line like the following if you want more information about what's returned:

```
print(json_data)
```

Again, there's more information on using this format in Chapter 7.

Processing text is far easier than processing audio, so you should now be able to integrate the output in your software. This example isn't yet complete, though. We're going to expand it so that you can ask it questions and, with a little luck, it should be able to answer them for you.

Asking the Program Questions

Answering questions is quite a challenging feature to add to a program, and would be a truly daunting task to code. Fortunately it's another area where you can get a little help. Wolfram Alpha is a web service that attempts to do just that. You can try it out in a web browser at www.wolframalpha.com. As you may have guessed, there's also an API to access it from a program.

Again, the code should be mostly familiar if you've read Chapter 7:

```
def wolfram_alpha(speech):
    url_section = urllib.parse.urlencode(dict(
        input=speech,
        appid=wolfram_alpha_app_id,
        ))

    url = http://api.wolframalpha.com/v2/query?' + url_section

    response = urllib.request.urlopen(url)

    tree = ElementTree.parse(response)
    root = tree.getroot()

    for node in root.findall('.//pod'):
        print(node.attrib['title'])
        for text_node in node.findall('.//plaintext'):
            if text_node.text:
                print(text_node.text)
        print("****")
```

The one part that you may not understand is the second half. Wolfram Alpha returns the results as an XML file, and this code uses an `ElementTree` from the `xml` module to parse this and extract the relevant information. We won't go into this in detail here as it's not relevant to the rest of the chapter, but should you need to look into it in the future, you can find more information in the `xml` module's documentation.

> **NOTE**   Before running this code, you need to get a Wolfram Alpha app ID. For this, you need to create an account at `https://developer.wolframalpha.com/portal/signup.html`. Once you have it, copy it to the appropriate place in the code.

Putting It All Together

You can combine these three functions (recording the sound, converting it to text, and getting answers to questions) to create a speech recognition oracle (which we call Pyri due to its similarity to a popular mobile-based application). You use the following code (it's on the website as `chapter9-pyri.py`). The functions discussed previously aren't repeated here, but you'll need to include them for the program to work.

> **NOTE**   Remember that most of the longer code examples in the book are available for download from the book's companion website at `www.wiley.com/go/python-raspberrypi`. To avoid potential typos, you can download and copy and paste the text into your IDE or code editor. The code for the following example is `chapter9-pyri.py`.

```python
import urllib.request
import json
import pyaudio
import wave
from xml.etree import ElementTree
import subprocess
import time

def record_sound(seconds, chunk_size, sample_rate, filename,
                 channels, format_type):
#Code give above

def google_speech_recognition(filename):
#Code given above
```

```
def wolfram_alpha(speech):
#Code give above


chunk_size = 512
sample_rate = 44100
seconds = 5
filename = "output.wav"
channels = 1
format_type = pyaudio.paInt16

url = "https://www.google.com/speech-api/v1/recognize?"
        + "client=chromium&lang=en-US"

wolfram_alpha_app_id = "PUT-YOUR-APPID-HERE"

record_sound(seconds, chunk_size, sample_rate,
             filename, channels, format_type)

subprocess.call(["sox", "output.wav", "-r16k", "-t",
                 "wav", "output-16k.wav"])
subprocess.call(["flac", "-5", "-f",
                 "output-16k.wav"],stdout=subprocess.PIPE )

time.sleep(2)

try:
    google_data = google_speech_recognition("output-16k.flac")
except urllib.error.HTTPError:
    print("voice recognition failure")
else:
    print(google_data)

    if google_data['status'] == 0:
        wolfram_alpha(google_data['hypotheses'][0]['utterance'])
    else:
        print("Voice recognition failed. Try again")
```

The final `try` block may be a little unfamiliar to you because it includes an `else` clause. This just runs after everything else in the block, but only if the original code doesn't raise an exception. In this case, that means as long as the Google request doesn't throw an `HTTPError`.

Before running the code, you'll need to make sure both of these are installed with the following:

```
sudo apt-get install sox flac
```

Then there are two system calls that convert the file to the appropriate format:

```
subprocess.call(["sox", "output.wav", "-r16k", "-t",
                "wav", "output-16k.wav"])
subprocess.call(["flac", "-5", "-f",
                "output-16k.wav"],stdout=subprocess.PIPE )
```

sox is also known as the "audio Swiss Army knife." It has loads of features for dealing with sound files. In this case, it's used to convert the file from a sample rate of 44,100 to 16,000. This is done with the -r16k option. The second line uses the flac program to encode the WAV file as a FLAC.

subprocess.call() is a feature we'll look at in more detail in the next chapter, but for now, we'll just say that it lets you run Linux commands from within Python.

Taking Things Further

If you feel like taking this example further, you could add it as a feature to the web browser you created in Chapter 4. Instead of displaying the text like it does here, it could take the browser directly to the relevant page.

You could also create a simple voice-driven menu so that you can use your program without a mouse or keyboard. For example, it could display a list of numbered options and the users simply need to say the number they want (a little like some telephone switchboards).

Making Movies

You should now have an idea of how to get started with audio on your Pi, so we'll move on to the second medium, video.

There are two types of cameras that you can attach to your Pi—USB webcams and the Raspberry Pi Foundation's camera module. We'll look at both here since they have different applications.

Using USB Webcams

Of the two, USB webcams are the best supported in Python. They also work the same on all computers, so we'll look at them first.

Oddly enough, the easiest way to capture images is using the PyGame module that you first looked at in Chapter 5. Previously, you used it to create a game, but the module mostly contains graphics features (which are often used in games), including ones to grab images from a webcam.

If you've already worked through Chapter 5, you'll have PyGame installed. If not, you'll need to do this now with the following:

```
sudo apt-get update
sudo apt-get install libsdl-dev libsdl-image1.2-dev \
   libsdl-mixer1.2-dev libsdl-ttf2.0-dev libsmpeg-dev \
   libportmidi-dev libavformat-dev libswscale-dev \
   mercurial python3-dev
```

Then grab the latest version of Pygame with:

```
hg clone <span cssStyle="font-family:monospace"><span
  cssStyle="font-family:monospace">https://bitbucket.org/pygame/
  pygame</span></span>
cd pygame
```

These two lines will download the current version of PyGame into a new directory called pygame, then move into it. Once it's there, you can build and install the module for Python 3 with:

```
python3 setup.py build
sudo python3 setup.py install
```

The simplest program is one that simply grabs a stream of images from the camera and displays them on the screen. Effectively, this turns your Raspberry Pi into a mirror. It's done as follows (the code is on the website as `chapter9-mirror.py`).

```
import pygame
import pygame.camera

pygame.init()
pygame.camera.init()

display = pygame.display.set_mode((640,480),0)
```

```
cam = pygame.camera.Camera("/dev/video0", (640,480))
cam.start()

while True:
    image = cam.get_image()
    display.blit(image, (0,0))
    pygame.display.flip()
```

As well as initialising PyGame, you also have to initialise the camera portion of the module. If you have just one camera connected, it should come up as /dev/video0; however, you may need to modify this if you have more than one camera.

Using the module then is as simple as calling the method get_image() on a camera object. This returns an image that can be used just like any other PyGame image. In this case, we'll just blit (draw) it to the main display, then call flip() to update the display (as covered in Chapter 5).

Once you have the image, you don't have to just spit it straight out to the screen. You can do other things with it as well. For example, there are some image effects you can apply, and you can send it to a file instead of to the screen.

Take a look at the following code (it's chapter9-mirror-lines.py on the website):

```
import pygame
import pygame.camera

pygame.init()
pygame.camera.init()
from pygame.locals import *

size = (320, 240)

display = pygame.display.set_mode(size,0)

cam = pygame.camera.Camera("/dev/video0", size)
cam.start()

inverse = pygame.Surface(size, pygame.SRCALPHA)
```

```
for i in range (1,50):
    image = cam.get_image()
    lines = pygame.transform.laplacian(image)
    inverse.fill((255,255,255,255))
    inverse.blit(lines, (0,0), None, BLEND_RGB_SUB)
    display.blit(inverse, (0,0))
    pygame.display.flip()

pygame.image.save(inverse, "/home/pi/test.png")
```

This has the same basic structure as the previous example, but with a few more operations. Firstly, it creates a new image called `lines`. This is made from a *laplacian* transform on the original image, which is a mathematical process that finds the edges in an image. The returned image will be white lines on black.

The program then inverts this image to create an image that's black lines on white. There isn't a method that just inverts the colours of an image, so to do this you have to create a white image and subtract the image from it (that is, call `blit()` with the special flag `BLEND_RGB_SUB`).

You may have noticed that this example doesn't have a `while` loop, but instead uses a `for` loop. This loop will execute 50 times and then exit. This should give you a few seconds of video (if you want to make it precise, you could update it with the timing functions used in Chapter 4). Once this is finished, it'll execute the final line, which saves the current inverted line image as a PNG file. This makes the program behave a little like a camera on a timer.

The final difference between this program and the first one is that it uses images that are a little smaller. The size is set in the `size` variable. This is because the transforms are quite computationally intensive, and reducing each axis of the image by half reduces the amount of processing by a quarter (because it is proportional to area). This makes the video far more responsive. You can change this to see how performance is affected.

Adding Computer Vision Features with OpenCV

PyGame is great for getting images into your computer, but isn't set up for doing much with them once it has them. There's another module called `OpenCV` that's designed for manipulating images. Unfortunately it didn't support Python 3 at the time of writing, although this should change in the future. Since it has some pretty interesting features that you can't easily get without it, we're going to cover it using Python 2. Hopefully, an update to Python 3 will be available soon, and then you shouldn't have any difficulty using it in the newer version of Python.

First, install it with the terminal command:

```
sudo apt-get install python-opencv libopencv-core-dev
```

The first example is the same as the first example with PyGame: a simple webcam viewer. This should give you a feel for how the library works:

```
import cv2

capture = cv2.VideoCapture(0)

while True:
    return_val, frame = capture.read()
    cv2.imshow('Face', frame)

    key = cv2.waitKey(5)
    if key == 113:
        break
```

This is structured roughly the same as with PyGame. You open the camera, then read a frame and display it. The final three lines listen for the users to press the q key (which corresponds to key 113), and exiting if they do.

OpenCV is a hugely powerful module for manipulating images. One of the most interesting features is object recognition. Your programs can identify certain parts of an image, for example an eye or a mouth.

This is all done with Haar cascades, which are saved as XML files. These are created from training sets of images that the computer compares to pick up similar objects. You can create your own using the opencv_traincascades program that runs on the Linux command line. However, you will need vast numbers of images (hundreds to get good results), both with the object you wish to recognise, and without it. There's a good tutorial on how to do this at http://docs.opencv.org/doc/user_guide/ug_traincascade.html.

We won't go into creating cascades, but OpenCV does come with some example ones installed and ready to go. The next example uses OpenCV bundles to recognise eyes and mouths. The code's on the website as chapter9-objectdetect.py.

```
import cv2

factor_down = 0.33
factor_up = 3

capture = cv2.VideoCapture(0)
```

```
eye_data = cv2.CascadeClassifier('/usr/share/opencv/haarcascades/'
                                 + 'haarcascade_eye.xml')
smile_data = cv2.CascadeClassifier('/usr/share/opencv/
  haarcascades/' +
  'haarcascade_mcs_mouth.xml')

while True:

    return_val, frame = capture.read()
    gray_frame = cv2.cvtColor(frame, cv2.COLOR_RGB2GRAY)
    small_gray_frame = cv2.resize(gray_frame, (0,0),
                       fx=factor_down, fy=factor_down)

    eyes = eye_data.detectMultiScale(small_gray_frame, 1.3, 5)

    for (eye_x, eye_y, eye_width, eye_height) in eyes:
        cv2.rectangle(frame, (eye_x*factor_up, eye_y*factor_up),
                      (eye_x*factor_up + eye_width*factor_up,
                      eye_y*factor_up+eye_height*factor_up),
                      (255,0,0),2)

    smiles = smile_data.detectMultiScale(small_gray_frame, 1.3, 5)
    for (smile_x, smile_y, smile_width, smile_height) in smiles:
        cv2.rectangle(frame, (smile_x*factor_up,
                      smile_y*factor_up),
                      (smile_x*factor_up + smile_width*factor_up,
                      smile_y*factor_up+smile_height*factor_up),
                      (0,255,0),2)
    cv2.imshow('Face', frame)

    key = cv2.waitKey(5)
    if key == 113:
        break
```

As you can see, loading the Haar cascades is simply a case of calling cv2.Cascade Classifier() with the cascade file as the sole parameter. This creates an object with a method called detectMultiScale(), which can be used to return a list of rectangles that match the cascade. There are a few more things going on here, though.

In the while loop, the program first captures a frame as in the first OpenCV example, and then it creates two new images—gray_frame and small_gray_frame. These, unsurprisingly, are a greyscale version of the initial frame and a smaller version of the grey frame. You need to do this is because object detection takes quite a bit of computing power, and while the Raspberry Pi is capable of doing it on a full size image, it runs slowly if it does. The smaller the images is, the less accurate the object recognition is. We found that shrinking the original image to a third of its size was a good compromise. You can play around with the values of `factor_down` and `factor_up` (they must always be equal to the reciprocal of the other) to see what works best for you.

TIP Remember that you can overclock your Pi using `raspi-config` in LXTerminal if you want better performance.

`detectMultiScale()` then returns the coordinates for all the rectangles that match the object, and the two for loops go through all of those returned and draws them on the image.

Taking Things Further

If you're prepared to take the time to create a set of training images, you can use this basic program in all sorts of programs. For example, you could create one that recognises the users rather than asking them to log in, or you could add OpenCV to a robotic buggy to make it understand simple signs.

Even without creating your own Haar cascades, you can add vision to your Pi. For example, you could use the hand Haar cascades and keep an eye on how the rectangles move. You could get it to watch for hand waving.

Using the Raspberry Pi Camera Module

USB webcams aren't your only option for adding images and video to your Raspberry Pi projects. In fact, they may not even be the most popular method for doing it. The Raspberry Pi Foundation released its own `camera` module, which plugs into the board. Here are some of the pros and cons of the `camera` module compared to a USB webcam.

Pros:

- Better resolution for still images than most webcams (five megapixels)
- Good command-line support for Linux
- Competitive price (£19; about $31)
- Infrared (night vision) version available

Cons:

- Less support in non-Pi specific programs and Python modules

- Limited to one camera per board

- Short cable (15cm), although it is possible, but not easy, to extend it

The choice comes down to the specific project you need the camera for.

Camera Module and OpenCV

OpenCV, which you saw in the previous section, won't work out of the box with the Raspberry Pi Foundation's `camera` module. However, you can modify OpenCV to work with it by following the instructions at `http://thinkrpi.wordpress.com/2013/05/22/opencv-and-camera-board-csi/`.

At the time of writing, there wasn't a Python module available for the Raspberry Pi camera board. One project that's working on it is available from `https://github.com/ashtons/picam`. It's still a little unstable. At the moment, the best approach is to use the command-line tool through Python to access the camera.

The first thing to do is make sure that the camera is connected and enabled. Open an LXTerminal session and enter:

```
raspistill -o test.png
```

This should display a preview of the camera output for a few seconds, then capture the result as `test.png`. If there are any problems, go back to the Raspberry Pi camera setup instructions at `www.raspberrypi.org/camera` and get this working before moving on.

This gives you the basic way of taking a picture with the command line. You can do the same in Python with:

```
>>> import subprocess
>>> subprocess.call(["raspistill", "-o", "test.png"])
```

If needed, you can then bring the image into Python by loading it as you would any other image. For example, with the image-loading features of PyGame that you used in Chapter 4.

`raspistill` allows you to set a wide range of options to control the way the image is captured. Enter `raspistill` at the command line for a full list of options. The options range from the simple, such as the size, to the more complex, such as metering mode or AWB.

As an example, the following code captures an image that's 200 by 200 pixels, has a high contrast, and uses the sketch image effect. In addition, it has no onscreen preview and a timeout of one millisecond.

```
raspistill -w 200 -h 200 -co 90 -n -t 1 -ifx sketch -o test.png
```

The result is a slightly cartoony image. This would be the perfect input to creating a time-lapse cartoon video, so that's exactly what we'll do with the next example (it's on the website as `chapter9-timelapse.py`).

```
import subprocess
import time

frames = 10


for i in range(1,frames):
    filename = "test" + format(i, "03d") + ".jpg"
    subprocess.call(["raspistill", "-n", "-t", '1', "-w", "200",
                     "-h', "200", '-co', "90", "-ifx", "sketch",
                     "-e", "jpg", "-e", "jpg", "-o", filename])
    print("taking photo", i)

print("Encoding. . .")
subprocess.call(["avconv", "-r", "5", "-i", "test%03d.jpg", "-r",
                 "24", "-s", "200x200",
                 "-vsync", "cfr" , "out.mpg"])
```

This code uses the `-e jpg` option on `raspistill`, which saves the image as a JPEG rather than as a PNG. This makes the conversion to a movie easier. Once it's taken all the images, it converts them to a movie using `avconv`. The key options here are the first `-r`. The number following this is the amount of images it will use to create one second of video. In this example, we've used five, but you can change this to whatever you like (the second `-r` is the frames per second in the final video). `-i test%03d.jpg` picks up files with names like `test001.jpg` and `test002.jpg`. This matches the line that creates the filename:

```
filename = "test" + format(i, "03d") + ".jpg"
```

These have to match each other so that the video encoder picks up the images that have been created. You can change test to anything you want, provided you change it in both places. If you want to take more than 999 images, you'll need to add more zeros. For example, if you wanted to take up to 99,999 images, you could change the threes in both lines to fives (the variable frames stores the number of frames captured (actually it will capture one less than this number, but we left it like this for simplicity).

-s 200x200 is the final dimension of the video in pixels. This doesn't have to match the size of the images. You can change out.mpg to whatever you wish to call the final video.

If you run this and create a video, you can then view the result with any standard video player such as VLC.

Creating Live Streams

The previous method works great if you want to create a video over a predetermined amount of time, but what if you want to keep a video going indefinitely? For example, what if you wanted to create a live video stream that you can watch over the Internet? Internet lore has it that the very first webcam was set up in Cambridge (the home of the Raspberry Pi) to allow people to keep an eye on a coffee pot, so they could time their visits to the canteen with a fresh brew. The following example re-creates that webcam.

In order to send data over the Internet, you'll need some form of server. There are a few that can do the job, but for the sake of familiarity, we'll use the Tornado server that you saw in Chapter 7.

The live stream can then be created with the following code. Before running it, you'll have to create the directory /home/pi/images with mkdir /home/pi/images.

```
import tornado.ioloop
import tornado.web
import subprocess
import time

class MainHandler(tornado.web.RequestHandler):
    def get(self):
        subprocess.call(["raspistill", "-w", "200", "-h", "200",
                         "-e", "jpg", "-n", "-t", "1", "-o",
                         "/home/pi/images/live.jpg"])
        time.sleep(2)
        self.write('<! DOCTYPE html><head>' +
                   '<META HTTP-EQUIV="refresh"' +
                   ' CONTENT="5"></head><body>' +
                   '<img src="/images/live.jpg"></body>')
```

```
class ImageHandler(tornado.web.StaticFileHandler):
    def set_extra_headers(self, path):
        self.set_header('Cache-Control',
                        'no-store, no-cache, must-revalidate,' +
                        ' max-age=0')

application = tornado.web.Application([
    (r"/", MainHandler),
    (r"/images/(.*)", ImageHandler, {"path":"/home/pi/images"})])

if __name__ == "__main__":
    application.listen(8888)
    tornado.ioloop.IOLoop.instance().start()
```

If this doesn't look familiar to you, pop back to Chapter 7 and have a look at the section on Tornado. There are, however, a few new things in here.

In essence, all this does is wait for a user to request the page with the live stream (this is simply the root, but you can update it to be wherever you want), then it takes a new picture. The web page is then served, and it includes the picture. To make it a live stream rather than just a live image, the web page it serves includes the tag <META HTTP-EQUIV="refresh" CONTENT="5">, which tells the web browser to automatically refresh the page every five seconds. It's not high-quality video, but it's enough to keep you updated on the amount of coffee in a pot.

The class ImageHandler extends tornado.web.StaticFileHandler. It does this so that it can change the default settings on caching. By default, Tornado will try to be efficient and not reserve images it's served before. That means if a web browser requests an image that Tornado has already sent to it, it'll just tell it to use the same image. Since the browser is constantly checking the image live.jpg, it would normally keep reserving the first image. By adding this header, you're telling it not to be so lazy and to actually reread the file each time.

This works, but it's not ideal. For example, it takes a new picture every time someone requests a page, but if a lot of people are constantly requesting pages, it'll get clogged up, as the camera can only take one picture at a time. Secondly, it doesn't store any of the pictures. This isn't a problem if you're just watching coffee, but if you're using this as a security camera for example, this could be an issue.

To get around this, you need to separate the section that takes the images, and the one that serves them. The following code will constantly take images so they can by amalgamated into a video, and at the same time, it keeps live.jpg updated with the latest. It's on the website as chapter9-live-take-pics.py:

```
import subprocess
import time
```

```
file_number = 0
dir = "/home/pi/images/"

while True:
    file_name = dir + format(file_number, "05d") + ".jpg"
    file_number = file_number + 1
    subprocess.call(["raspistill", "-w", "400", "-h", "400", "-e",
                     "jpg", "-n", "-t", "1", "-o", file_name])
    subprocess.call(["cp", "-f", file_name, dir + "live.jpg"])
    time.sleep(2)
```

The next piece of code starts the previous script automatically, and displays the latest image just as the previous example did. It's on the website as chapter9-live-image-server.py.

```
import tornado.ioloop
import tornado.web
import subprocess

class MainHandler(tornado.web.RequestHandler):
    def get(self):
        self.write('<! DOCTYPE html><head>' +
                   '<META HTTP-EQUIV="refresh"' +
                   ' CONTENT="5"></head><body>' +
                   '<img src="/images/live.jpg"></body>')

class ImageHandler(tornado.web.StaticFileHandler):
    def set_extra_headers(self, path):
        self.set_header('Cache-Control',
                'no-store, no-cache, must-revalidate, max-age=0')

application = tornado.web.Application([
    (r"/", MainHandler),
    (r"/images/(.*)", ImageHandler, {"path":"/home/pi/images"})])

if __name__ == "__main__":
    subprocess.Popen(["python3", "chapter 9-live-take-pics.py"])
    application.listen(8888)
    tornado.ioloop.IOLoop.instance().start()
```

This uses subprocess.Popen() to create a new process that lets both of the programs run at the same time (more on this next chapter).

Taking Things Further

There are still a few problems though. This code will simply run constantly until it fills up the SD card with images. At this point, the Pi will probably crash. If you want to take things further, there are a few things you could do. For example, every certain amount of time (maybe every day or every 20,000 images), you could convert the images into a video, and then delete the images. For extra bonus points you could make the archive videos available online.

To make it more secure, you could constantly upload the videos to a central server that's offsite. This means that if your Pi is stolen or destroyed, you still have access to the surveillance footage.

If you are deploying this on a publicly accessible web server, you should implement some security so only authorised people are able to view the footage online. Take a look back to Chapter 7 for details on how to do this.

Summary

After reading this chapter, you should understand the following a bit better:

- PyAudio is a great module for bringing sound into Python programs.

- The `wave` module lets you output WAVE files.

- There aren't great Python tools for everything in audio, but that doesn't cause a problem because you can use the Linux command-line tools such as `sox` and `flac` to fill in the gaps.

- You can also use web services such as Google's speech recognition to add even more audio features.

- There are two options for adding cameras to your Pi: USB webcams and the Raspberry Pi Foundation's `camera` module.

- USB webcams work best with standard Python tools such as PyGame and OpenCV.

- The `camera` module works with OpenCV, but it also has its own set of command-line tools for grabbing images and videos.

- OpenCV can be used to add computer vision features such as object recognition.

- A web server such as Tornado can be used to serve streams of images on the Internet.

Chapter 10
Scripting

THERE ARE LOADS of different tasks that you need to perform on a computer to keep it running properly. For example, you need to back up your data regularly just in case there's a problem. Other tasks can depend on exactly what you use your computer for. You might need something to keep your music collection in order, or sort photos. This chapter looks at how you can use Python to make your life easier by automating these housekeeping jobs so that your computer keeps running with minimal intervention.

This requires a lot of interaction with the underlying operating system, so the first thing to do is learn a little about Linux.

Getting Started with the Linux Command Line

By this point, you're probably fairly familiar with general use of Raspbian. Raspbian brings together several distinct parts to create an operating system. Firstly, there's the Linux kernel. This is the bit that makes everything work at the lowest level. It's constantly running and manages the hardware and memory and controls how other programs run. Then there's the command line and a wide range of tools. These provide an entirely text-based way of using Raspbian, and it's an area that you'll be looking at in more detail in this chapter. The chances are, you probably don't use this too much at the moment; instead, you probably interact with the desktop environment, which is another distinct section of Raspbian. The default GUI is LXDE, and on top of this there are a wide range of graphical programs.

If you've mostly used Windows, the first big difference you'll notice will probably be the file-system. You won't find a C drive (or for that matter, any other lettered drive) on your Raspberry Pi. Instead, everything is built into a single hierarchy that starts at / (known as the *root*). Before getting started with Python scripting, you'll need to know where everything is in this filesystem, so open LXTerminal (the window that contains the text-based way of using Raspbian) and enter the following:

```
cd /
ls
```

The first line changes the directory to / (the root), then the second lists everything in the current directory. You should get output like this (see Figure 10-1):

```
bin   dev   home   lost+found   mnt   proc   run    selinux   sys   usr
boot  etc   lib    media              opt   root   sbin   srv              tmp   var
```

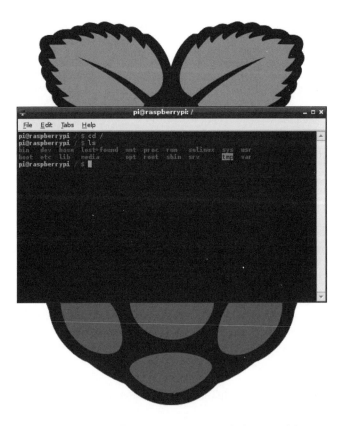

FIGURE 10-1: LXTerminal allows you to interact with the powerful Linux command-line environment.

These are the directories in the root (if there were any files, they'd be listed here as well, but there aren't any in this folder). If you use a different Linux system, you'll find a similar set of directories in /. Most of these directories you'll never need to touch. Raspbian will look after them for you, and keep everything up to date. The ones that you're likely to use are /home, where the users' home directories are kept, /media, where removable devices such as USB memory sticks will be found, and /etc, where system-wide application settings are kept.

It's important to realise that this filesystem doesn't directly correspond to a filesystem that's stored on a disk in the same way it does in Windows. So, for example, /home/pi is stored on the SD card. However, if you were to put in a USB memory stick called MyStick, you'll find it at /media/MyStick.

/sys and /proc don't exist on any disk. They're virtual filesystems that are created to look like normal directories and files, but are just the system's way for displaying information. For example, if you type:

```
cat /proc/cpuinfo
```

cat is a command that outputs the contents of one of more files, and /proc/cpuinfo contains the technical details of the CPU. You should get something like this:

```
pi@raspberrypi /proc $ cat /proc/cpuinfo
Processor: ARMv6-compatible processor rev 7 (v6l)
BogoMIPS: 697.95
Features: swp half thumb fastmult vfp edsp java tls
CPU implementer: 0x41
CPU architecture: 7
CPU variant: 0x0
CPU part: 0xb76
CPU revision: 7

Hardware: BCM2708
Revision: 000d
Serial: 0000000074f3d523
```

The environment in LXTerminal is known as *Bash*. It's a powerful environment and even has its own programming language. If you want to learn more about Raspbian and Linux in general, Bash is a good place to start, and there are loads of resources (such as www.linuxcommand.org). However, this is a book about Python, so we'll leave it here and let interested readers learn on their own.

Using the Subprocess Module

The easiest way to interact with the underlying system from Python is to use the subprocess module. We used this in Chapter 7, so you may already be a little familiar with it. Open up a Python interpreter (if you're already using LXTerminal, you can do this just by typing python3), and enter the following:

```
>>> import subprocess
>>> subprocess.call("ls")
```

As you can see, using subprocess.call(), you can run any command on the underlying OS. If there are spaces in the command you want to run, you need to separate the command into a list of strings. For example, the command cat /proc/cpuinfo becomes:

```
>>> subprocess.call(["cat","/proc/cpuinfo"])
```

This is all well and good, but all this really does is provide a more verbose way of running commands. After all, you could just have easily run the same commands in LXTerminal. As we said at the start, the aim of this chapter is to automate general tasks, and to do that you're going to need to read in the outputs so that you can manipulate them.

For example, cat /proc/cpuinfo returns a load of information, most of which you probably don't want to know. The following program strips out all the information except the line that tells you the type of processor the computer is running.

```
import subprocess

p = subprocess.Popen(["cat", "/proc/cpuinfo"],
                     stdout=subprocess.PIPE)

text = p.stdout.read().decode()

for line in text.splitlines():
    if line[:9] == "Processor":
        print(line)
```

This uses subprocess.Popen() rather than subprocess.call(). Doing this gives you much more control over what's going on because it creates a new object that you can use to get the information you want.

Whenever a command runs on a Linux machine, there are two pieces of output: stdout and stderr. Stdout (or standard out) is where all the normal output goes. For example, when you run a Python program, any print() statements go to stdout. Stderr (or standard error) is where the system sends error messages. If you're running something in LXTerminal, both of these go to the screen, but when you're scripting things, it can be useful to split them up. That way, if you're running a lot of commands, you can send any error messages to one place so that you can see instantly if something's gone wrong without having to check through all the output.

The parameter stdout=subprocess.PIPE tells Python to keep stdout in the object we're creating rather than sending it to the screen. Since you're not telling it what to do with stderr, it will, by default, send that to the screen. So, if you change the line to:

```
p = subprocess.Popen(["cat", "/proc/cpuinfozzz"],
                     stdout=subprocess.PIPE)
```

The error message will be printed on the screen even though it doesn't get printed in any print() statement.

If needed, you can also capture the stderr of a command. For example, take a look at the following program, which displays the contents of a file that the user enters:

```
import subprocess

f_name = input("Enter a filename: ")

p = subprocess.Popen(["cat", f_name ], stdout=subprocess.PIPE,
                     stderr=subprocess.PIPE)

text = p.stdout.read().decode()
error = p.stderr.read().decode()

print(text)

if len(error) > 0:
    print("*****ERROR*****")
    print(error)
```

Command-Line Flags

Linux commands often take flags. These flags come after the main command and are ways to tell it what to do. For example, in LXTerminal, try running the following:

```
ls
ls -a
ls --all
```

ls lists the contents of the current directory. By using the flag -a, you're telling it to list everything in the directory (usually ls omits files and directories that start with a '.'). --all is the same as ls -a. Many commands have two versions of each flag—a short version that starts with - and a long version (often easier to remember) that starts with --. To get more information on how to use ls, run it with either the flag -h or -help.

Flags can also take values, as you'll see in a minute.

If you're developing scripts, you should try to follow these conventions whenever possible. There's a module named optparse that can help. The previous example can be made to take its input from a flag rather than a prompted user input. Take a look at the following:

```python
import subprocess
from optparse import OptionParser

parser = OptionParser()

parser.add_option("-f", "-file", dest="filename",
                  help="The file to display")

options, arguments = parser.parse_args()

if options.filename:
   p = subprocess.Popen(["cat", options.filename ],
                          stdout=subprocess.PIPE,
                          stderr=subprocess.PIPE)

   text = p.stdout.read().decode()
   error = p.stderr.read().decode()
else:
   test = ""
   error = "Filename not given"
```

```
if len(error) > 0:
    print("*****ERROR*****")
    print(error)
else:
    print(text)
```

As you can see, this creates an `OptionParser` object. In this example, there's only one option, but you can add as many as you like by having more calls to `parser.add_option()`. The first two parameters to this are the short and long versions of the flag. `dest="filename"` means that the value of the flag is stored in the attribute called `filename` of the options that are returned.

Note that the parser automatically creates the flags `-h` and `--help`, and builds the help text up from the `help=` parameters in `add_options()` calls.

If you save the previous code as `print-file.py`, you can run it in LXTerminal by cding to the directory it's saved in and entering `python3 print-file.py -f /proc/cpuinfo`. You can view the help with `python3 print-file.py --help`.

Regular Expressions

All this is, though, is a Python wrapper around `cat` that just does what the original does. It doesn't actually add anything.

Let's add a feature that lets the users specify which lines of the file they want to display.

Python (and many other programming languages) has a feature called *regular expressions*. This slightly oddly named feature (often shortened to *regex*) enables you to specify bits of text to match.

They do this with special characters. The most common special character is `*`. This means, match the preceding character zero or more times. For example: `do*g` will match `dg`, `dog`, `doog`, and so on. The character `+` will match the preceding character one or more times. For example, `do+g` will match `dog`, `doog`, `dooog`, and so on, but not `dg`. `do?g`, on the other hand will match `dg` or `dog` only.

A period will match any character other than a new line, so `.*` will match any line, while `.+` will match any line that isn't empty.

You can group characters together, so `d[io]g` will match `dig` and `dog`, and `d[io]*g` will match `dg`, `dog`, `dig`, `doog`, `dioioioig`, and anything like that.

We'll look at a few more features of regular expressions a bit later on, but for now let's get started with using them. The following code is on the website as `chapter10-regex.py`.

```python
import subprocess
from optparse import OptionParser
import re

parser = OptionParser()

parser.add_option("-f", "-file", dest="filename",
                  help="The file to display")

parser.add_option("-r", "-regex", dest="regex",
                  help="The regular expression to search for")
options, arguments = parser.parse_args()
if options.filename:

    p = subprocess.Popen(["cat", options.filename ],
    stdout=subprocess.PIPE, stderr=subprocess.PIPE)

    text = p.stdout.read().decode()
    error = p.stderr.read().decode()
else:
    test = ""
    error = "Filename not given"

if len(error) > 0:
    print("*****ERROR*****")
    print(error)
else:
    for line in text.splitlines():
        if not options.regex or (options.regex
            and re.search(options.regex, line)):
            print(line)
```

This gets the regular expressions from the module re. There are two main ways of using regular expressions: re.match() and re.search(). The first one tries to match the regular expression from the start of the string, while the second one tries to find text anywhere in the string that matches the regular expression. This program does the latter because we wanted to make it as easy as possible to match lines.

There is a slightly convoluted condition in the `if` line:

```
if not options.regex or (options.regex
        and re.search(options.regex, line)):
```

This is to handle the case whereby the user hasn't entered a `-r` or `-regex` flag. It says to print the line if either there isn't a `regex` flag, or there is a flag and the line matches.

To match the first example, run it with:

```
python3 chapter.py -f /proc/cpuinfo -r Processor
```

Linux systems keep log files that register various events. These can be useful in diagnosing problems, but they can also get huge and be hard to work with. They're all located in the `/var/log` folder. `syslog` holds much of the general information about what's been going on. For example, if you're having some difficulty with a USB device, running the following log file list all the times Raspbian registered a new USB peripheral (either hub or device):

```
python3 chapter10-regex.py -f /var/log/syslog -r"USB.*found"
```

In this case, putting the regular expression in quote marks isn't necessary, but sometimes the Linux shell will try to process special characters before they're passed to Python. Using double quote marks stops that from happening, so it's a good habit to get into when putting regular expressions on the command line.

Let's return to features of regular expressions:

- `[^abc]` matches every character except a, b, and c, so `d[^o]g` matches dig, dxg, and dag but not dog.

- `[a-c]` matches the characters a through to c, so `d[a-j]g` matches dag, dbg, and dig, but not dkg or dog.

- `{a, b}` matches the preceding character anywhere between a and b times, so `do{2,4}g` matches doog, dooog, and doooog, but not dog or dooooog.

In addition, there are a series of special letters that, when preceded by a slash, take on a special meaning. Table 10-1 lists these special letters.

Table 10-1   **Escaped Characters in Regular Expressions**

Character	Description
\n	The newline character
\t	Tab
\d	Any digit
\D	Anything except a digit
\s	Any whitespace such as a space, Tab, or newline
\w	Any alphanumeric character
\W	Any non-alphanumeric character

Obviously, this can lead to some problems if you want to match a \ character. For this, or any other time where you want to match a special character (such as ., * or +), you can *escape* them with a \. Therefore, \\w matches \w and \w matches any alphanumeric character.

This can create a problem when entering strings in Python, since slashes need to be escaped there as well. For example:

```
>>> print("\\")
\
>>> print("\\\\")
\\
```

NOTE	This isn't a problem in this example because you've been passing the strings into Python, but if you're creating strings for regex matching in Python itself, you'll need to remember to double the amount of slashes you want to use in the regex.

Testing Your Knowledge

We've covered quite a log of regular expression information in quite a short space. To make sure everything is sinking in, take a look at the following exercise.

Take the following file:

```
aaa
a10
10
Hello
Helllo
Helloo
```

Which regex will match which lines? Try to work it out, then run the previous program on them to find out (you'll need to create a text file in Leafpad or download it from the website, where it's called chapter10-regex-test). For example, to check the first one, run:

```
python3 chapter10-regex.py -f chapter10-regex-test -r"."
```

Remember that the program uses re.search() not re.match()

- .
- \d
- \D\d
- 1{3,4}
- e*
- e+
- [Ha]
- \d{2,3}
- 1?

Scripting with Networking

We looked at networking in Chapter 7, and we're not going to repeat ourselves here. Instead, we're going to look at ways you may need to use the network when scripting. The most common thing you'll need to do is copy files between two computers. There is an excellent module for this called Fabric; however, at the time of writing, it doesn't support Python 3. This is likely to change, but not in the immediate future.

In the absence of a module to handle the process, you could create the Python code from scratch and copy everything across. This is certainly possible, but it'll be quite long winded. There is a Linux command-line program called scp (secure copy) that does this, and you've already seen how to run command-line programs.

There is a slight problem though. When you run scp normally, it'll ask you for your password. This will cause a problem when scripting in Python because you can't easily tell it to answer questions. scp does, though, allow you to set it up with certificates so that if you're logged in as an authorised user on one machine, you can log in without a password on another.

`scp` can be used to copy information between Linux computers (such as Raspberry Pis), so it will work between two Raspberry Pis, or between a Pi and a Linux server. Other (non-Linux) servers may also support it, but you'll have to ask your system administrator to set it up.

The first thing you need to do is log into the machine you want to transfer information to and run the following on the Linux command line, such as in LXTerminal. If you have only one Linux machine, you can try this out with a single computer, so run these commands on the same machine. If you only have remote access to this machine, you can do this via `ssh`.

```
ssh-keygen -t rsa
```

This will create two files in the `.ssh` folder in your home directory, called `id_rsa` and `id_rsa.pub`. These contain the public and private keys. `id_rsa.pub` is the public key, and you'll need to copy it across to the computer you wish to log in from. You can do this with a USB memory stick, cloud storage (such as Dropbox or Google Drive), or even email, but since we're talking about `scp`, you could do it with that. The format of an `scp` command is:

```
scp location1 location2
```

It simply copies the file from `location1` to `location2`. If one of the locations is a normal file path, such as `/home/pi/.ssh/id_rsa.pub`, then `scp` deals with it on the local machine. However, if the location is in the form `user@machine:/home/pi`, then `scp` tries to log in as a user on the remote machine. `machine` can either be an IP address or a host-name. Typically with Pis, it'll be a IP address. So, if the IP address of the machine you want to copy your `id_rsa.pub` file is `192.168.0.10`, and you want to use the user `pi`, the command would be

```
scp /home/pi/.ssh/id_rsa.pub pi@192.168.0.10:/home/pi
```

If you're trying this out on a single machine, you don't actually have to move the file, but just to try out `scp`, you can use the machine `localhost`. Therefore, the copy command is

```
scp /home/pi/.ssh/id_rsa.pub pi@localhost:/home/pi
```

Then you just need to copy the contents of the file into the `authorized_keys` file by logging into the machine you just copied the file to and running:

```
cat /home/pi/id_rsa.pub >> /home/pi/.ssh/ authorized_keys
```

That's been a little fiddly, but you should now be able to copy files from this machine to the other one (but not the other way around) without using a password. To try it out, enter the following:

```
touch test
scp test user@machine:/home/pi/
```

Where user, machine, and /home/pi are changed as appropriate. The first line simply creates an empty file called test. If everything works correctly, you won't need to enter a password.

With all that set up, you can copy files between machines using subprocess.call(). For example:

```
subprocess.call(["scp", "file1.py", "pi@localhost:/home/pi"])
```

Bringing It All Together

At the start of the chapter, we promised some Python that can make your regular computer chores easier, and while we've shown you lots of cool Python, we haven't fulfilled that promise yet. Now we will. In this section, we're going to create a Python program that can help you keep backup copies of your most useful files so that if disaster strikes, and your SD card breaks, you can get your data back.

We'll do this using most of what we've covered so far in this chapter, and one more module as well, os. This provides access to some of the operating system's functionality. Take a look at the following code (there's an explanation after it) The code's on the website as chapter10-backup.py:

```
import os
import tarfile
from optparse import OptionParser
from time import localtime
import datetime
import subprocess
import re

parser = OptionParser()

parser.add_option("-f", "--file", dest="filename",
                  help="filename to write backup to (if no option
                  is give, backup will be used)", metavar="FILE")
parser.add_option("-p", "--path", dest="path",
```

```
                        help="path to backup (if no option is give, ~
                        will be used)")
parser.add_option("-v", "--verbose", action="store_true",
                        dest="verbose", default=False,
                        help="print status messages to stdout")
parser.add_option("-i", "--images", action="store_true",
                        dest="images", default=False,
                        help="backup image files")
parser.add_option("-c", "--code", action="store_true", dest="code",
                        default=False,
                        help="backup code files")
parser.add_option("-d", "--documents", action="store_true",
                        dest="documents", default=False,
                        help="backup document files")
parser.add_option("-a", "--all", action="store_true", dest="all",
                        default=False,
                        help="backup all filetypes (this overrides
                        c, d & i)")
parser.add_option("-m", "--mtime", dest="mtime", default=False,
                        help="backup files modified less than this many
                        days ago")
parser.add_option("-r", "--regex", dest="regex",
                        help="only back up filenames that match this
                        regex")
parser.add_option("-s", "--server", dest="server", default=False,
                        help="copy backup file to this remote point
                        (should be an scp location)")

options, arguments = parser.parse_args()

if options.filename:
    backup_file_name = options.filename + '.tar.gz'
else:
    backup_file_name = "backup.tar.gz"

backup_tar = tarfile.open(backup_file_name, "w:gz")

file_types = {"code":[".py"],
              "image":[".jpeg", ".jpg", ".png", ".gif"],
              "document":[".doc", "docx", ".odt", ".rtf"]}
```

```
backup_types = []
all_types = False

if options.images:
  backup_types.extend(file_types["image"])
if options.code:
  backup_types.extend(file_types["code"])
if options.documents:
  backup_types.extend(file_types["document"])

if len(backup_types) == 0 or options.all:
  all_types = True
if options.mtime:
    try:
        mtime_option = int(options.mtime)
    except ValueError:
        print("mtime option is not a valid integer.",
              "Ignoring option")
        mtime_option = -1
else:
    mtime_option = -1

if options.path:
    if os.path.isdir(options.path):
        directory = options.path
    else:
        print("Directory not found. Using ~")
        directory = os.getenv("HOME")
else:
    directory = os.getenv("HOME")

for root, dirs, files in os.walk(directory):
    for file_name in files:
        if not options.regex or re.match(options.regex, file_name):
            name, extension = os.path.splitext(os.path.join(root,
                                                file_name))
            if (extension in backup_types) or all_types:
                modified_days = (datetime.datetime.now() -
                                 datetime.datetime.fromtimestamp(
                                 os.path.getmtime(
                                 os.path.join(root,
                                 file_name)))).days
```

```
                if mtime_option < 0 or modified_days <
                                      mtime_option:
                    if options.verbose:
                        print("Adding ",
                                os.path.join(root,file_name),
                                "last modified", modified_days,
                                "days ago")
                    backup_tar.add(os.path.join(root,file_name))
    if options.server:
        subprocess.call(["scp", backup_file_name, options.server])
```

As you can tell from the numerous `parser.add_option()` calls, you can change this program to work the way you want it to. Its basic function is to copy files into a `tar.gz` file, which is a type of compressed archive that's popular on Linux systems. This file can then be copied automatically to a safe location on a separate server. Should anything then happen to the original files, you can resurrect them from this backup.

If you run `python3 chapter10-backup.py -help`, you'll get the following, which describes what it does:

```
Usage: chapter10-backup.py [options]

Options:
  -h, --help            show this help message and exit
  -f FILE, --file=FILE  filename to write backup to (if no option
                        is given, backup will be used)
  -p PATH, --path=PATH  path to backup (if no option is given, ~
                        will be used)
  -v, --verbose         print status messages to stdout
  -i, --images          backup image files
  -c, --code            backup code files
  -d, --documents       backup document files
  -a, --all             backup all filetypes (this overrides c, d &
                        i)
  -m MTIME, --mtime=MTIME
                        backup files modified less than this many
                        days ago
  -r REGEX, --regex=REGEX
                        only back up filenames that match this
                        regex
  -s SERVER, --server=SERVER
                        copy backup file to this remote point
                        (should be an scp location)
```

The basic usage is

```
python3 chapter10-backup.py -f backup.tar.gz -p /home/pi -s \
pi@192.168.0.10:/home/pi/backups/
```

This tells the program to go through /home/pi and every subdirectory looking for files. It does this using the os.walk() function. This simply returns a collection of directories and files that you can move through using a for loop. This is done in the lines:

```
for root, dirs, files in os.walk(directory):
    for file_name in files:
```

The first line will go through every directory in turn and return the path to that directory (root), the subdirectories (dirs), and the files (files). Since this program only cares about files, there is only one inner loop that iterates through all the files. os.walk() automatically goes through all the subdirectories, so you don't need to direct it to do that.

There are then some options you can choose to limit which files get selected. The basic ones limit it by filetype. -i, -c, and -d limit it to just images, code, and documents, respectively, while -a overrides these and selects all files (the default). These don't select perfectly, but work based on the dictionary of filetypes:

```
file_types = {"code":[".py"],
              "image":[".jpeg", ".jpg", ".png", ".gif"],
              "document":[".doc", "docx", ".odt", ".rtf"]}
```

If one or more of these is selected, it'll only back up files that end with extensions in the appropriate list. The program finds the file extension in the line:

```
name, extension = os.path.splitext(root, file_name)
```

The function os.path.splitext() (note that's split-ext not split-text) splits the filename into its two basic components, and returns these as two separate values. The first is the main part of the filename (which is captured in the name variable), and the part that comes after the final. (which is captured in the extension variable). All that's left to do is check whether the extension is in the list backup_types, which we made by joining the lists of specified types. If you use these options, you should make sure that the entries in the list cover all the file types you actually want to back up.

The -r or --regex flag can be used to specify regular expressions that filenames must match to be included in the backup. This is in the line:

```
if not options.regex or re.match(options.regex, file_name):
```

Note that this uses re.match() rather than re.search(). This means that the entire filename must match the regular expression. For example, the regex ".*\.py" will match all files with the extension .py (which is equivalent to using the -c flag).

The final option you can use is -m or --mtime, which is short for modified time. In other words, it backs up all files that were modified more recently than this number of days. It does this with the rather convoluted line:

```
modified_days = (datetime.datetime.now() -
                datetime.datetime.fromtimestamp(
                os.path.getmtime(
                os.path.join(root,file_name)))).days
if mtime_option < 0 or modified_days < mtime_option:
```

The part of this that does most of the work is os.path.getmtime(). This takes a filename complete with a path (that is, it needs /home/pi/filename rather than just filename), and it returns the timestamp when the file was last modified.

os.path.join() takes two arguments, a path and a filename, and it joins them to create what the previous function needs (you can't just join two strings together because sometimes paths have a / on the end and sometimes they don't).

The timestamp returned by os.path.getmtime() isn't a regular date, but the number of seconds since January 1st 1970 (this was the standard for Unix systems, and is used on Linux systems as well). Therefore, to get the number of days between now and when the file was last changed, we first have to convert it into a Python datetime using datetime.datetime.fromtimestamp( ), and then take it off the current time.

With all that done, all that's left is to see if the result is less than the number of days given as an option. The initial clause in the if (mtime_option < 0) is because the program sets mtime_option to -1 if there's a problem with what the user entered, or if there isn't an mtime option.

These are all the options that limit whether a file is selected. Once they've all been checked, the only thing left to do is add it to the tar file. This is done using the module tarfile, which provides a really simple way to handle these archives. You just need to open the file at the start. This is done with the line:

```
backup_tar = tarfile.open(backup_file_name, "w:gz")
```

The second parameter (w:gz) specifies that the file should be opened for writing and that it's a gzipped (that is, compressed) file. The appropriate files can then be added to this archive with:

```
backup_tar.add(os.path.join(root,file_name))
```

You should recognise the code that uses scp to copy the file to a remote server if the option is specified.

This program is one example of a script that can help keep your computer in order. It makes the task of creating backups trivial; however, you still have to remember to run it to create said backups. Python can't help you here, but there's a Linux feature called crontab that takes care of running programs at specific times. Because all the options of this program are on the command line, all you have to do is decide what you want to run and set chrontab to start it at the appropriate time.

There are two main options for crontab: -l displays the list of the programs it currently has set to run, and -e opens up a text editor where you can edit what programs run when. Each task to run is on a separate line, and consist of five numbers or asterisks separated by spaces followed by the command. The five numbers relate to the minute of the hour, hour of the day, day of the month, month of the year, and day of the week the command should run, and an asterisk means any. Take, for example, the following (as a single line):

```
0 0 1 * * python3 /home/pi/chapter10-backup.py -s
pi@192.168.0.10:/home/pi/backups
```

This will take a backup of your home directory (the default) at midnight on the first of every month. The following will run every day at midday:

```
12 0 * * * python3 /home/pi/chapter10-backup.py -s
pi@192.168.0.10:/home/pi/backups
```

Working with Files in Python

In this chapter, you've seen a lot of ways to deal with files. However, you haven't yet actually opened any of them in Python to read or write data to (except the `tar` archive, but that was a special case). In this section, you'll see how to store information in text files, and then read it back.

This is actually really easy. All you need to do is call the `open()` function. For example, to open the file `myfile.txt` and print out every line, you need the following:

```python
file_a = open("myfile.txt", encoding="utf-8")

for line in file_a:
    print(line.strip())

file_a.close()
```

The `open()` function creates a file object. It can take a number of parameters. The essential one is the filename, and encoding is a particularly useful one since it tells Python what format the file is in. Most text files are `utf-8`, and that's the one you should use when creating your own files.

> **NOTE** Note that you can't use `file` as a variable name because it's used for other things in Python.

Once you've opened the file, you can loop through it with a `for` loop. The only slightly unusual thing here is the `.strip()` that we've called on `line`. This is because each line of the file contains a newline character which will be printed, and the `print` function then adds its own newline, so without this you'd get a blank line between each of the printed lines.

Once you've opened a file, you should always close it. There is another way you can write this code so that it automatically closes. That is

```python
with open("myfile.txt", encoding="utf-8") as file_a:
    for line in file_a:
        print(line.strip())
```

The two pieces of code do exactly the same thing. The `with` block will automatically close the file when the code block ends, so it's useful if you're prone to forgetting to close files.

Writing to files is almost as easy. You just need to add a `mode="w"` to the parameters of `open()`, then you can write. Take a look at the following:

```
with open("myfile.txt", mode="w", encoding="utf-8") as file_a:
    for letter in "abcde':
        file_a.write(letter + "\n")

with open("myfile.txt", encoding="utf-8") as file_a:
    for line in file_a:
        print(line.strip())
```

This will overwrite `myfile.txt`. However, if you want to add to the end of the file, you can use `mode="a"` (append). This will leave the original text intact and add new information to the bottom of the file.

Summary

After reading this chapter, you should understand the following a bit better:

- The Raspberry Pi runs a version of Linux.

- Linux has a different filesystem to Windows, based around the root directory, `/`.

- Linux has an entirely text-based mode.

- You can run commands on this text-based mode using the `subprocess` module.

- Commands in Linux can output to `stdout` and `stderr`.

- When writing scripts in Python, it's useful to get all the input as command-line flags if possible.

- Regular expressions are a way of matching patterns of text.

- `scp` can be used to copy files between computers.

- There are loads of functions in the `os` module to help you interact with the operating system (far more than we could cover here; take a look in the Python documentation for more information).

- The `open()` function can be used to open files for reading or writing.

Chapter 11
Interfacing with Hardware

UNLIKE MOST COMPUTERS, a Raspberry Pi has a series of *General Purpose Inputs and Outputs* (GPIOs) that allow you to interact with the world outside. These are the metal pins that stick up next to the SD card. You can use them a bit like programmable switches to turn things on and off, or you can use them to get information from other sources. In short, they allow you to expand your Pi in any way you want. They're widely used by digital artists to create interactive displays and by robot builders to bring their creations to life. With a bit of imagination, there really is no limit to what you can achieve with the Pis GPIOs and a few components.

Since this chapter is all about controlling things outside of the Pi, you will need a bit more equipment to try the examples here. It needn't be expensive though, and you can get started for just a few pounds. Even as you improve, most of the bits you'll need are cheap and easily available both online and in hobbyist stores.

Setting Up Your Hardware Options

Before jumping in and building circuits, the first thing you'll need is a way of connecting to the GPIO pins on the Pi. Since you can't just connect wires straight to the pins (actually you can solder directly onto them, but it's not recommended), there are a few options for accessing them, covered in the next sections.

Female to Male Jumper Wires

These are probably the simplest option. They simply fit over the top of the GPIO pins and allow you to then connect them to a solderless breadboard. This is the simplest way to get access to the GPIOs. It's also the method you'll see in the pictures of this book. It's fine for connecting a few pins, but it can get a little confusing if you're accessing a lot of pins at once. Take a look at Figure 11-1.

FIGURE 11-1: These jumper wires have a female end that slots over the GPIO pins and a male end that you can fit into the solderless breadboard.

Pi Cobbler

The Pi Cobbler is a really simple design that takes the GPIO pins and connects them to a header that can be pushed into a solderless breadboard (see Figure 11-2). It doesn't add anything that you don't get by using jumper wires, but it's a bit tidier and it's less likely to get into a confusing knot of wires.

FIGURE 11-2: The Pi Cobbler gets all the GPIO pins onto the breadboard without risk of tangled wires or confusion.
© Adafruit Industries

Solderless Breadboard

You'll probably need one of these whichever option you go with. It's a way of connecting components to build circuits quickly, and allowing them to be taken apart again when you're finished. They come in different sizes, but they all follow the same basic layout. Down the long sides there are two parallel lines of pins that can be used as positive and negative rails. In between these, there are two banks of pins with a gap in the middle. These are connected in strips perpendicular to the long edge (see Figure 11-3). In the pictures, we'll be using a small solderless breadboard that doesn't have the positive and negative rails; however, you can do them on whatever size board you have. If you are interested in electronics, it's well worth getting a full-sized one as it will become the core of many of your projects.

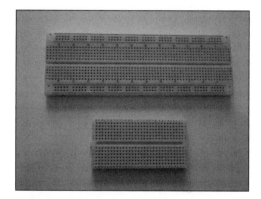

FIGURE 11-3: With solderless breadboards, you can easily prototype circuits, and then dismantle them and build new circuits using the same components.

You can push most components straight into the holes, and make connections using either male-male jumpers, or pieces of single-core wire.

Stripboards and Prototyping Boards

Once you've prototyped your circuits on a solderless breadboard, you may wish to build them on a stripboard. This will permanently join all the components together, and is far more durable than a solderless breadboard. These are a little beyond the content in this chapter, but if you want to take things further, you'll probably soon find yourself using these.

An alternative is the prototyping board. This simply contains lots of holes you can solder into. There are no connections between the holes so you have to solder on whatever connections you want.

PCB Manufacturing

The most advanced option involves making your own PCBs (Printed Circuit Boards). There are a number of options for doing this, including commercial printing. This is for the final stage when you have a complete design. If you want to go down this route, Fritzing is an excellent resource (see `http://fritzing.org`). They produce software to help you design the boards, and a service to print them.

Getting the Best Tools

You won't necessarily need any tools to build simple circuits (as long as you have male-male jumpers for the breadboard), but there are a few that'll make life easier for you.

Wire Cutters/Strippers

These are pretty self-explanatory. You'll need these (they usually come as a single tool) if you're planning on using single-core wire to make connections. However, if you have a set of jumpers for your breadboard, these aren't necessary.

Multimeters

These devices give you the ability to check a range of different things, including the voltage, current, and resistance. It you're having problems with a circuit, they're invaluable tools to help you find out what's wrong. Without one, it's hard to tell if a particular connection is conducting well, or if a component is broken. They're also a lazy way of checking the value of a resistor (discussed later in this chapter).

Soldering Irons

Soldering irons are for creating permanent connections between two components or between one component and a circuit board. You'll need one if you're using stripboard, or if you buy a Raspberry Pi add-on that needs soldering together. We won't cover soldering in this chapter, but if you need to do it, there's an excellent guide called "Soldering Is Easy" at `http://mightyohm.com/files/soldercomic/FullSolderComic_EN.pdf`.

All of these tools are shown in Figure 11-4.

FIGURE 11-4: A set of tools for building your own hardware. None of them is essential for the projects in this chapter, though.

Hardware Needed for this Chapter

We've tried hard to keep the hardware for this chapter as simple, as easy to get, and as cheap as possible. In order to follow along, you'll need at least the following:

- Light emitting diode (LED)
- Resistors: 220 ohm, 1.1K ohm, and 6.2K ohm
- Solderless breadboard (any size should do)
- Jumpers for the breadboard (or single-core wire and a wire cutter)
- A way of connecting the breadboard to the Pi — either female-to-male jumpers or a Pi Cobbler
- MCP3008 chip
- Push switch
- Light-dependent resistor (LDR)

Each of these is discussed in the following sections.

The First Circuit

Before getting too far into the details of circuitry, let's create a simple circuit. You'll need a breadboard, an LED, a 220 ohm resistor, and some way of connecting the GPIOs to the breadboard (either female-male jumpers or a Pi Cobbler).

This circuit is simply going to let you turn an LED (a type of light) on and off from Python. LEDs are a bit like mini light bulbs except for two things: firstly, they're much more power-efficient, so they shouldn't get too warm when running normally, and secondly they will only run one way round. That is, they have a positive leg and a negative leg, and the positive has to be connected to the positive and vice versa. The base of the LED should be round with a small flat section on one side. The flat side is next to the negative leg.

The resistor is there to stop too much power flowing through the circuit. As a general rule, you should always have at least one resistor of at least 220 ohms in a circuit; otherwise, you risk damaging your Pi and the other components. We'll look at this in a bit more detail later.

In this circuit, the resistor doesn't have to be 220 ohms; anywhere between 220 and 470 should be fine (you can try it with higher values, but the LED will be dim).

Resistors are colour-coded so you can tell their values. There are typically four or five bands of colour (a 220 ohm one will usually have four) and this should be red, red, black, and then silver or gold. Again, we'll discuss what this means a bit later.

The resistor and LED should be connected on the breadboard, as shown in Figure 11-5. The positive leg of the resistor (that is, the one not next to the flat side) should be the one that connects to the resistor.

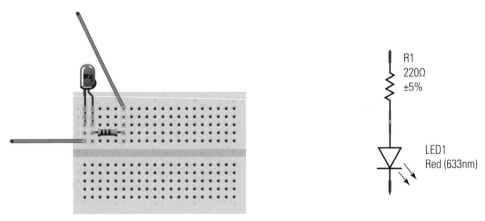

FIGURE 11-5: Two diagrams for the circuit. The left one shows how to physically connect it while the right one shows how it's linked together.

In order to make sure the circuit works, connect the wire from the resistor to one of the 3.3v pins on the Raspberry Pi (see Figure 11-6), while the lead coming from the LED should go to a ground pin. If it's connected properly, the LED should light up.

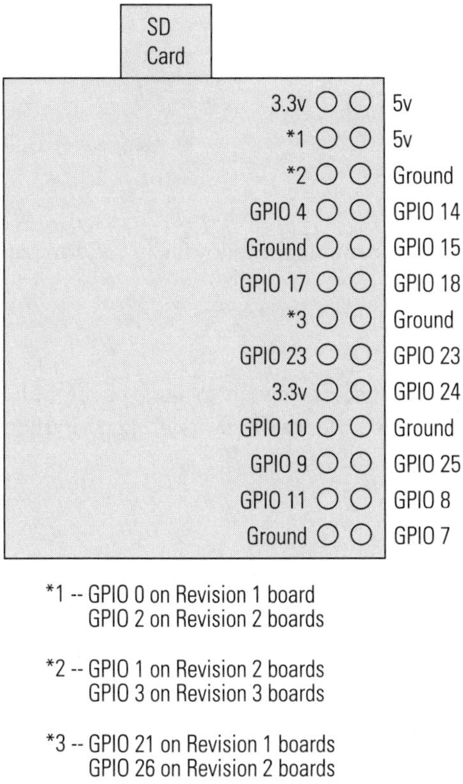

```
SD
Card
            3.3v  O O  5v
              *1  O O  5v
              *2  O O  Ground
          GPIO 4  O O  GPIO 14
          Ground  O O  GPIO 15
         GPIO 17  O O  GPIO 18
              *3  O O  Ground
         GPIO 23  O O  GPIO 23
            3.3v  O O  GPIO 24
         GPIO 10  O O  Ground
          GPIO 9  O O  GPIO 25
         GPIO 11  O O  GPIO 8
          Ground  O O  GPIO 7
```

*1 -- GPIO 0 on Revision 1 board
      GPIO 2 on Revision 2 boards

*2 -- GPIO 1 on Revision 2 boards
      GPIO 3 on Revision 3 boards

*3 -- GPIO 21 on Revision 1 boards
      GPIO 26 on Revision 2 boards

FIGURE 11-6: Raspberry Pi pin layout. Don't try to work out a logic for the pin numbering; there is none.

This, though, is just using the Raspberry Pi as a power source. In order to be able to control the circuit from Python, you first need to install the RPi.GPIO module. First make sure you have pip (a tool to help you access modules) installed with the following command (in LXTerminal, not in Python):

```
sudo apt-get install python3-pip
```

Then get the library with this command (also in LXTerminal):

```
sudo pip-3.2 install RPi.GPIO
```

When you're working with the GPIO pins, you have to access the Raspberry Pi at a low level. Because of this, you can't run the Python scripts normally. Instead, you need to run them with superuser permissions. This sounds fancy, but in fact it just means prefixing commands with sudo. So, for example, if you want to run a script in LXTerminal, you need to run:

```
sudo python3 your-script.py
```

Alternatively, you can start a Python shell with:

```
sudo python3
```

Or you can start IDLE 3 with superuser permissions by running the following in LXTerminal:

```
sudo idle3
```

Once you've installed RPi.GPIO, you just need to connect the circuit to a one of the GPIO pins. Disconnect the pin from 3.3v and connect it to pin 22. Once this is done, open a Python session (don't forget sudo!) and enter the following:

```
>>> import RPi.GPIO as GPIO
>>> GPIO.setmode(GPIO.BCM)
>>> GPIO.setup(22, GPIO.OUT)
>>> GPIO.output(22, True)
>>> GPIO.output(22, False)
>>> GPIO.output(22, True)
>>> GPIO.output(22, False)
```

As you can see, setting the pin to True turns the LED on, while False turns it off. Figure 11-7 shows the running circuit.

FIGURE 11-7: The fully connected circuit on a small, solderless breadboard.

About Circuits

In essence, a circuit contains three things — a source of power, something that does something, and a place for the power to go (that is, a ground). Circuits always have to have all three. Nothing will happen if you connect a power source, but no ground. If you just connect a power source to the ground, then you have what's called a short circuit and it can draw a very large current and damager the power supply (see the section "Protecting Your Pi").

Circuits can vary from the very simple (like the one you made here) to the hugely complicated (such as a computer), but they all follow the same principles.

In this chapter, we only have space to talk about the basics of using the Raspberry Pi's inputs and outputs, but if you're interested in circuits, you can take it as far as you want to go.

If you want to take this further, the Penguin Tutor website has a good course to help you understand a little more about what's going on: `www.penguintutor.com/electronics/`.

Protecting Your Pi

In general, it's very hard to physically damage a computer by programming. You might be able to corrupt some files (although even this is rare), but generally, no matter how much you mess things up, simply reinstalling the operating system will sort things out. However, when you're adding things to the GPIO, you're sending power directly to the CPU, and you can damage it. There are two properties of electricity that can cause problems, *voltage* and *current*.

With voltage, the rule is simple and very important. NEVER CONNECT MORE THAN 3.3 VOLTS TO A GPIO PIN. That's very important, which is why we're shouting. Quite a lot of hobby electronics components are designed to run at 5v because other processors run at that voltage level. However, if you connect these directly to the Pi, it can cause irreparable damage to the board. The result is known as *bricking* the Pi because afterwards its only use is as a brick.

CAUTION   Never connect more than 3.3 volts to a GPIO pin!

You'll notice that the Raspberry Pi has a 5v pin. This is only there to power external circuits that don't come back to the Pi. If you need to connect a 5v device to the GPIO ports, you'll need a *logic-level converter*. These are available for a few pounds and convert 5v signals into 3.3v and vice versa.

Whereas voltage can be thought of as the amount of energy electricity has, *current* is the amount of it that's flowing through the wires. The two are connected by Ohm's law, which states:

Voltage = Current × Resistance

Or, to put it another way:

Current = Voltage / Resistance

Current is measured in amps, voltage in volts, and resistance in ohms. In the previous circuit, there were 3.3 volts and 220 ohms, so that meant:

Current = 3.3 / 220 = 0.015A or 15mA

When using a Raspberry Pi, you must never draw more than 16mA from any one pin, or 50mA from all the GPIO pins combined. That means that you can light up only three LEDs at a time (or use more resistance to decrease the amount of current each one draws). It also means that you should never connect a GPIO pin to a circuit unless there is at least 220 ohms of resistance in it. If you're ever unsure about resistors, always err on the side of caution and use larger ones than you have to.

Technically, this isn't actually correct because LEDs are a little different from many other components. This circuit will draw less power than that. However, unless you understand voltage drop on LEDs, it's best to stick with these guidelines.

If you need to draw more current, or just want to protect your Pi in case you accidentally draw more current, you can use an expansion board that has buffered input/output ports such as the PiFace, or alternatively, use a buffer-integrated circuit (IC or chip) to protect the GPIO ports.

Power Limits

The amount of current your Pi can supply is also limited by the amount of current it can get. Some power supplies will struggle to deliver much power, especially if there are several other things attached to the Pi like optical mice and USB memory. If you find that your Raspberry Pi becomes unstable or starts turning itself off when you're using GPIOs, then insufficient power may be the problem.

To combat this problem, you can upgrade to a power supply that can provide more current, or reduce the amount of current your Pi draws. Things like reducing overclocking in `raspi-config` and removing non-essential peripherals will help.

Getting Input

In the previous example, you used the GPIOs to turn an LED on and off. This was the output side of GPIO — now it's time to look at the input. You'll also use the previous circuit, so leave it connected, but add a button.

The push button switch is a really simple component. When it's open (that is, not pressed) it doesn't connect the two pins, so no current can pass. When it's pressed, it connects the two pins and therefore acts just like a wire.

As you've seen, you'll need one resistor to stop too much current from flowing through the circuit. Just to be extra safe, we used a 1.1K ohm resistor here.

However, if you just connected a power supply to a resistor, to a button, to the GPIO, then when the switch is open, there won't be a circuit. If there's not a circuit, then the GPIO isn't on or off (or `True` or `False`, if you prefer). You need to ensure that there's a circuit that ties the GPIO pin to the ground (and therefore `False`) when the switch is open. This is known as a pull-down resistor because it pulls the GPIO down to 0v if there's nothing else connected to it. It needs to have quite a high value compared to the other resistor to ensure that enough of the electricity goes to the GPIO when the switch is closed. We used a 6.2K ohm resistor, but a 10K ohm one would work just as well.

Take a look at Figure 11-8 to see how to connect it. Note that the resistor between the GPIO and ground is the larger of the two. The button should, as the diagram shows, be connected between a 3.3v power source and GPIO 4.

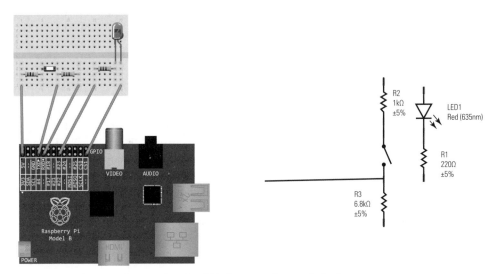

FIGURE 11-8: A circuit diagram that should help you understand what's going on.

Once it's set up, the following code will create a simple reactions game. It'll wait a random amount of time before turning the LED on. Then you have to press the button as soon as you can and it'll then tell you your reaction time. It's on the website as `chapter11-reaction.py`. Figure 11-9 shows the game in action.

FIGURE 11-9: You can expand this simple circuit to fit a wide range of projects.

```
import RPi.GPIO as GPIO
import time
import random
from datetime import datetime

GPIO.setmode(GPIO.BCM)
GPIO.setup(22, GPIO.OUT)
GPIO.setup(4, GPIO.IN)

GPIO.output(22, False)
random.seed()

while True:
    time.sleep(random.random()*10)
    start = datetime.now()
    GPIO.output(22, True)
    while not GPIO.input(4):
        pass
    print("Your reaction time: ",
          (datetime.now() - start).total_seconds())
    print("Get ready to try again.")
    GPIO.output(22, False)
```

Expanding the GPIO Options with I2C, SPI, and Serial

When you're connecting two computers together, you can use an Ethernet network. This is a series of standards that define things such as the physical cable you use, and the way your computer addresses other computers on the network. As long as all the computers are compatible with Ethernet, they should all be able to talk to each other.

There are also communications protocols designed for working with smaller pieces of hardware, such as different chips. There are three main ones we'll look at in this chapter—SPI, I2C, and Serial.

The SPI Communications Protocol

SPI or Serial Peripheral Interface uses four wires to provide a two-directional communication channel between two or more devices—a master (usually the Raspberry Pi) and one or more slaves (typically chips). The four wires include a clock wire that keeps everything in time, the Master Out Slave In (MOSI), Master In Slave Out (MISO), and a Slave Select (SS).

Simply connect the pins from the Raspberry Pi to the corresponding pins on the slave, and you should be ready to go.

There are a wide range of expansion options for SPI, for example, analogue input.

Raspberry Pis have a range of inputs and outputs, but they're all digital. That is, they can only read on or off. That's fine for some things, such as buttons and controlling LEDs, but sometimes you'll need to read or write data on a scale. For example, you might want to read data from a sensor such as a light or temperature sensor. These don't give on-or-off values, but a range.

Values like this (that fall within a range) are known as *analogue values* (as opposed to digital). In order to read them, you'll need an analogue-to-digital converter (ADC). For this chapter, we're using an MCP3008, which is a chip that provides eight analogue channels and communicates with the Raspberry Pi using SPI.

Figure 11-10 shows what the pins on the MCP3008 do, and Figure 11-11 shows how to connect the circuit.

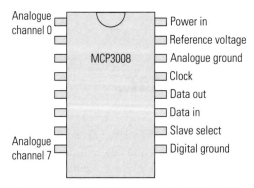

FIGURE 11-10: The eight pins on the left input 0 to 7, while the pins on the right are to control the chip. This diagram is based on looking down from the top. You should see a semicircle cut into the plastic case. This should match the one in the diagram.

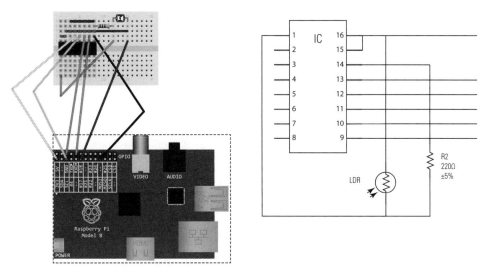

FIGURE 11-11: How to wire the circuit. You can change which GPIO pins the pins on the MCP3008 connect to by altering the appropriate values in the code.

The code for it is as follows. You'll find it on the website as `chapter11-spiadc.py`. Figure 11-12 shows the connected circuit.

FIGURE 11-12: The MCP3008 being used to convert the analogue signal from the LDR to a digital signal for the Raspberry Pi.

```
import time
import RPi.GPIO as GPIO
GPIO.setmode(GPIO.BCM)

# read SPI data from MCP3008 chip, 8 possible adc's (0 thru 7)
def readadc(adcnum, clockpin, mosipin, misopin, cspin):
```

```python
        if ((adcnum > 7) or (adcnum < 0)):
                return -1
        GPIO.output(cspin, True)

        GPIO.output(clockpin, False)  # start clock low
        GPIO.output(cspin, False)     # bring CS low

        commandout = adcnum
        commandout |= 0x18  # start bit + single-ended bit
        commandout <<= 3    # we only need to send 5 bits here
        for i in range(5):
                if (commandout & 0x80):
                        GPIO.output(mosipin, True)
                else:
                        GPIO.output(mosipin, False)
                commandout <<= 1
                GPIO.output(clockpin, True)
                GPIO.output(clockpin, False)

        adcout = 0
        # read in one empty bit, one null bit and 10 ADC bits
        for i in range(12):
                GPIO.output(clockpin, True)
                GPIO.output(clockpin, False)
                adcout <<= 1
                if (GPIO.input(misopin)):
                        adcout |= 0x1

        GPIO.output(cspin, True)

        adcout >>= 1        # first bit is 'null' so drop it
        return adcout

SPICLK = 4
SPIMISO = 17
SPIMOSI = 18
SPICS = 23

# set up the SPI interface pins
GPIO.setup(SPIMOSI, GPIO.OUT)
GPIO.setup(SPIMISO, GPIO.IN)
GPIO.setup(SPICLK, GPIO.OUT)
GPIO.set'up(SPICS, GPIO.OUT)

ldr_adc = 0;
```

```
last_read = 0
tolerance = 5

while True:
        # we'll assume that the light didn't change
        input_changed = False
        # read the analog pin
        ldr_value = readadc(ldr_adc, SPICLK,
                            SPIMOSI, SPIMISO, SPICS)
        ldr_movement = abs(ldr_value - last_read)

        if ( ldr_movement > tolerance ):
              input_changed = True

        if ( input_changed ):
              print('Light = ', int(ldr_value))
              last_read = ldr_value

        # hang out and do nothing for a half second
        time.sleep(0.5)
```

Don't worry too much about how the `readadc()` function works. It manipulates the individual bytes and sends and receives them down the MOSI and MISO wires. You can simply take it and use it to read the other ports on the ADC if you want to add more. Support for SPI is planned for the `RPi.GPIO` library, but at the time of writing, hadn't been implemented. You can see how the project's progressing at `http://code.google.com/p/raspberry-gpio-python/`.

The main loop then uses this function to get the value of the ADC connected to the LDR and (if it's changed by more than the threshold), print its value onto the screen.

The I2C Communications Protocol

Inter-Integrated Circuit (I2C or I²C, pronounced "I squared C") is a more powerful protocol than SPI. It still uses four wires, but one of them is the power line, and another is the ground, so there are only two data wires. Up to 127 devices can be connected to an I2C bus, and it has addressing capabilities rather than the rather simplistic slave select on SPI.

Quick2wire makes a series of I2C boards that expand the functionality of the Pi. You don't need these boards to use I2C, although they do make the process a bit easier. They also make a Python module that can communicate over I2C regardless of whether you're using their boards. You can find it at `https://github.com/quick2wire/quick2wire-python-api`.

Like SPI, support for I2C is planned for `RPi.GPIO`. Again, follow the website for up-to-date information.

The Serial Communications Protocol

The previous two methods are generally used for sending binary data between devices. Serial communication, on the other hand, is generally used for sending text back and forwards (although there are exceptions in both cases).

Serial communications are supported by the `pyserial` module that you can get with the following command:

```
sudo pip install pyserial
```

Once the `pyserial` module is installed, you just have to create a serial connection, then you can use `write()` and `read()` methods to send and receive data. For example, the following code will send the message "Hello" out of the serial port. It was created to work with a Ciseco PiLite, which will then scroll the letters across the screen.

```
>>> import serial
>>> pilite = serial.Serial("/dev/ttyAMA0", baudrate=9600)
>>> pilite.open()
>>> pilite.write(bytes("Hello", "utf-8"))
```

Taking the Example Further

If you feel like taking this example further, try the following ideas.

Arduino

If you're interested in hobby electronics, perhaps the most useful kit is an Arduino. These are microcontroller boards slightly larger than Raspberry Pis. They have far more GPIOs (the exact number depends on the model), as well as analogue inputs and in some cases analogue outputs as well.

Perhaps the most useful thing about Arduinos, though, is the number of expansion boards (known as *shields*) that can slot onto them. With these you can quickly create powerful hardware with little (if any) wiring.

It is perfectly possible to connect your Raspberry Pi GPIOs to an Arduino to get them to talk via I2C or SPI, although most Arduino models run at 5v, so you'll need to use logic-level converters. They can also communicate over the USB using a serial connection.

Some people consider Arduinos to be overkill when connected to a Pi, and it's true that almost anything you can do with an Arduino, you can also do with a Pi. However, the sheer amount of existing Arduino hardware and code makes them very useful companions to Raspberry Pis.

Perhaps the biggest drawback for readers of this book is that they're programmed in a dialect C++ rather than Python. The language has a different layout, but it's based on the same general principles. If you've read this far into the book, you shouldn't have too much difficulty picking up basic C++, although we won't deal with it here.

PiFace

The PiFace is an expansion board that slots straight onto the GPIO pins of the Raspberry Pi and is a really useful addition to the GPIO. As well as buffering the input and output (and so protecting your Pi and providing up to 500mA of current), it also has a pair of relays that can be used to drive higher powered components such as motors.

It's the same size as the Raspberry Pi, and fits neatly over the top. It's a great choice for getting started with simple robotics. It's around £25 ($41) so, while not as cheap as getting the components yourself, it's a great value for its ease of use and the range of projects it supports. Figure 11-13 shows the PiFace connected to a "Model A Pi."

FIGURE 11-13: The buffered outputs of the PiFace mean you can control far more without worrying about the small current limits on the Raspberry Pi.

Gertboard

The Gertboard is the Goliath of the Raspberry Pi GPIO options. It crams just about everything you could want into a board. It has the similar ATMega chips to Arduinos for learning microprocessing, a motor controller, digital-to-analogue converters, analogue-to-digital converters, push buttons, and a whole bunch of LEDs. Of course, all this comes at a cost, not just in terms of price (expect to pay a little under £60/$98), but also in terms of size, which could make it unsuitable for many projects where this is important (such as with robotics).

It is perhaps best thought of as a board for learning about electronics and control, and once you have a good idea what's going on, you can design a smaller circuit for implementing your project.

The fact that it's designed by the Raspberry Pi Foundation's hardware supremo Gert Van Loo means you can trust that it's been built by someone who really knows the Raspberry Pi inside and out (literally).

Wireless Inventor's Kit

Everything we've done here so far has used wires to connect various components. For most projects, this is fine. However, some projects require a bit more freedom. Ciseco has put together a Wireless Inventor's Kit, which contains everything you need to get started with simple radio communications and the Raspberry Pi.

It uses a radio system that's designed to work at a lower level than WiFi networking, and it's best used to connect sensors to your Pi remotely, or to use your Pi to control circuits from a distance.

Trying Some Popular Projects

You can create almost anything with a handful of components and a Raspberry Pi, but to get you started, the following sections include a few ideas.

Robots

These can range from simple wheeled devices powered by two motors, to vastly complex humanoid walking robots, to the bizarre such as those that move like snakes or spiders. To work with robots, you'll need to learn how to control motors (the GPIOs don't provide enough power to do this straight from the pin). The PiFace has a pair of relays, which is one option for getting started.

You'll also probably need some servos. *Servos* are a bit like motors, but can be turned a few degrees at a time. There are also a vast array of sensors that can be hooked up to your Pi to help your creation see the world around them.

Home Automation

Imagine a world where you can control your heating and lights from your smartphone. It's not an impossible dream—it can be achieved with a Raspberry Pi, some circuitry, and Python. Chapter 7 showed you how to control a Python program from the web, so combined with what you've learned here, you should be able to make this dream a reality.

Burglar Alarms

Maybe these are less glamorous than home automation, but they might keep you safe. With a Raspberry Pi's camera and a few things like passive infrared (PIR) movement sensors, you should be able to create your very own Fort Knox.

Digital Art

Art doesn't have to be lifeless painting in dusty rooms. Nor does it have to be sculptures or poetry or dance. It can be anything you want it to be. One of the emerging forms is digital art, which uses some form of computing to add a new dimension to an installation. It could be, for example, to add shifting light patterns, or pressure sensitive pads to create feedback for people touching it. You can let your imagination run wild, and then use a Raspberry Pi to give life to your imagination's creation.

Summary

After reading this chapter, you should understand the following a bit better:

- The pins that stick up from one corner of the Raspberry Pi are General Purpose Input and Outputs (GPIOs) that can be programmed from within Python.

- The `RPi.GPIO` library offers a simple interface for switching the pins on and off, or reading values from them.

- You have to be careful when working with GPIOs because sending too much voltage, or drawing too much current, can cause irreparable damage to your Pi.

- You can expand your Pi by adding devices using protocols such as SPI, I2C, and Serial, all of which can be programmed from Python.

- One example of this is the MCP3008 chip, which has eight analogue-to-digital converters that can be read via SPI.

- Your Pi can control circuits of almost any complexity. The only limit is your imagination.

Chapter 12
Testing and Debugging

THERE ARE ALWAYS times when your code won't do what it should be doing. You see the inputs and work through the code, but somehow, it spits out an output that just shouldn't be possible. This can be one of the most infuriating parts of programming.

Investigating Bugs by Printing Out the Values

There are loads of ways to find out exactly what's happening, but one of the simplest is judicious use of print() statements. By using these to print out the value of every variable, you can usually get to the bottom of what's going on.

Take a look at the following code for a simple menu system. It doesn't produce any errors, but whatever input you give it, it always says "Unknown choice". (It's on the website as chapter12-debug.py):

```
choices = {1:"Start", 2:"Edit", 3:"Quit"}
for key, value in choices.items():

    print("Press ", key, " to ", value)



user_input = input("Enter choice: ")



if user_input in choices.values():

    print("You chose", choices[user_input])
```

```
else:

    print("Unknown choice")
```

Perhaps you've seen the problem already, but if you haven't, what's the best way to find it? The problem is that the if statement isn't correctly identifying when the user_input is valid, so add some print() statements to see what's happening:

```
choices = {1:"Start", 2:"Edit", 3:"Quit"}

for key, value in choices.items():

    print("Press ", key, " to ", value)


user_input = input("Enter choice: ")


print("user_input: ", user_input)

print("choices: ", choices)

print("choices.values(): ", choices.values())


if user_input in choices.values():

    print("You chose", choices[user_input])

else:

    print("Unknown choice")
```

Straight away you should see the problem: choices.values() should be choices. keys(). The code was checking the wrong part of the choices dictionary. Make the change in the code and try running it again. With that bug fixed, everything should be fine.

Oh no, it still doesn't work! There must be another bug. Have another look at the output from the print statements:

```
user_input:  1

choices:  {1: 'Start', 2: 'Edit', 3: 'Quit'}

choices.values():  dict_values(['Start', 'Edit', 'Quit'])
```

Can you see why it's failing? After the value of variable, the second most important thing is the data type of that value, so expand the print statements to include more details about what's going on there:

```
print("user_input: ", user_input)

print("choices: ", choices)

print("choices.values(): ", choices.values())

print("type(user_input): ", type(user_input))

for key in choices.keys():

    print("type(key): ", type(key), "key: ", key)
```

If you run this, it should output:

```
Press  1  to  Start

Press  2  to  Edit

Press  3  to  Quit

Enter choice: 1

user_input:  1

choices:  {1: 'Start', 2: 'Edit', 3: 'Quit'}

choices.values():  dict_values(['Start', 'Edit', 'Quit'])

type(user_input):  <class 'str'>
```

```
type(key):   <class 'int'> key:   1

type(key):   <class 'int'> key:   2

type(key):   <class 'int'> key:   3
```

```
Unknown choice
```

Now you can see that the cause of the problem is that `user_input` is a string, but the keys of choices are integers. The easiest way to solve this is to change the invocation of choices to make the keys strings:

```
choices = {"1":"Start", "2":"Edit", "3":"Quit"}
```

Now the basic logic of the program is working as expected; however, it still spits out loads of extra text that the user doesn't want to see. Obviously you could just delete the `print()` statements, but they may be useful again in the future. You can keep them in the code, but have a flag that can be set to turn them off and on like as follows:

```
debug = True



choices = {"1":"Start", "2":"Edit", "3":"Quit"}

for key, value in choices.items():

    print("Press ", key, " to ", value)



user_input = input("Enter choice: ")



if debug:

    print("DEBUG user_input: ", user_input)

    print("DEBUG choices: ", choices)

    print("DEBUG choices.values(): ", choices.values())
```

```
print("DEBUG type(user_input): ", type(user_input))

for key in choices.keys():

    print("DEBUG type(key): ", type(key), "key: ", key)



if user_input in choices.keys():

    print("You chose", choices[user_input])

else:

    print("Unknown choice")
```

If you encounter any problems in the future, all you need to do is change the debug variable to True. Prefixing all the lines with DEBUG also makes it easy to see which output is normal, and which is debugging.

Finding Bugs by Testing

Debugging is the process of getting rid of problems in your programs. It can be quite challenging, but it can be even more difficult to find the problems in the first place. This might sound silly, but it's true. As a program gets larger, the number of different ways it can be used increases, and the more different ways something can be used, the more places there are to check for bugs.

Imagine, for example, a word processor that has options for style, page layouts, file formats, layout managers, and so on. Bugs could lurk in any of these areas, so it's important for the developers to check to make sure everything's running as it should. They could even hide in combinations; for example, a problem may occur only if a particular font is used with a particular layout.

Checking Bits of Code with Unit Tests

The most basic form of testing programs is the *unit test*. This is where you take one small piece of code and make sure it's behaving as it should. Typically, these are used to check that individual methods and functions are working properly.

Essentially, all a unit test does is run a piece of code with a particular set of inputs and check that their outputs are correct.

Take, for example, a function that takes a string of characters and returns a string with the same letters, but converted to uppercase. This could be implemented and tested as follows:

```python
def capitalise(input_string):

    output_string = ""

    for character in input_string:

        if character.isupper():

            output_string = output_string + character

        else:

            output_string = output_string + chr(ord(character)-32)

    return output_string
```

```python
print(capitalise("helloWorld"))
```

This should behave as expected. It works because the UTF-8 character encoding that Python uses stores characters as numbers, and uppercase letters are 32 places below their lowercase counterparts.

In this example, we've used a simple test case, and we're printing it to the screen to check manually. We can get Python to check the test case for us using the `unittest` module in the following code:

```python
import unittest
```

```python
def capitalise(input_string):

    output_string = ""

    for character in input_string:

        if character.isupper():
```

```
            output_string = output_string + character

        else:

            output_string = output_string + chr(ord(character)-32)

    return output_string


class Tests(unittest.TestCase):

    def test_1(self):

        self.assertEqual("HELLOWORLD", capitalise("helloWorld"))


if __name__ == '__main__':

    unittest.main()
```

This does more or less what the previous code did. If you run it, it'll check one string to make sure "helloWorld" goes to "HELLOWORLD". At this level, it's not much better or worse than just having a print statement.

When you run unittest.main(), Python runs every method in subclasses of unittest. TestCase that start with test_. In this case it's just test_1. The real advantage of using unit tests is that you can combine lots of tests in order to check at a glance whether things have worked properly.

You can add a second test case that checks that the string "hello world" capitalises to "HELLO WORLD":

```
    def test_2(self):

        self.assertEqual("HELLO WORLD", capitalise("Hello World"))
```

If you run this, you should get the following output:

```
FAIL: test_2 (__main__.Tests)

-------------------------------------------------------------
```

```
Traceback (most recent call last):

  File "capitalise.py", line 17, in test_2

    self.assertEqual("HELLO WORLD", capitalise("Hello World"))

AssertionError: 'HELLO WORLD' != 'HELLO\x00WORLD'

- HELLO WORLD

?        ^

+ HELLOWORLD

?        ^
```

Oh dear, it looks like the test failed. You can see that the space wasn't properly dealt with. If you go back to the original code, you can see that the problem is that everything that isn't an uppercase character gets 32 taken off its UTF-8 value. Since space isn't uppercase, this happens to it too, but this isn't what the program should do.

Test cases should be designed to try a wide range of valid inputs. For example:

```
class Tests(unittest.TestCase):

    def test_1(self):

        self.assertEqual("HELLOWORLD", capitalise("helloWorld"))


    def test_2(self):

        self.assertEqual("HELLO WORLD", capitalise("Hello World"))


    def test_3(self):

        self.assertEqual('!!"£$%^&*()_+-=',

                         capitalise('!!"£$%^&*()_+-='))
```

```
def test_4(self):

    self.assertEqual("1234567890", capitalise("1234567890"))



def test_5(self):

    self.assertEqual("HELLO WORLD", capitalise("HELLO WORLD"))

def test_6(self):

    self.assertEqual("`¬#~'@;:,.<>/?",
                     capitalise("`¬#~'@;:,.<>/?"))
```

If you run these, you'll see that most fail. The problem is a flaw in the program logic. The code leaves it alone if it's an uppercase letter and changes it otherwise. However, what you want is for the code to change it if it's a lowercase letter, and leave it alone otherwise.

If you change the `capitalise` function to the following, it'll do this:

```
def capitalise(input_string):

    output_string = ""

    for character in input_string:

        if character.islower():

            output_string = output_string + chr(ord(character)-32)

        else:

            output_string = output_string + character



    return output_string
```

Now if you run the code, you should find that it passes all the tests.

By default, `unittest` will give you details only if one or more tests fail. Otherwise, it just returns an overall OK. For most purposes, this is what you want, but you can specify how verbose you want the output to be in two ways. If you're running the script from the command line, you can add the -v flag for more output. So, for example, if you've saved the program as `capitalise.py`, you can run the tests with verbose output using:

```
python3 capitalise.py -v
```

Alternatively, you can specify that you want a more verbose output in the code itself by changing:

```
if __name__ == '__main__':

    unittest.main()
```

to:

```
if __name__ == '__main__':

    unittest.main(verbosity=2)
```

Before going any further, we should point out that the `capitalise()` function is here for this example. If you actually need to capitalise text, you should use `upper()` method of the string class. For example:

```
>>> 'hello world'.upper()
```

Getting More Assertive

All these tests have a call to `self.assertEqual()`. This line tells the unit test module what the output of the test should be. That is, the test should pass if the two values passed are the same, and fail if they're different. This covers a large proportion of cases, but you may wish to check different things. There are a number of different `assert` methods that you can use in your tests.

These check that various structures are the same:

- `assertSequencesEqual(sequence1, sequence2)`
- `assertListEqual(list1, list2)`
- `assertTupleEqual(tuple1, tuple2)`
- `assertSetEqual(set1, set2)`
- `assertDictEqual(dict1, dict2)`

With these structures, you may want to check that the value is in the structure rather than if two structures are the same. The following methods check if a value is in a structure:

- `assertIn(value, structure)`
- `assertNotIn(value, structure)`

Strings are a special type of structure and have their own method:

- `assertMultiLineEqual(string1, string2)`

You can also check values using tests other than equality using these assert methods:

- `assertNotEqual(value1, value2)`
- `assertGreater(value1, value2)`
- `assertGreaterEqual(value1, value2)`
- `assertLess(value1, value2)`
- `assertLessEqual(value1, value2)`

There are also a few that allow a margin of error:

- `assertAlmostEqual(value1, value2)`
- `assertNotAlmostEqual(value1, value2)`

These check that the two values differ (or not) by less than 0.000001. These are useful if you're testing floating-point functions that might have small rounding errors that are acceptable.

You can also test anything that you can reduce to a `True` or `False` value using:

- `assertTrue(value)`
- `assertFalse(value)`

Whatever you want to check, each `test_` method should have one `assert` method call that is used to determine the success or failure of that particular test.

You can use these unit tests in a number of ways. There is a style of development called test-driven development that says that the tests are the first thing you should write and then you use those tests as the specifications for the code. Most programmers, though, write the tests towards the end of development to make sure everything's working properly.

Using Test Suites for Regression Testing

Writing programs isn't usually a single effort. You don't usually sit down, create software, and then stop and go on to do something else. Instead, you generally code some of the features, distribute it to users, then fix bugs and add new features in later versions.

There is a risk of breaking things that once worked as you add new features, so it's important to test not only newly created things, but also older things that have worked. Testing older code is called *regression testing*, and having a properly ordered set of tests makes it really easy.

To make sure that you're not introducing bugs into previously working code, you should rerun the tests after you make any changes. However, as your programs become bigger, you'll end up with more and more tests. Eventually, you'll get to the point where it's not practical to run every test every time. You can group tests together into test suites. These allow you to test just particular areas of your program at a time.

Using the previous code, you can change the final code block to:

```python
if __name__ == '__main__':

    letters_suite = unittest.TestSuite()

    symbols_suite = unittest.TestSuite()

    letters_suite.addTest(Tests("test_1"))

    symbols_suite.addTest(Tests("test_2"))
```

```
symbols_suite.addTest(Tests("test_3"))

symbols_suite.addTest(Tests("test_4"))

symbols_suite.addTest(Tests("test_5"))

symbols_suite.addTest(Tests("test_6"))

all_suite = unittest.TestSuite()

all_suite.addTest(letters_suite)

all_suite.addTest(symbols_suite)

unittest.TextTestRunner(verbosity=2).run(all_suite)
```

This bit of code by itself does exactly what the previous code block did. That is, it runs all the tests. However, it has grouped them into different test suites. There's `letters_suite` that runs the test that checks letters, `symbols_suite` that runs the tests that check symbols, and `all_suite` that combines both of them. You can use the final line to run any of these three suites.

Using this code, you should find it quite easy to build a simple testing menu to help you make sure that everything's running smoothly.

Testing the Whole Package

Unit testing is great because you can automate it, and quickly check that everything's running properly. However, it doesn't cover everything. Even though everything seems to work properly by itself, you may still find that there are problems when everything comes together.

In commercial software development, after the unit tests have been done, the code will be passed to the quality assurance team to make sure everything's working fine. This team will outline a series of test cases that cover how the software will be used. It should check every aspect of the program and test it with a variety of inputs to make sure it behaves as expected. This is sometimes done manually with testers interacting with the software just as users would, and sometimes by specialist testing software that can simulate mouse and keyboard input.

Of course, it's unlikely that you'll have a quality assurance team to help you with your software, but there are some things you can take from the professional approach. You should be methodical. Before you start testing, make a list of everything that the program does, and come up with test input and expected outputs. You can then go through this list and make sure it's all functioning correctly.

It's probably a bit excessive to do this after every code change, but you should do it periodically, and especially before any big releases.

Making Sure Your Software's Usable

By the time you've finished a program, you know everything there is to know about it. You know how to interact with it, how to get the best out of it, and what all the various options are. Your users, however, don't have any of this knowledge. Your software has to help them understand it and provide enough information for them to know what to do. After all, it doesn't matter how awesome your features are if the users don't know how to invoke them.

User testing is the area of testing devoted to making sure this is possible. In an ideal world, you'd get a room full of people, sit them down in front of your software, and ask them to perform certain tasks and see how they get on. Again, you're unlikely to be able to do this. Sometimes you may be able to persuade a friend or relative to help you out, but the more programs you create, the fewer volunteers you seem to find. The only real solution to this is to listen to people using the software, and make sure to ask for feedback.

How Much Should You Test?

There's an old saying about software bugs that goes, "Absence of proof isn't proof of absence." Basically, no matter how much you test your software, there's no way of ever proving that there aren't any bugs in it. In fact, it's almost impossible to write software that doesn't have any bugs in it. The purpose of testing isn't to make perfect software, but to make software that's good enough. What "good enough" means will vary from project to project. The more important the software, the more you should test it, but all software deserves at least some testing. It's not as glamorous as implementing new features, but most of the time it is more important to have a few features that are properly tested than have loads that are buggy, so it's worth spending some time writing unit tests and making sure everything's working properly. After all, it could well be your data that the program loses when there's a problem.

Summary

After reading this chapter, you should understand the following a bit better:

- Debugging is the process of removing any problems from the code.

- Judicious use of `print()` statements can help you find out what the problems are.

- It sometimes helps to have a way of switching these `print()` statements on and off so you can reuse them if you find more problems.

- Testing is the process of finding bugs in code.

- Unit tests are the most basic form of testing and can be automated using the `unittest` module.

- Test cases can be grouped together into test suites to help you test particular areas of a program.

- It's easy to accidentally introduce new bugs when you add features, so you should always regression test after you make changes to your code.

- Unit tests won't pick up all problems though, so you should also test at a complete-system level.

- Usability problems are also bugs, so you need to listen to your users to make sure they are addressed.

This brings us to the end of the book. Hopefully, you're now confident and knowledgeable enough to create your own programs. Don't worry if you feel you don't know everything about every aspect of Python, very few people do. If you ever get stuck, you can always refer back to this book, or the Python documentation at `http://docs.python.org/3/`.

Hopefully you've seen that programming isn't overly complex, and if you break up a problem into small steps, it's usually quite straightforward to code. The main thing to remember is that programming should be fun! Find an area that interests you and explore it. Despite its small size, there's very little you can't do with a Raspberry Pi.

Index